Computer Networking:
Internet Protocols In Action

Jeanna Matthews

Clarkson University

WILEY
John Wiley & Sons, Inc.

ACQUISITIONS EDITOR	Bill Zobrist
SENIOR PRODUCTION EDITOR	Lisa Wasserman
COVER DESIGNER	Harry Nolan
COVER IMAGE	©Digital Vision/Getty Images

This book was set in 10/12 Roman by the author and printed and bound by Malloy Lithographing. The cover was printed by Phoenix Color Corp.

This book is printed on acid free paper. ∞

To order books or for customer service, please call 1-800-CALL WILEY (225-5945).

Library of Congress Cataloging in Publication Data:
Matthews, Jeanna
Computer Networking: Internet Protocols in Action / Jeanna Matthews.
    p. cm.
ISBN 978-0-471-66186-3 (pbk.)
1. Computer Networks. I. Title.

TK5105.5.M3965   2005
004.6'2—dc22   2004059089

ISBN 978-0-471-66186-3

Printed in the United States of America

10 9 8 7 6 5

Preface

INTRODUCTION

With clear, straightforward text and engaging examples, this book brings an active style of learning to the study of computer networking. It can be used as a primary textbook to accompany lecture material or as a companion text to provide hands-on assignments. It is also an ideal guide to self-study for the computing professional. In fact, this book can help any interested readers look under the hood of the network they use every day and become a more informed network consumer.

The book consists of a set of exercises, each of which involves analyzing traces of actual network activity. Important concepts are presented in the context of actual traces of real-world scenarios. Readers learn the details of networking protocols in the best ways possible—by seeing them in action!

Well-chosen examples make it clear how the details of networking protocols are relevant to everyday life. For example, security issues are highlighted throughout the book. Readers will see what is sent over the network when they browse the web or shop online. They will see what a home wireless network looks like to someone driving by if WEP is not enabled. These and many more concrete illustrations help readers understand how to secure their networks against attack.

Anywhere people are learning about computer networking, this book will help them learn by doing rather than simply hearing information. The material contained in this book has been used with both undergraduate and Master's level courses in computer networking. It has been used successfully in short courses with high school students. It has been used to accompany networking courses tailored to computer science students, electrical and computer engineering students and business students. Students have used it as the basis for independent study courses and working professionals have used it to brush up on their knowledge of computer networking. We sincerely hope that these exercises will make computer networking come alive for you too!

GETTING THE MOST OUT OF THE BOOK AND CD

PACKET TRACES

This book is based on the premise that the best way to understand network protocols is to see them in action. Each exercise is accompanied by one or more packet traces that allow you to do just that. To get the most out of this text, you should open these traces as they are discussed. The following symbol will appear in the margins whenever a new trace file is discussed, and the name of the trace file will be given (e.g. **exampleFileName.cap**).

The traces themselves can be found on the attached CD. From the table of contents, choose the title of an exercise you are currently reading, and you will see a list of trace files referenced in that exercise.

These trace files are in a standard packet capture format referred to as pcap format. They can be viewed with various network analysis applications. The application we use in this text is an open source application called Ethereal. It is an easy-to-use GUI application available for many platforms, including Windows, Linux and Solaris.

In the first section ("Getting Started"), we will discuss the basics of packet capture in Ethereal. Before beginning this section, we recommend that you install Ethereal on a local computer. You can install the latest version of Ethereal from **http://www.ethereal.com/ download.html**. We have also included an installer for Windows on the attached CD.

You will probably want to capture traces of your own network activity in addition to the traces we have provided. It is fun to see your own traffic captured and to understand the characteristics of your local network. We certainly encourage you to do so, but it is important that you familiarize yourself with the policies set by your local network administrator. For example, capturing packets is often forbidden on shared campus network segments. You will appreciate why as you do the exercises in this book.

ORGANIZATION OF THE TEXT

The book is organized into six main sections: an introductory section that covers the basics of using Ethereal to examine traces of network activity, four sections covering a layer of the network protocol stack (application, transport, network and link layer), and finally one section on security.

The exercises are organized in a top-down fashion, but care has been taken to assure they can also be used to accompany a bottom-up presentation of the protocol stack. Both approaches to using this text are show in the figure labeled "Alternate Pathways". In either case, we recommend beginning with Section 1 (Getting Started) and ending with Section 6 (Security). We also recommend that the exercises within each section be done in order.

Each exercise begins with an introduction covering the required background material so this book can be used as a stand-alone set of exercises or to accompany a class of computer networking that consists of additional lecture presentations and readings from a textbook.

The introduction is followed by a configuration section. Here we describe how we set up the hardware and software before we begin capturing a trace of network activity. Even though you are not taking the traces on your own, we want to give you enough information to know how to do so. This section will typically contain a network diagram.

The next section is the experiment section. This is the longest part of the exercise. In this section, we describe how we took the trace and step you through the initial analysis of the trace. In each exercise, we ask you to open the trace from the accompanying CD and follow along. You can read the text of the exercise without doing this but you will learn a great deal more if you follow along. This section will contain screenshots of using Ethereal to analyze certain aspects of the trace.

The experiment section is followed by a set of questions. Some questions can be answered simply by reading the exercise, some require you to open traces from the accompanying CD and analyze them, some require you to do some research on the Internet.

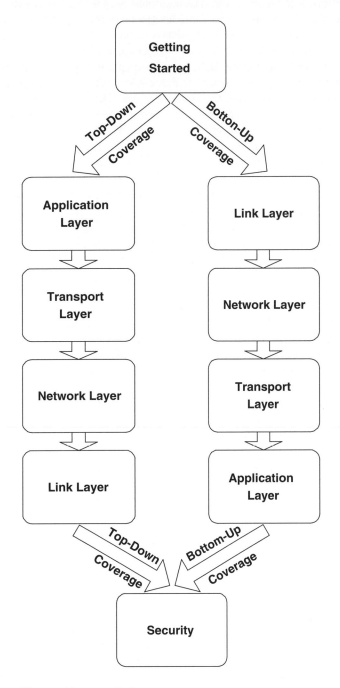

Figure: Alternate Pathways

Questions that require a significant amount of external investigation and open-ended discussion questions are grouped into a separate discussion and investigation section.

The last section of each exercise is a resources section. It contains a list of pointers to on-line materials that will be useful to you in your further study of networking. In some cases, we provide specific URLs, and in others, we specify a list of recommended search terms to use with your favorite search engine. We highly encourage you to consult these resources. The most important thing you can take away from this book or any course in networking is a solid understanding of how to use the on-line resources available to answer questions and solve problems you encounter. We also encourage you to search the Internet on your own for more information. There is a wealth of information available that can clarify and enhance your study of computer networking.

The accompanying CD contains the actual traces, source code and binaries for the Ethereal software used in the exercise. An instructor's CD is also available and contains answers to many of the questions.

WHY THIS BOOK

As an instructor of computer networking, I have struggled to find an efficient and easy to manage way to bring hands-on exercises to my students. At first, I believed this required a lab full of networking equipment, so I set about collecting routers, switches, hubs, PCs and the lab space to house them. I was able to provide a great learning experience for a small number of students, but the experience did not scale to the size of a typical undergraduate class. It was too expensive to outfit a laboratory large enough to hold the entire class and holding many small lab sections became an administrative nightmare. Even the lab space required for a small class required significant time to maintain, upgrade, and manage.

I found myself facing an unpleasant decision—teach computer networking in a pure lecture style without the hands-on exercises that I (and my students) loved or continue to invest huge amounts of time in funding and managing the facilities required to support them. At that point, I took a good look at the exercises I was using. Nearly all of them involved three parts: 1) configuring the hardware and software to prepare for a networking experiment, 2) performing the experiment and capturing a trace of the activity, and 3) analyzing the trace to understand the subtleties of what had happened. It occurred to me that most of the real learning was occurring in step 3 when students analyzed the traces they had captured.

I decided to try a new approach. I would describe the experiment in detail to the students and then distribute a trace of the experiment that I had taken for them to analyze. I was thrilled with the results! I could maintain a single set of networking equipment on which I could take the traces. I could write an answer key that referred to specific packet numbers because all students looked at the same trace. Even campus system administrators that had been nervous about students collecting packet traces were happy because I collected the traces myself and distributed them to the students.

I have tested this method in large classes (150) and small classes (10). I have used it at both a small university (Clarkson, 3,000 students) and a large university (Cornell, 20,000 students). I have used it with a master's level networking class and short courses in networking for high school students. I have universally found it to provide 95 percent of the benefit with a fraction of the headaches.

Students routinely report that exercises based on network traces are their favorite part of the class, and that they help cement their understanding of the lecture material. They say this style of assignment encourages them to do additional research on their own to understand each detail of the traces. Students often take their own traces and come to me with wonderful in-depth questions about what they see.

As I used this approach to teaching networking, I found that while the tasks necessary to support it (taking traces, describing the experimental set-ups, writing questions and answers, etc.) were much easier than maintaining a lab, they were quite time consuming. For example, when posting online for students, it can be tricky to ensure that the traces do not capture any private data that should not be revealed. I decided to write a book that would remove these obstacles for other instructors wanting to add a hands-on component to their computer networking courses. This book and its accompanying CD are the result.

CONTACTING THE AUTHOR

We hope that you will find this book an easy way to add a fun, hands-on component to your study of computer networking. We would love to hear about your experiences using these exercises in a formal course or as the basis for self-study. You are welcome to send comments or suggestions to the author at:

Dr. Jeanna Matthews
8 Clarkson Avenue, MS 5815
Potsdam, NY 13699
jnm@clarkson.edu

Acknowledgments

There are many people who contributed to the development of this book. I would like to thank Paul Crockett, my first editor at John Wiley & Sons, for believing in this project and helping to make it a reality. I would also like to thank Senior Editorial Assistant, Simon Durkin, for his many contributions to this book. Executive Editor Bill Zobrist oversaw the final changes to the text and made some excellent suggestions on the introductory material. Senior Editorial Assistant, Bridget Morrisey oversaw the production of the CD. Senior Production Editor, Lisa Wasserman, sheparded the book through the copy-editing and proofreading phases.

I would like to thank my husband Leonard Matthews for his patience and support during this process and my children Robert and Abigail for giving me up to the office more often than they wanted.

I have been developing the exercises that would become this book through several years of teaching computer networking. Hundreds of students in my classes have completed similar exercises and their feedback has been invaluable in developing the text. I would like to thank each student who asked a new question, suggested a new exercise, or answered a question differently yet correctly.

I would like to specifically recognize some students by name: Niranjan Srinivasan, Chong-Suk Yoon, Dachao Wang, Nidthida Perm-Ajchariyawong, and Tingyan Yuan helped me assemble the first small set of formal exercises. Eric Kobelski and Scott Mead collected the wireless and FDDI traces used in this text. Steve Evanchik collected the SMTP and POP traces. Kandiah Mathavan, Eric Kobelski, Scott Mead, Jason Herne and Nate Dudek helped me to capture RIP and OSPF traces. Kandiah Mathavan, Todd Deshane, and Patricia Jablonski helped to capture EIGRP and BGP traces. Todd Deshane, Anthony Peltz, and Tim Fanelli provided me with access to several machines that they administered. Leslie Cherian helped me with the index.

Students in CS 454/554 at Clarkson University in the Spring 2004 semester provided excellent feedback on a beta version of this text. Patty Jablonski, in particular, made a detailed editing pass that was invaluable in fixing many errors. Eli Dow, Dalia Solomon, Corey Girard, Creighton Long, and Tim Fanelli also made excellent suggestions.

I would also like to thank the Ethereal developers for producing a tool that is ideal for hands-on exploration of computer networking and for releasing it open source.

Most importantly, thanks be unto God for his unspeakable gift (II Corinthians 9:15)!

Contents

Section 1: Getting Started

Introduction

Throughout this book, you will learn about the network protocols on which the Internet is based by examining traces of real network activity. To do this, we will use an open source network protocol analyzer called Ethereal. This section is designed to provide you with everything you need to get started.

We begin with an exercise that uses Ethereal to capture and examine a short trace taken on a network with very little activity. This exercise will introduce you to the basic features of Ethereal.

With the basics of Ethereal in place, we will move on to an overview of the layered protocol stack in the Internet. Later sections of the book focus on each layer in detail. However, an overview is essential for understanding the context in which each layer occurs.

The third exercise in this section examines a more complicated network trace containing interleaved threads of activity. It shows you how to use filters to identify and understand each individual thread of network activity.

Getting Started: Exercise **1.1**

Examining a Quiet
Network with Ethereal

INTRODUCTION

If you use network software like web browsers or e-mail clients, then you know they require a network connection to work properly. However, do you know what kind of messages they send over the Internet? For example, what does your computer say to a remote web server in order to retrieve a web page and how does your computer direct your e-mail to the person to whom you have addressed it?

You can examine the details of network conversations using a tool called a *network protocol analyzer*. A network protocol analyzer is a piece of software that can record each packet sent over the network and display them in a human-readable format. On a busy network, this can be a lot of information so network protocol analyzers typically provide summary statistics about all packets and allow users to filter out unwanted data or search for specific packets of interest.

Throughout this book, we are going to use an open source network protocol analyzer called Ethereal. This first chapter will give you a basic introduction to Ethereal. Once you have mastered the basics of Ethereal, we will be ready to use it as a tool for exploring the details of network protocols like HTTP, SMTP, TCP, UDP, IP and many more.

You will learn the most from each exercise if you install Ethereal on your local computer and follow along as you read. Ethereal is available for most platforms, including Windows, Mac, and Unix/Linux. We have also included the source code and some binaries on a companion CD. You can also install the latest version directly from the Ethereal web site, **http://www.ethereal.com**. The version on the CD will match the dialogs used in the book. If you upgrade to a later version, they may not.

In this first exercise, we will examine a packet trace captured from a "quiet network." We will show you how to capture your own traces (if you have permission to do so on your local network). We will also show you how to examine the details of each individual packet in the trace and how to view summary statistics about the entire trace.

CONFIGURATION

Each exercise in this book will begin by describing the network configuration in which the experiment is performed. This experiment was performed on a private home network. A single PC running Windows was connected to a cable modem router. Before beginning the experiment, all applications using the network (ex. web browsers, e-mail clients, etc) were closed.

Figure 1.1.1: Exercise Configuration

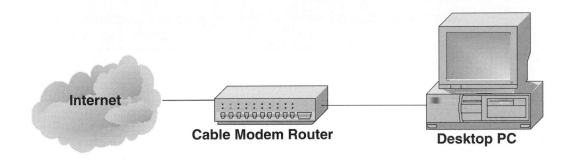

Internet

Cable Modem Router   **Desktop PC**

EXPERIMENT

We begin by starting Ethereal. To capture a trace, we choose Start from the Capture menu and use the Capture Options Dialog to specify desired aspects of the trace. In Figures 1.1.2 and 1.1.3 we show both the Capture Menu and the Capture Options Dialog.

Figure 1.1.2: Capture Menu

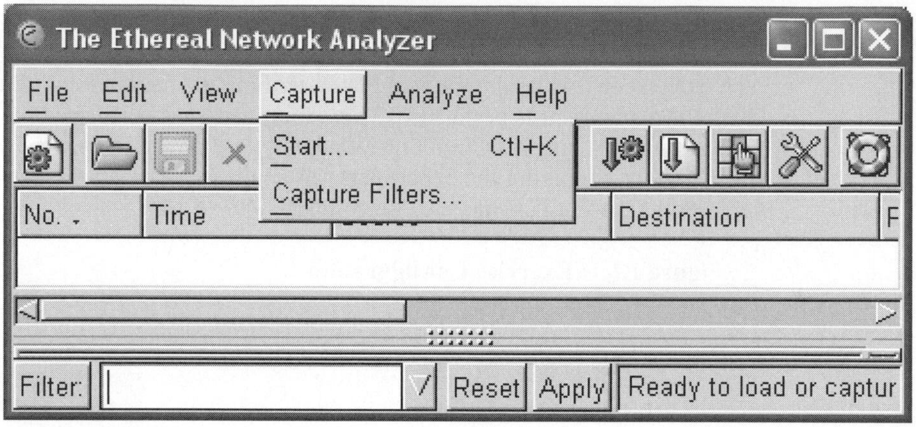

Figure 1.1.3: Capture Options Dialog

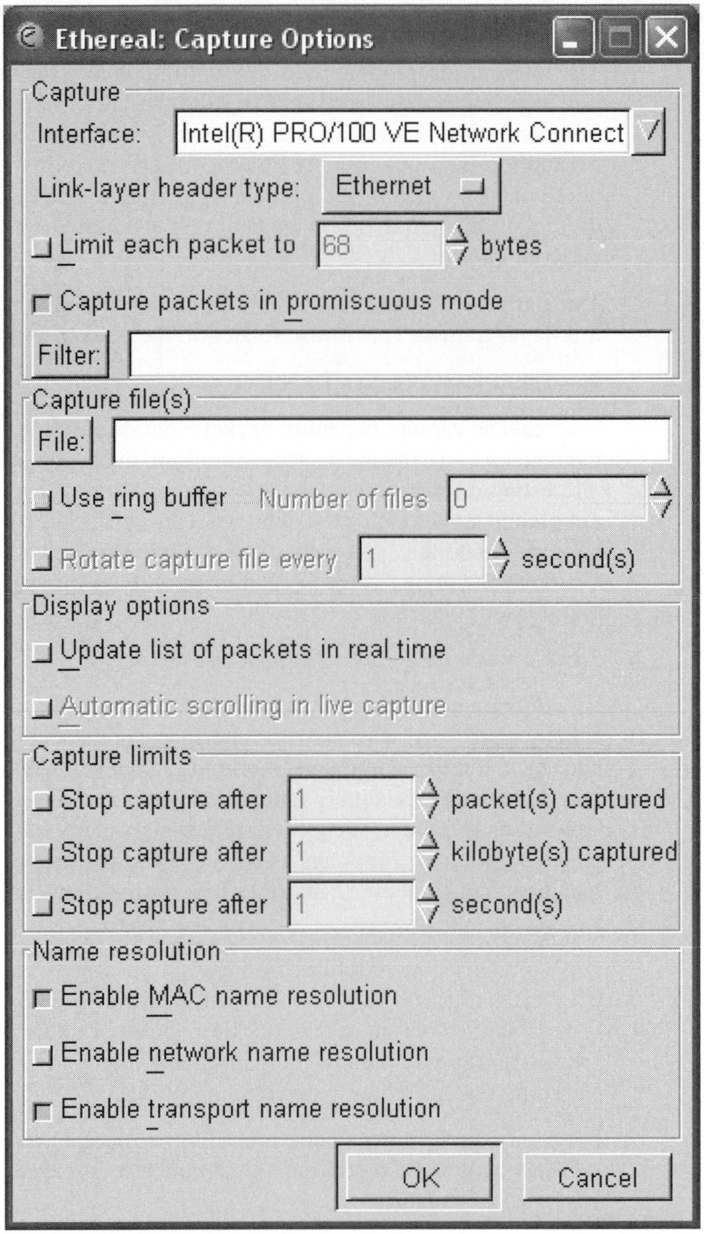

USING THE CAPTURE OPTIONS DIALOG

We aren't using all of the options available from the Capture Options Dialog for this exercise, but we provide a brief overview of each one.

1. **Interface and Link-layer Header Type**

The Interface drop-down list allows you to choose the interface for which you want a packet trace taken. For example, if your machine has both an Ethernet interface and a wireless interface, you must choose which interface to monitor. If you choose the Ethernet interface, only traffic sent over the wired connection will be recorded. If you start a capture and see no traffic or do not see the traffic you expect, then you may need to choose a different network interface.

The Link-layer Header Type Field represents how Ethereal will interpret the link-layer frames. This is also related to the type of interface.

2. **Limit Each Packet To N Bytes**

Ethereal can capture the entire packet – data and headers and all. Typically, the data takes up the most space, but often, the headers contain the most interesting information (source, destination, type of packets, etc.). If you are not planning to examine the data, you can save space by capturing only the headers. To do this, you compute the maximum length in bytes of the headers you are interested in examining and use this option to capture only that portion of each packet.

3. **Capture Packets In Promiscuous Mode**

If your computer is on a shared network segment, like a wireless LAN or an Ethernet hub, then your network interface can detect all packets, even those addressed to other computers. Normally, however, packets destined for other computers are simply ignored. If you place your network interface in "promiscuous mode," then it will report all packets even those not addressed to your computer. You need administrative privileges on a machine to put a network interface into promiscuous mode.

When you capture packets in promiscuous mode on a shared network, you may capture sensitive information being transmitted by others. Therefore, it is essential that you have the permission of the network administrator and preferably the consent of network users before capturing packets in promiscuous mode. Many companies and universities expressly prohibit capturing traces on their networks.

For each exercise in this book, we will provide you with captured traces that you can analyze. You are free to open the traces we have provided without any special privileges.

4. Filter

You can limit the amount of data captured by specifying a capture filter. Only packets matching the filter criteria will be recorded. For example, you could capture only packets sent to and from the IP address 192.168.0.1 with the following filter: `host 192.168.0.1`. Ethereal filters are quite powerful, but require learning a simple filter language.

In addition to capture filters, you can use a different language to specify display filters that limit the packets displayed while still recording all packets. For example, you can display only packets sent to and from IP address 192.168.0.1 with the following filter: `(ip.dst eq 192.168.0.1) || (ip.src eq 192.168.0.1`. You can use the same language to associate colors with various filters. This technique can be used to highlight some packets while still displaying all of them.

5. Capture Files

You can specify that the captured packets be saved directly to a file rather than saved in memory. If you choose "Use ring buffer," packets will be written into multiple files, switching files when each becomes full or after a specified number of seconds. These controls are important when capturing large or long running traces.

6. Display Options

By default, packets are not displayed as they are captured because when network activity is high it can be difficult for the display to keep up. You can choose to see the packets updated in real time and, if so, you can have the display scroll to the last captured packet automatically.

7. Capture Limits

You can stop the trace manually with the Stop button on the Capture Summary Screen. You can also use these options to request that the trace stop after a certain number of packets are captured, after the trace reaches a certain size, or after a specified amount of time.

8. Name Resolution

You can request that Ethereal translate various numbers in the packets into human readable names where possible. With MAC addresses translation enabled, Ethereal will translate a portion of this address into the Manufacturer's name. With network address translation enabled, Ethereal will attempt to translate the network address (an IP addresses such as 201.100.0.1) into a host name like www.foo.org. It does this by contacting the local DNS server and requesting a translation. This causes additional network traffic and can result in delays. With transport name resolution enabled, Ethereal will translate well-known port numbers into their corresponding protocols. For example, port 80 would be translated into http.

For this exercise, we specify our Ethernet interface and choose "Update list of packets in real time." We leave all other options set to their defaults, as shown in the Capture Option Dialog (Figure 1.1.3).

When we choose Ok, Ethereal begins to capture packets and a capture summary window appears. Each time a packet is transmitted over the Ethernet, it is added to the packet totals in the capture summary window. Since we choose "Update list of packets in real-time," each new packet is also added to the list of packets in the main window. To end the capture, we click stop in the Capture Summary Window. In this experiment, we capture 30 seconds of data.

Figure 1.1.4: Captured Packets Statistics

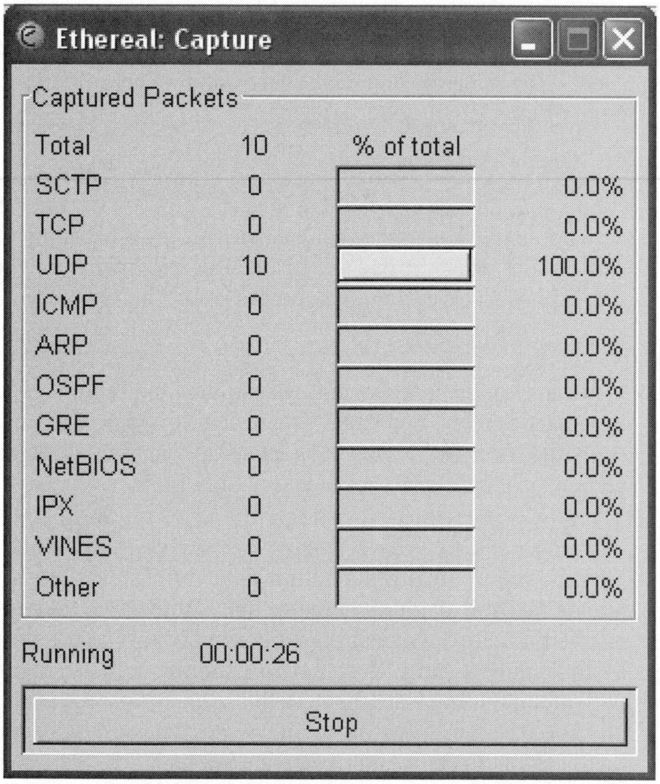

Ethereal: Capture			
Captured Packets			
Total	10	% of total	
SCTP	0		0.0%
TCP	0		0.0%
UDP	10		100.0%
ICMP	0		0.0%
ARP	0		0.0%
OSPF	0		0.0%
GRE	0		0.0%
NetBIOS	0		0.0%
IPX	0		0.0%
VINES	0		0.0%
Other	0		0.0%
Running	00:00:26		
Stop			

EXAMINING A SHORT TRACE

With our capture complete, we save the resulting trace to the file **quietNetwork.cap** (Save from the File menu). You can open this same file from the accompanying CD and follow along.

In this experiment, we are looking at the network traffic that remains after we close all applications we expect to be using the network. Besides a good exercise for exploring Ethereal, this is an important type of capture for network administrators. An otherwise quiet network is an ideal place to look for suspicious activity. For example, a computer infected with a computer virus may send packets to attack other computers without the knowledge of the computer's owner.

We capture only 21 packets in 30 seconds. A busy network could have hundreds in that same time. In the upper pane of the main window, we see a list of the 21 packets we captured. Each packet is given a number in the trace itself and several important details are displayed including the time the packet was sent (relative to the time of the first packet in the trace), the address of the machine that sent the packet (source), the address to which the packet was sent (destination), the protocol (or language being spoken in the payload of the packet), and finally some information about the contents of the packet.

Figure 1.1.5: Quiet Network Capture

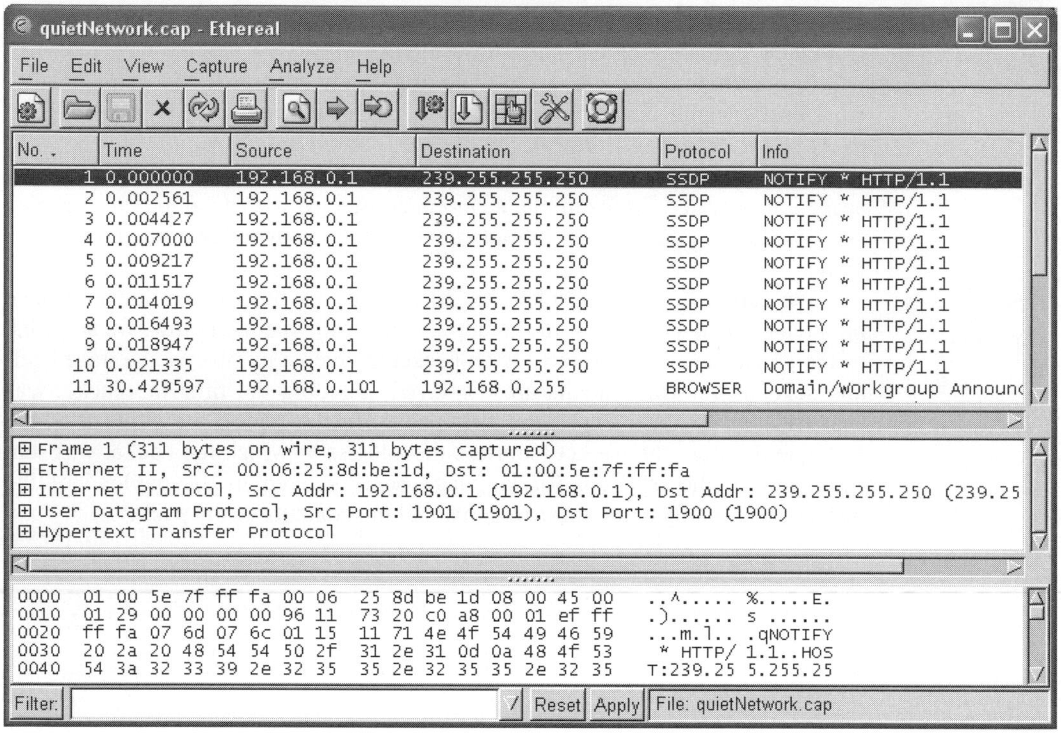

```
quietNetwork.cap - Ethereal                                          _ □ ☒

 File  Edit  View  Capture  Analyze  Help

 [⚙] [📁] [💾] [✖] [↻] [🖨] [🔍] [➡] [⇥]  [📲] [⬇] [⊞] [✂] [◎]

No. .   Time       Source          Destination        Protocol  Info
    1 0.000000    192.168.0.1     239.255.255.250     SSDP      NOTIFY * HTTP/1.1
    2 0.002561    192.168.0.1     239.255.255.250     SSDP      NOTIFY * HTTP/1.1
    3 0.004427    192.168.0.1     239.255.255.250     SSDP      NOTIFY * HTTP/1.1
    4 0.007000    192.168.0.1     239.255.255.250     SSDP      NOTIFY * HTTP/1.1
    5 0.009217    192.168.0.1     239.255.255.250     SSDP      NOTIFY * HTTP/1.1
    6 0.011517    192.168.0.1     239.255.255.250     SSDP      NOTIFY * HTTP/1.1
    7 0.014019    192.168.0.1     239.255.255.250     SSDP      NOTIFY * HTTP/1.1
    8 0.016493    192.168.0.1     239.255.255.250     SSDP      NOTIFY * HTTP/1.1
    9 0.018947    192.168.0.1     239.255.255.250     SSDP      NOTIFY * HTTP/1.1
   10 0.021335    192.168.0.1     239.255.255.250     SSDP      NOTIFY * HTTP/1.1
   11 30.429597   192.168.0.101   192.168.0.255       BROWSER   Domain/Workgroup Announc

⊞ Frame 1 (311 bytes on wire, 311 bytes captured)
⊞ Ethernet II, Src: 00:06:25:8d:be:1d, Dst: 01:00:5e:7f:ff:fa
⊞ Internet Protocol, Src Addr: 192.168.0.1 (192.168.0.1), Dst Addr: 239.255.255.250 (239.25
⊞ User Datagram Protocol, Src Port: 1901 (1901), Dst Port: 1900 (1900)
⊞ Hypertext Transfer Protocol

0000  01 00 5e 7f ff fa 00 06  25 8d be 1d 08 00 45 00   ..^..... %.....E.
0010  01 29 00 00 00 00 96 11  73 20 c0 a8 00 01 ef ff   .)...... s ......
0020  ff fa 07 6d 07 6c 01 15  11 71 4e 4f 54 49 46 59   ...m.l.. .qNOTIFY
0030  20 2a 20 48 54 54 50 2f  31 2e 31 0d 0a 48 4f 53    * HTTP/ 1.1..HOS
0040  54 3a 32 33 39 2e 32 35  35 2e 32 35 35 2e 32 35   T:239.25 5.255.25

Filter:                                              / Reset Apply  File: quietNetwork.cap
```

LIST, PROTOCOL, AND RAW PANES

Ethereal can be used to further dissect each packet. When a packet is highlighted in the upper pane of the main window, the two lower panes fill with greater detail about the chosen packet. We will call the top pane the *trace list pane* or simple the *list pane*. We will call the middle pane the *protocol layer pane* or simply the *protocol pane*. We will call the bottom pane the *raw packet pane* or simply the *raw pane*.

To illustrate the function of these three panes, we highlight the first packet in the list pane. As we do so, the protocol pane and the raw pane fill with details of the first packet.

The protocol pane shows each protocol layer of the selected packet: the physical layer frame, the Ethernet frame and its headers, the Internet Protocol (IP) datagram and its headers, the User Datagram Protocol (UDP) datagram and its headers, and finally the Hypertext Transfer Protocol (HTTP) notify message.

For each protocol, you can expand the information even further. For example, if you expand the Internet Protocol Layer, you can see each field in the IP header including the version, the header length, the differentiated services field etc.

Figure 1.1.6: The Protocol Pane

```
⊞ Frame 1 (311 bytes on wire, 311 bytes captured)
⊞ Ethernet II, Src: 00:06:25:8d:be:1d, Dst: 01:00:5e:7f:ff:fa
⊟ Internet Protocol, Src Addr: 192.168.0.1 (192.168.0.1), Dst Addr: 239.255.255.250 (239.255.255.250)
     version: 4
     Header length: 20 bytes
   ⊞ Differentiated Services Field: 0x00 (DSCP 0x00: Default; ECN: 0x00)
     Total Length: 297
     Identification: 0x0000 (0)
   ⊞ Flags: 0x00
     Fragment offset: 0
     Time to live: 150
     Protocol: UDP (0x11)
     Header checksum: 0x7320 (correct)
     Source: 192.168.0.1 (192.168.0.1)
     Destination: 239.255.255.250 (239.255.255.250)
⊞ User Datagram Protocol, Src Port: 1901 (1901), Dst Port: 1900 (1900)
⊞ Hypertext Transfer Protocol
```

The raw pane shows each byte of the data contained in the packet. This allows you to look at the data transmitted without interpretation. It is shown in hex on the left and in ASCII on the right.

Notice that when we select the Internet Protocol layer in the protocol pane, the IP header section of the raw packet is highlighted in the raw pane. In this case, "45 00 01 29 00 00 00 00 96 11 73 20 c0 a8 00 01 ef ff ff fa" translates into all the Internet Protocol information displayed in the protocol pane. At the very least, this level of detail can help you appreciate the GUI display capabilities of Ethereal!

Figure 1.1.7: The Raw Pane

```
0000    01 00 5e 7f ff fa 00 06   25 8d be 1d 08 00 45 00    ..^..... %.....E.
0010    01 29 00 00 00 00 96 11   73 20 c0 a8 00 01 ef ff    .)...... s ......
0020    ff fa 07 6d 07 6c 01 15   11 71 4e 4f 54 49 46 59    ...m.l.. .qNOTIFY
0030    20 2a 20 48 54 54 50 2f   31 2e 31 0d 0a 48 4f 53     * HTTP/ 1.1..HOS
0040    54 3a 32 33 39 2e 32 35   35 2e 32 35 35 2e 32 35    T:239.25 5.255.25
0050    30 3a 31 39 30 30 0d 0a   43 61 63 68 65 2d 43 6f    0:1900.. Cache-Co
0060    6e 74 72 6f 6c 3a 6d 61   78 2d 61 67 65 3d 31 32    ntrol:ma x-age=12
0070    30 0d 0a 4c 6f 63 61 74   69 6f 6e 3a 68 74 74 70    0..Locat ion:http
0080    3a 2f 2f 31 39 32 2e 31   36 38 2e 30 2e 31 3a 35    ://192.1 68.0.1:5
0090    36 37 38 2f 72 6f 6f 74   44 65 73 63 2e 78 6d 6c    678/root Desc.xml
00a0    0d 0a 4e 54 3a 75 75 69   64 3a 75 70 6e 70 2d 49    ..NT:uui d:upnp-I
00b0    6e 74 65 72 6e 65 74 47   61 74 65 77 61 79 44 65    nternetG atewayDe
00c0    76 69 63 65 2d 31 5f 30   2d 30 30 39 30 61 32 37    vice-1_0 -0090a27
00d0    37 37 37 37 37 0d 0a 4e   54 53 3a 73 73 64 70 3a    77777..N TS:ssdp:
00e0    61 6c 69 76 65 0d 0a 53   65 72 76 65 72 3a 4e 54    alive..S erver:NT
00f0    2f 35 2e 30 20 55 50 6e   50 2f 31 2e 30 0d 0a 55    /5.0 UPn P/1.0..U
```

TRACE SUMMARY STATISTICS

Now, let's return to the list pane and examine the 21 packets we captured at a higher level.

Twenty of the packets are from source IP address, 192.168.0.1 to destination IP address 239.255.255.250. These 20 packets all list SSDP or the Simple Service Discovery Protocol as their protocol. SSDP is a protocol used for network devices to discover one another. In this case, they are broadcast by the Linksys cable modem router (239.255.255.250 is actually a multicast address). Notice that the cable modem router actually sent 2 groups of 10 identical messages approximately 30 seconds apart (from the timestamps, you can see 10 packets sent from time 0 to time 0.021 and 10 packets sent from time 30.99 to 31.02). If you look inside the Hypertext Transfer Protocol section of one of these packets, you will see that it is announcing it is an available Internet Gateway Device.

We have discussed the 20 SSDP packets in the **quietNetwork.cap** trace. The one remaining packet, packet 11, is sent from IP address 192.168.0.101 to the broadcast address, 192.168.0.255. 192.168.0.101 is the address of the desktop machine. It is announcing its membership in the Domain/workgroup MSHOME.

You can group the 20 packets together by clicking on the "Protocol" heading in the list pane. This sorts the list of packets by protocol. You can click on any of the headings to request a different sort order.

These two types of announcements are just two examples of the type of network activity that occurs even when you are not aware that your computer is using the network. You might be surprised to learn about all the different types of activity on your network that you did not even know existed!

You can view a summary of the trace by choosing Summary from the Analyze menu. It will report a number of useful statistics like the total number of bytes of traffic, the traffic rate, and the average packet size. You may also want to experiment with some of the other analysis tools in the Analyze menu including the Protocol Hierarchy Statistics and the Statistics menu.

Figure 1.1.8: Trace Summary Statistics

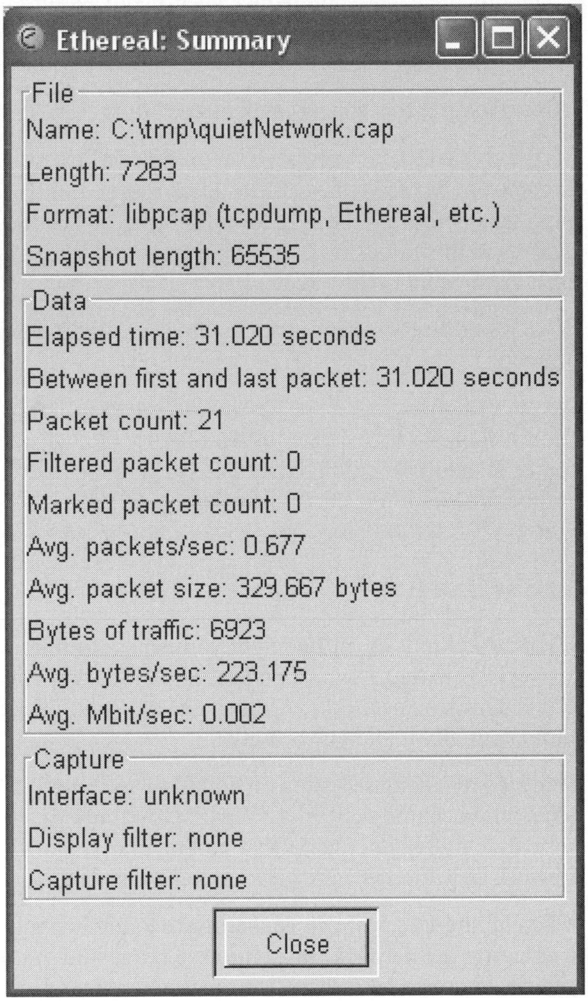

```
Ethereal: Summary                    [_][□][X]

 File
 Name: C:\tmp\quietNetwork.cap
 Length: 7283
 Format: libpcap (tcpdump, Ethereal, etc.)
 Snapshot length: 65535

 Data
 Elapsed time: 31.020 seconds
 Between first and last packet: 31.020 seconds
 Packet count: 21
 Filtered packet count: 0
 Marked packet count: 0
 Avg. packets/sec: 0.677
 Avg. packet size: 329.667 bytes
 Bytes of traffic: 6923
 Avg. bytes/sec: 223.175
 Avg. Mbit/sec: 0.002

 Capture
 Interface: unknown
 Display filter: none
 Capture filter: none

               [  Close  ]
```

QUESTIONS

Answer the following questions about the file **quietNetwork_15 minutes.cap**

1. How many seconds does Ethereal report the trace to be? What are two different ways to determine this?

2. When this trace was captured we specified a capture limit of 15 minutes. Give a reasonable explanation for the trace to report less than 15 minutes.

3. How many packets appear in this trace?

4. In **quietNetwork.cap**, we saw 2 types of packets SSDP announcements from the cable modem router and Domain/Workgroup announcement from the Windows PC. Do you see these same types of packets in this trace? If so, give the packet number of the first one of each that occurs in the trace.

5. What other protocols appear in the trace? (Hint: try sorting by protocol.)

6. In **quietNetwork.cap**, we saw only two different source IP addresses, 192.168.0.1 and 192.168.0.101. Do we see any additional source IP addresses in this trace? If so, give the address and the packet number at which it occurs.

DISCUSSION AND INVESTIGATION

1. What other kinds of traffic might you expect to find on a "quiet network" (i.e. one in which no user is deliberately running an application that is using the network)? Consider both useful background activity and potentially malicious activity?

2. Many system administrators do not allow users to run programs like Ethereal on shared networks. Why do you think this is? Investigate the policies for all the networks that you regularly use. Can you find a network on which you are allowed to take traces?

3. When taking traces, it can be important to understand with whom you are sharing the network. In addition to requesting permission for tracing, knowing who shares your network can help you understand the traffic that you capture and diagnose network performance problems. Make a diagram showing one or more of the local networks you use regularly. How many machines are present on the local network? Are the connections wireless or wired? What type of device do they connect to (hub, switch)?

4. If you have permission, take a trace on a local network. How many source IP addresses and destination IP addresses do you see? Can you identify each machine? Is the network you are tracing "quiet"? Make a list of questions (5–10) you have about the traffic. You could revisit periodically as you complete more exercises in this book.

5. Investigate Snort, an excellent open source network intrusion detection system (**http://www.snort.org**). You can use Snort to monitor your local network for suspicious traffic patterns. Snort users write rules that specify what suspicious traffic is using the same type of information captured by Ethereal (source and destination IP address, protocol, etc.) From what you have learned in this exercise, discuss how Snort might work and propose some simple rules that might detect malicious activity.

RESOURCES

- Ethereal Documentation, **http://www.ethereal .com**
- SSDP, **http://www.upnp.org/download/draft_cai_ssdp_v1_03.txt**
- Snort, **http://www.snort.org**
- Web search: Network Protocol Analyzers

Getting Started: Exercise 1.2

Protocol Layering

INTRODUCTION

Computer communication, much like human communication, relies on mutually agreed upon patterns of interaction called *protocols*. A protocol defines the format, content, and order of messages used by communicating entities to accomplish a specified task. For example, the Hypertext Transfer Protocol or HTTP defines the set of messages exchanged between a web browser and a web server when transmitting a web page.

Computer communication is accomplished with a set of protocol layers, each layer accomplishing a portion of the required tasks. For example, in the case of a web browser and web server, HTTP is not the only protocol required. HTTP relies on the Transmission Control Protocol or TCP to ensure reliable delivery of the web page despite data loss that might occur in the network. In turn, TCP relies on the Internet Protocol or IP to route the packet through the network from the machine running the web browser to the machine running the web server.

Together, these protocol layers form the *network protocol stack*. The International Organization for Standardization (ISO) defined a standard seven-layer protocol stack called the Open Systems Interconnection (OSI) model. In this model, each layer provides a service to the layer above it and relies only on the layer below it. Logically, each layer interacts with its peer layer on the remote computer through an agreed upon protocol. The protocol stack in the Internet operates in a similar way, but uses only four of the seven layers. These four layers: application, transport, network, and link layer are described in detail next.

Figure 1.2.1: Layered Protocol Stacks

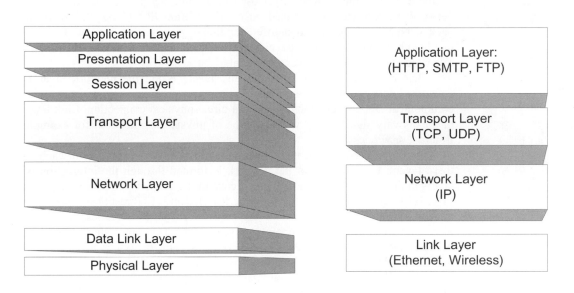

a) OSI Seven Layer Model   b)Internet Protocol Stack

Application layer protocols arc at the top of the stack. As their name suggests, they are most closely related to the function of the network application. For example, if the application is web browsing then the application layer protocol directly supports the retrieval of web pages, and if the application is an e-mail client then the application layer protocol directly supports the transmission of e-mail. Application layer protocols are not concerned with the specific data transferred (e.g. the contents of a web page or the contents of an e-mail). Instead, they provide a framework for exchanging any user-defined data.

Below the application layer is the transport layer. Transport layer protocols are not directly related to the application's functionality. Rather, they are concerned with transporting generic application data between applications running on different machines in the network. From the perspective of the transport layer protocol, it does not matter what application layer protocol the applications are exchanging. The most common transport layer protocols are the Transmission Control Protocol (TCP) and the User Datagram Protocol (UDP). TCP provides reliable, in-order data delivery regardless of any loss or reordering of data in the network. UDP, on the other hand, is an unreliable transport protocol.

Below the transport layer is the network layer. Network layer protocols are concerned with delivering data from one machine in the network to another. End-to-end delivery typically involves many intermediate transmissions or "hops" between the source machine and the destination machine. The Internet Protocol or IP is the network layer used in the Internet. It provides best effort delivery between endpoints based on the destination IP address placed in the packet. Network protocols that offer additional guarantees (in order delivery, bandwidth guarantees, etc.) have been designed, but the success of IP has relegated them to specialized environments.

Below the network layer is the link layer. While the network layer is concerned with end-to-end data delivery, link layer protocols are concerned with communication between machines with a direct physical connection. Link layer protocols vary significantly with the type of physical connection, for example Ethernet or wireless.

On a typical computer, there are entities that "speak" protocols in each of these layers. Each packet on the network is formed through the interaction of layers in the protocol stack. For a specific example, when a web server responds to an HTTP get request over the network, it forms an HTTP response containing a valid HTTP response code and the actual web page. It passes this entire message to TCP layer in the operating system. The TCP layer views the entire message including the HTTP response codes as data. It divides this data into segments, adding a TCP header to each one and passes each segment to the IP layer. The IP layer treats each segment including the TCP headers as data. It divides this data into datagrams and adds an IP header to each one and passes it to the device driver of the device used to transmit the data. This device driver will treat the IP datagram as data, add its own headers and transmit the final frame with the physical device. This final packet is what we see captured by a network protocol analyzer.

In this exercise, we will explore the concept of the protocol layering. We will practice decomposing each packet into its various protocol layers and isolate headers from the application layer, transport layer, network layer, and link layer. In future exercises, we will concentrate on the details of specific protocols. Most protocols used in the Internet are open protocols, meaning that the full specification is available to anyone as opposed to proprietary protocols for which the definitions are kept secret. To learn the details of Internet protocols, one consults a set of documents called *Requests For Comments* or RFCs. For example, the Transmission Control Protocol (TCP) is defined in RFC 793.

Link-layer standards, like the Ethernet standard, are published by Institute of Electrical and Electronics Engineers (IEEE). For example, IEEE 802.3 is the "CSMA/CD Access Method and Physical Layer Specification" on which Ethernet is based. Unlike RFCs, however, these documents must be purchased. They are publicly available in the sense that anyone can purchase them, but they are not freely available. At the time of this writing, IEEE is making older versions of some of the 802 standard documents available for free download through a program called GetIEEE802. The GetIEE802 website states that this is a pilot program and may be discontinued if supported by company sponsors.

In this exercise, we focus on identifying the headers from various protocol layers found in captured packets. We will explore each layer in detail in sections throughout the book.

CONFIGURATION

This experiment was performed on a private home network. A single PC running Windows was connected to a cable modem router. On the PC, a Mozilla web browser was started.

Figure 1.2.2: Exercise Configuration

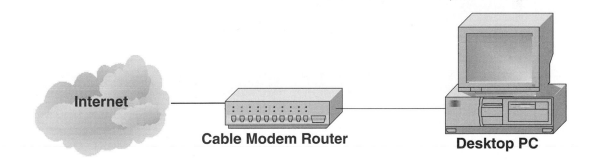

Internet — **Cable Modem Router** — **Desktop PC**

EXPERIMENT

We started Ethereal on the PC and began capturing a trace. In the web browser, we opened the URL advertised by the cable modem router itself (http://192.168.0.1:5678/rootDesc.xml). We saved this trace in the file **simpleHttp.cap**. You should open this file found on the accompanying CD and follow along.

PROTOCOL HIERARCHY STATISTICS

This trace contains only 26 packets, but it has examples of several important protocols. Begin by selecting the Protocol Hierarchy Statistics from the Analyze menu. It lists all the protocols used in a packet in the order in which they occur in the protocol stack. The columns "Packets" and "Bytes" list information for all packets in which the specified protocol occurs. The columns "End Packets" and "End Bytes" reflect only those packets in which the specified protocol is the last (i.e. most deeply nested) protocol in the packet.

It shows that 100% of the frames captured are Ethernet frames at the link layer and use the Internet Protocol (IP) at the network layer. This is not surprising as we are capturing on an Ethernet interface and IP is the standard network layer protocol in the Internet. At the transport layer, we see the packets divided between TCP and UDP. All UDP packets contain the application layer protocol HTTP. The TCP packets are further decomposed into packets that contain actual data. Interestingly, the TCP data is not recognized as HTTP even though it is. I suspect this is because a nonstandard port number 5678 was used instead of the typical HTTP port 80.

Figure 1.2.3: Protocol Hierarchy Statistics

Protocol	% Packets	Packets	Bytes	End Packets	End Bytes
⊟ Frame	100.00%	26	8238	0	0
⊟ Ethernet	100.00%	26	8238	0	0
⊟ Internet Protocol	100.00%	26	8238	0	0
⊟ Transmission Control Protocol	61.54%	16	4902	10	566
Data	23.08%	6	4336	6	4336
⊟ User Datagram Protocol	38.46%	10	3336	0	0
Hypertext Transfer Protocol	38.46%	10	3336	10	3336

Ethereal: Protocol Hierarchy Statistics — Close

TCP CONNECTION

Examine the TCP connection shown in packets 1 through 16. The purpose of this connection to transfer the XML page from the web server on the Linksys cable modem router to the web browser on the PC. Many connection devices like routers run a web server that allows an administrator to configure and manage the device. In this case, rootDesc.xml is a file describing itself as a Universal Plug and Play device offering particular services.

Interestingly, the file rootDesc.xml is only 3459 bytes in size while the Protocol Hierarchy Statistics report 4902 bytes transferred over the connection. As we could see from the Protocol Hierarchy Statistics, 10 of the 16 packets contain no data. These ten packets are required by the TCP protocol to setup and maintain the connection and account for 566 bytes. (We will study these portions of TCP in Section 3.) The Data is reported as 4336 bytes. This Data is both the actual rootDesc.xml file and the HTTP headers. In total, the overhead of all protocol layers is 1443 bytes or 41.1% of the actual file transferred. This is a good illustration of the overhead associated with the protocol stack.

Not surprisingly, the packets that have no data are much smaller than those with data. For each packet, we can note the frame size in the protocol pane. Packets without data are between 54 and 62 bytes. Packets with data are between 75 and 1200 bytes.

If we examine only the six packets with data (4,5,6,8, 9, and 11), we see that the first packet is from the PC with the web browser. It is the client and it is making an HTTP request of the web server. The next packet contains the HTTP headers of the server's response, and the final four contain the actual rootDesc.xml file. If you examine the Data section of these packets, you can see the contents of the HTTP conversation and the actual file transferred. For example, below we show the data section of packet 11. If you compare this to the end of the file itself, you will see the same text.

Figure 1.2.4: Simple HTTP Connection

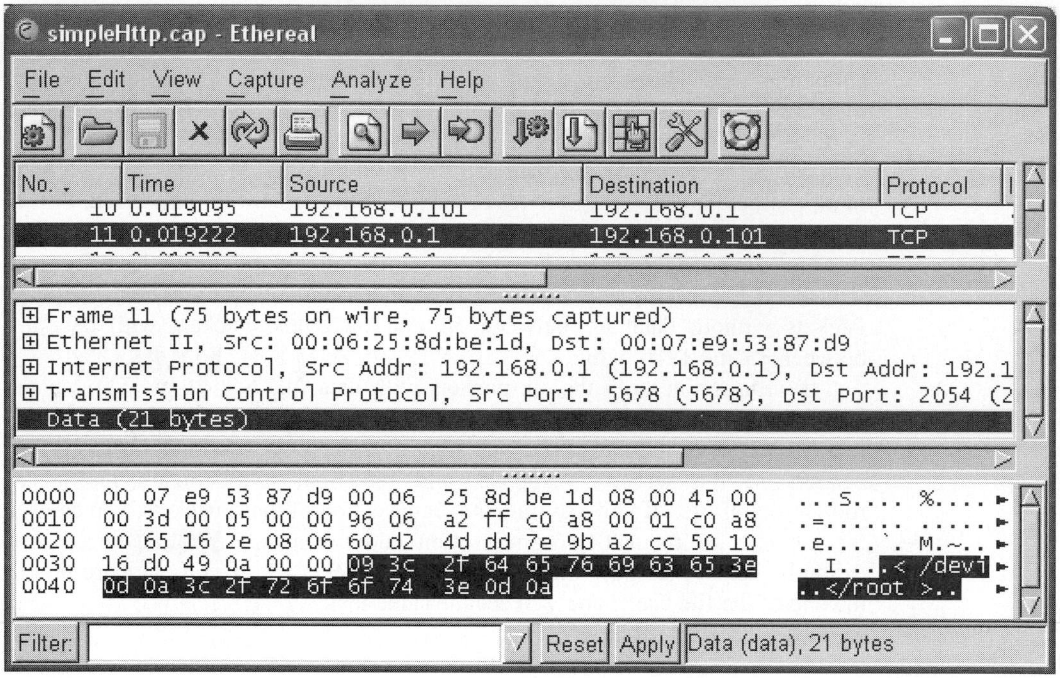

```
 simpleHttp.cap - Ethereal                                    _ □ X

 File   Edit   View   Capture   Analyze   Help

 [icons toolbar]

 No.    Time          Source              Destination         Protocol
   10  0.019095      192.168.0.101       192.168.0.1         TCP
   11  0.019222      192.168.0.1         192.168.0.101       TCP
   12  0.019788      192.168.0.1         192.168.0.101       ---

 ⊞ Frame 11 (75 bytes on wire, 75 bytes captured)
 ⊞ Ethernet II, Src: 00:06:25:8d:be:1d, Dst: 00:07:e9:53:87:d9
 ⊞ Internet Protocol, Src Addr: 192.168.0.1 (192.168.0.1), Dst Addr: 192.1
 ⊞ Transmission Control Protocol, Src Port: 5678 (5678), Dst Port: 2054 (2
   Data (21 bytes)

 0000  00 07 e9 53 87 d9 00 06  25 8d be 1d 08 00 45 00   ...S.... %....
 0010  00 3d 00 05 00 00 96 06  a2 ff c0 a8 00 01 c0 a8   .=...... ....
 0020  00 65 16 2e 08 06 60 d2  4d dd 7e 9b a2 cc 50 10   .e....`. M.~..
 0030  16 d0 49 0a 00 00 09 3c  2f 64 65 76 69 63 65 3e   ..I....< /devi
 0040  0d 0a 3c 2f 72 6f 6f 74  3e 0d 0a                  ..</root >..

 Filter:                                    √  Reset Apply Data (data), 21 bytes
```

FRAME LAYER

Now let's open each of the other protocol layers of packet 11 beginning with the "Frame" layer. This represents the entire packet as it appears on the wire. Notice that when the Frame layer is selected in the protocol pane, the entire packet is highlighted in the raw pane. Each of the pairs in the highlighted section represents one byte. For example, the first three bytes are "00 07 e9." If you count them, there are indeed 75 highlighted pairs. In the Frame layer, Ethereal reports the actual capture time, the time delta relative to the first packet and the previous packet, the frame number, the packet length, and the capture length. The packet length and capture length are the same unless "Limit each packet to X bytes" was chosen in the capture options.

Figure 1.2.5: Frame Length

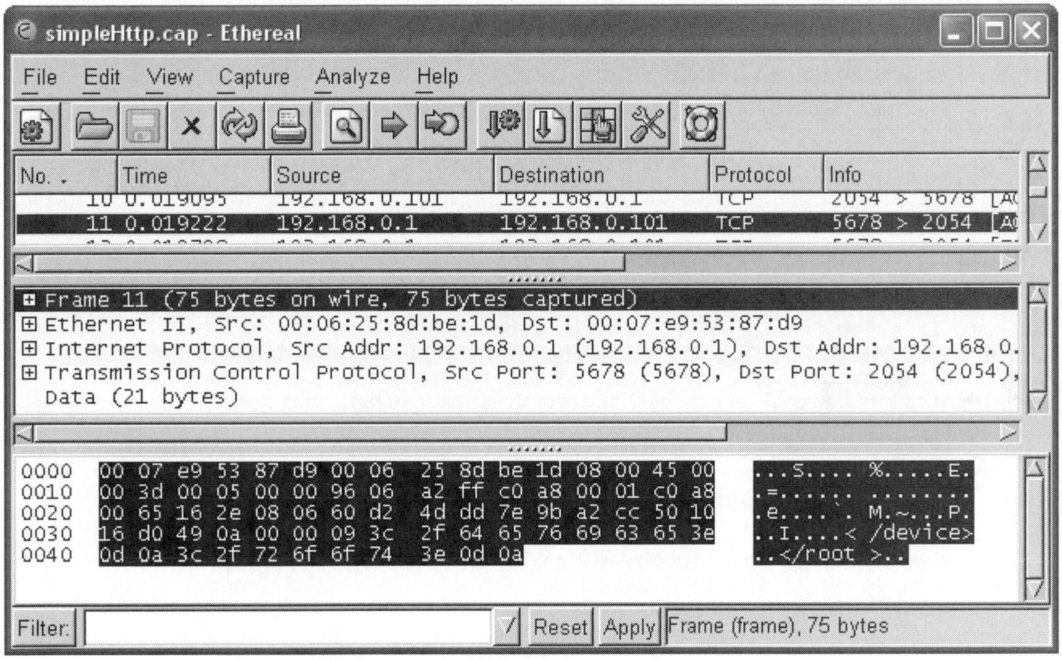

ETHERNET LAYER

Next, select the Ethernet layer for packet 11 in the protocol pane. The Ethernet header as with many protocol headers is specified as a sequence of bit fields rather than as text fields. This makes the ASCII section of the raw pane relatively useless. However, compare the contents of the protocol pane to the highlighted data. Notice that the first 6 pairs (00 07 e9 53 87 d9) match the Destination address and that the second 6 pairs (00 06 25 8d be 1d) match the Source address.

Finally the type (08 00) indicates that the data in the Ethernet frame should be passed to an entity on the destination that is registered to speak IP (i.e. the IP layer in the operating system). It is this type that allows Ethernet to be used with multiple network layer protocols if desired. When the type is 0x0800, it will be passed to the IP layer, and when the type is another value it will be passed to a different layer.

The Ethernet header occupies 14 bytes, 6 bytes for each address and 2 bytes for the type. We can see this both because it is reported in the lower right corner, and because there are 14 highlighted pairs in the raw pane. The other 61 bytes of the packet including the IP and TCP headers are the data of the Ethernet frame.

Figure 1.2.6: Ethernet Header

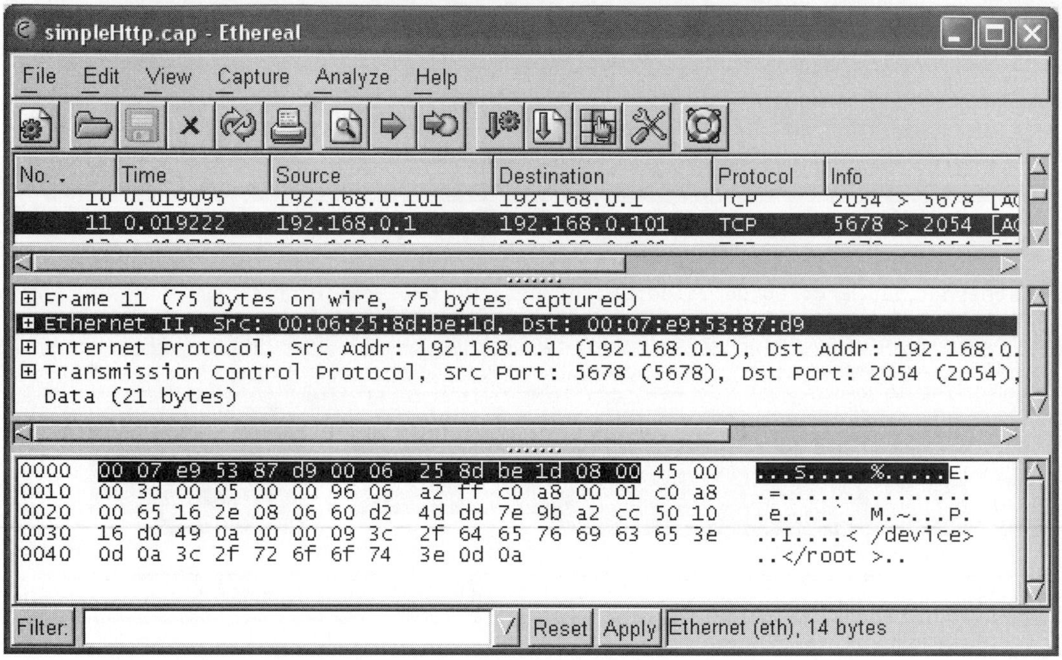

In some cases, there is an Ethernet trailer in addition to a header. You can see an example of this in packet 2.

You can highlight each element of the Ethernet header separately. When you do, it displays its size in the lower right. It also shows a name (e.g. eth.src) that can be used to write display filters. For example, we could display only packets sent to 00:07:e9:53:87:d9 with the following filter: `eth.src eq 00:07:e9:53:87:d9`. You can find more information on capture and display filters in Exercise 1.3.

Figure 1.2.7: Simple Filter

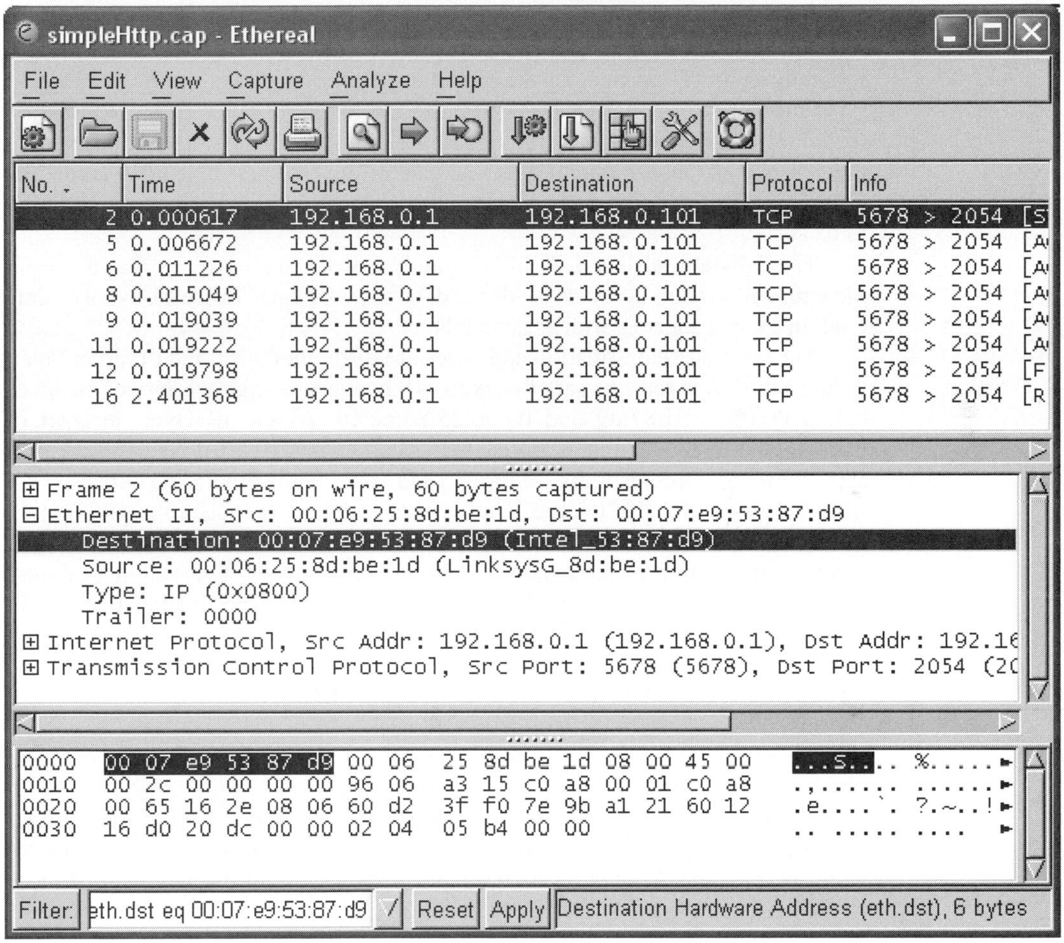

```
simpleHttp.cap - Ethereal                                    [_][□][X]

File   Edit   View   Capture   Analyze   Help

[toolbar icons]

No. .    Time         Source            Destination       Protocol  Info
     2 0.000617   192.168.0.1      192.168.0.101     TCP      5678 > 2054 [S
     5 0.006672   192.168.0.1      192.168.0.101     TCP      5678 > 2054 [A
     6 0.011226   192.168.0.1      192.168.0.101     TCP      5678 > 2054 [A
     8 0.015049   192.168.0.1      192.168.0.101     TCP      5678 > 2054 [A
     9 0.019039   192.168.0.1      192.168.0.101     TCP      5678 > 2054 [A
    11 0.019222   192.168.0.1      192.168.0.101     TCP      5678 > 2054 [A
    12 0.019798   192.168.0.1      192.168.0.101     TCP      5678 > 2054 [F
    16 2.401368   192.168.0.1      192.168.0.101     TCP      5678 > 2054 [R

⊞ Frame 2 (60 bytes on wire, 60 bytes captured)
⊟ Ethernet II, Src: 00:06:25:8d:be:1d, Dst: 00:07:e9:53:87:d9
    Destination: 00:07:e9:53:87:d9 (Intel_53:87:d9)
    Source: 00:06:25:8d:be:1d (LinksysG_8d:be:1d)
    Type: IP (0x0800)
    Trailer: 0000
⊞ Internet Protocol, Src Addr: 192.168.0.1 (192.168.0.1), Dst Addr: 192.16
⊞ Transmission Control Protocol, Src Port: 5678 (5678), Dst Port: 2054 (20

0000  00 07 e9 53 87 d9 00 06  25 8d be 1d 08 00 45 00   ...S... %.....
0010  00 2c 00 00 00 00 96 06  a3 15 c0 a8 00 01 c0 a8   .,.....  ........
0020  00 65 16 2e 08 06 60 d2  3f f0 7e 9b a1 21 60 12   .e....`. ?.~..!
0030  16 d0 20 dc 00 00 02 04  05 b4 00 00               .. ..... ....

Filter: eth.dst eq 00:07:e9:53:87:d9  √  Reset  Apply  Destination Hardware Address (eth.dst), 6 bytes
```

INTERNET PROTOCOL LAYER

Next, select the Internet Protocol layer for packet 11 in the protocol pane. The IP header is 20 bytes – 1 byte for version number, 1 byte for header length, 1 byte for the differentiated services field, 2 bytes for total length, 2 bytes for identification, 1 byte for flags, 2 bytes for a fragment offset, 1 byte for the "time to live" field, 1 byte for protocol, 2 bytes for a checksum of the header, and four bytes each for the source and destination addresses. We will discuss each of the elements of the IP header in later exercises, but there are a few fields worth pointing out now.

The 1-byte header length field is provided because the IP header is variable length. For all packets in this trace however it is always 20 bytes.

The 1-byte protocol field is set to 0x06 for TCP. This serves the same function as the Type field in the Ethernet header. It allows multiple transport layer protocols to be used with IP because it tells the IP layer on the destination machine which entity to pass the remainder of the packet on to after processing the IP headers. Choose one of the UDP packets (e.g. packet 17) and examine the protocol field in the IP header. You will see that for UDP the protocol field is set to 0x11.

The 2-byte total length field accurately reflects the 61 bytes that make up the entire IP packet, 20 bytes header and 41 bytes of data. These 41 bytes of data contain TCP headers as well as actual data.

The source and destination addresses are different than at the Ethernet layer. At the Ethernet layer, this set of packets is a conversation between two machines called 00:07:e9:53:87:d9 and 00:06:25:8d:be:1d. At the IP layer, this set of packets is a conversation between two Internet hosts called 192.168.0.1 and 192.168.0.101. Interestingly, both IP addresses and Ethernet addresses are intended to be globally unique. The Ethernet address reflects a unique number given to the network interface hardware by the manufacturer. The IP address reflects the position of the machine in the global Internet. The Ethernet address does not change unless you replace the physical device. The IP address however will change if the computer is moved to a different location in the Internet.

TRANSPORT CONTROL PROTOCOL LAYER

Finally, select the Transport Control Protocol layer for packet 11 in the protocol pane. The TCP header is 20 bytes (like the IP header) including 2 bytes each for source and destination port number, 4 bytes for sequence number, 4 bytes for an acknowledgment number, 1 byte for header length, 1 byte for flags, 2 bytes for window size, and 2 bytes for a checksum. Again we will discuss each of these fields in detail in later exercises, but will highlight a few fields in this exercise. The "next sequence number" field displayed by Ethereal is not actually contained in the TCP header but rather can be computed from the sequence number and the length fields.

The 1-byte header length field is included because the TCP header is variable in size like the IP header. It is variations in the size of the TCP header that cause the overall variation in size of those packets that contain no data. For example, notice that in packet 1 the TCP header is 28 bytes while in packet 2 the TCP header is 24 bytes.

The TCP header does not contain unique source and destination addresses like the Ethernet and IP headers. It does however contain source and destination port numbers. The source port number refers to an application end point on the source machine. It is unique on the source machine but not unique in the network. Similarly, the destination port number refers to an application end point on the destination machine. You can think of the IP address as the house number of a large apartment building and the port number as the number of each apartment. The people living in each apartment might all live at 100 Main Street, but to reach a particular person you must specify their apartment number. Similarly, many applications may be running on a single machine with the IP address 123.45.34.10, but to reach the correct application you must use the correct port number.

PACKET OVERVIEW

Overall, in packet 11, there are 21 bytes of data (32%) and 54 bytes of various protocol headers (68%). However, this packet has a small amount of data because it is the tail end of the file. Packets with more data have the same size headers but a lower percentage of header overhead. For example, packet 6 also has 54 bytes of protocol headers, but is less than one percent headers.

UDP PACKETS

Examine one of the UDP packets, packet 17 for example. The Ethernet and IP headers are similar. The UDP header is only 8 bytes. It contains a subset of the fields in the TCP header – 2 bytes each for source and destination port, 2 bytes for length, and 2 bytes for a checksum.

   TCP has a larger header and therefore higher header overhead. It uses the additional space to record information that supports reliable data delivery by detecting losses and retransmitting the lost data. UDP has lower per packet overhead, but applications that use UDP must be prepared to deal with losses on their own. This explains why 10 identical UDP packets are sent in less than a tenth of a second.

QUESTIONS

Answer the following questions about the file **simpleHttp.cap**

   1. Which Ethernet address and IP address belong to the PC? To the cable modem router? How do you know?

	Ethernet Address	IP address
PC		
Cable router		

2. Consider packet 5. How large is the Ethernet header? How large is the entire Ethernet frame? How large is the IP header? The IP datagram? The TCP header? The TCP segment? You may want to consider drawing a picture of the packet with each of these pieces identified.

3. In packet 11, we saw that the actual portion of the packet that contained file data was 21 bytes long. Was this 21 bytes part of the Ethernet Frame? The IP datagram? The TCP segment? Why or why not?

4. If we had wanted to use the "Limit packet to X bytes" option for this particular capture, what is the lowest we could set X to and still capture all the transport layer headers? All the application layer protocol messages? Explain your answer.

5. What is the largest possible IP packet? (Hint: How big is the total length field in the IP header?) How did you determine this?

6. If you can, experiment with capturing traces using Limit packet to X bytes. What does the Ethereal display look like if you truncate the packet in the middle of the IP header?

DISCUSSION AND INVESTIGATION

1. Packet 4 uses the HTTP GET method. Use the RFC-Editor (See the Resources section below) to find the RFC that defines the Hypertext Transfer Protocol (HTTP/1.1) and find the specification of the GET method. What was the number of the RFC and what section number contains this information? What about the NOTIFY method used in packets 17 through 26, can you find this in the same RFC? If not, where would you find its definition?

2. In an earlier question, you were asked to determine the lowest number of bytes we could capture from each packet and still capture all the transfer headers for one specific trace. This is relatively easy to determine from a given trace. However, determining this value for any possible trace would require consulting the RFCs for TCP and IP to determine the maximum possible header size for each protocol. Consult RFC 793 (TCP) and 791 (IP) and determine this value. How does this compare to Ethereal's default value for "Limit packet to X bytes"? Speculate on the reason for any difference.

3. Browse through the RFCs (**http://www.rfc-editor.org**) and also the GetIEEE802™ information (**http://standards.ieee.org/getieee802**). How do the documents vary in length? Presentation? Style? Ease of use?

4. Take a trace on a local network for which you have the system administrator's permission. Make a list of questions about the contents (5 to 10 questions). For each one, say how you would expect to search for an answer in either the RFCs or the GetIEEE802™ information.

5. Investigate the Internet Standards Process (**http://www.ietf.org/rfc/rfc2026.txt**, **http://www.ietf.org/**). How do new protocols or changes to existing protocols become standards in the Internet? Who participates in the process? How are decisions made and disagreements resolved? Similarly, investigate the IEEE standards process (**http://standards.ieee.org/**) and answer the same set of questions.

6. Investigate the role of the session and presentation layers in the Open Systems Interconnection (OSI) seven-layer model proposed by the International Organization for Standardization (ISO). Are these functions missing from the Internet or are they incorporated in other layers?

7. Investigate the history of the standards process that produced the OSI seven-layer model.

8. Investigate the role of proprietary protocols in the Internet (proprietary instant messaging protocols, video/audio streaming protocols and others).

9. Discuss what it means to be an open protocol as opposed to a proprietary protocol. In some sense are the IETF protocols more open than the IEEE protocols? What are the impacts on society of these two styles of open protocols and of proprietary protocols? What impact do open protocols have on innovation, security, competition, etc.?

RESOURCES

- RFC-Editor, **http://www.rfc-editor.org**

- Internet Engineering Taskforce (IETF), **http://www.ietf.org**

- Internet Standards Process, **http://www.ietf.org/rfc/rfc2026.txt**

- IEEE Standards Association, **http://standards.ieee.org**

- GetIEEE802™, **http://standards.ieee.org/getieee802**

- ICQ, **http://en.wikipedia.org/wiki/ICQ**

- Web search: Proprietary Protocol

Getting Started: Exercise 1.3

Examining a Busy Network Using Filters

INTRODUCTION

On a busy network, a network protocol analyzer can capture hundreds or thousands of packets every second. This can lead to information overload for both the analyzer program and for the human user.

For each packet that appears on the network, the analyzer program must at a minimum copy the contents into memory. Depending on the capture options chosen by the user, it may also need to write it into a file or display it in the GUI. It may perform various translation activities such as looking up port numbers in a hard-coded table of well-know port numbers or issuing network queries to translate IP addresses found in the trace into human-readable machine names. Ethereal will do some preliminary characterization of the packet's contents in order to update the packet totals on the capture summary screen.

With higher data rates, the analyzer may have a difficult time performing each of these tasks before the next packet arrives. If it is busy when the next packet arrives, it may not be able to copy it into memory and the packet would be "dropped." Dropped packets are not recorded in the trace even though they appeared on the network. These dropped packets can make analyzing the trace difficult.

Depending on the network data rate and the speed of the computer, it may be necessary to take steps to minimize dropped packets. One logical choice is to disable real-time display and translation. These activities can always be performed later when analyzing the trace. Another good approach for large or long running traces is to avoid the overhead of the Ethereal's GUI entirely by using `tethereal`, a command line version of Ethereal. `tethereal` and a man page describing its use are typically installed with Ethereal itself.

Sometimes it is necessary to trace on an idle machine rather than on one of the machines generating the network traffic. When the analyzer program shares the computer (memory, CPU time, network bandwidth and other resources) with other applications, it can lead to dropped packets, and it can also disturb timing of the network activity itself. Tracing on an idle machine allows the truest capture with the fewest dropped packets.

Another issue for long running traces is limiting the amount of data captured. If you expect to capture a large amount of data, the first thing to do is to specify that the data be saved directly to a file or files to avoid using a huge amount of memory for the capture. You can also limit the portion of each packet captured. Depending on the purpose of the capture, you may be primarily interested in the protocol header sections of each packet and by discarding the data sections, you can dramatically reduce the size of the trace. Ethereal also allows you to reduce the size of the trace by specifying a *capture filter*. A capture filter is an expression that specifies which packets should be recorded; all other packets are simply discarded. The language used for Ethereal capture filters comes from a program called `tcpdump`, a command line based network protocol analyzer.

Even with these steps to limit the data captured, packets may be dropped on a highly utilized network. Also, Ethereal may not perform well for a large capture file even if it can keep up with the data rate. On a busy network, a good rule of thumb is to begin with a short capture (one minute or less). If the capture proceeds smoothly but the trace did not show you the network activity of interest, try incrementally longer traces.

Just as large traces can cause problems for the analyzer program, they are also difficult for users to examine. Finding the packets of interest among thousands of captured packets can be like finding a needle in a haystack without tools to help manage the large volume of data. Ethereal allows users to specify *display filters* that limit the packets displayed to those packets matching a user-specified expression. Display filters are similar in principle to capture filters, but they only change how the trace is displayed rather then changing the contents of the trace. Users can also specify *color filters*. Color filters display matching packets in a specified color rather than removing nonmatching packets from the display. Display filters and color filters use the same expression language. However, capture filters use a different language.

CONFIGURATION

This experiment was performed on a private home network. A single PC running Windows was connected to a Linksys cable modem router. Before beginning the experiment, several network applications were started including a Secure Shell (SSH) session and a web browser.

Figure 1.3.1: Exercise Configuration

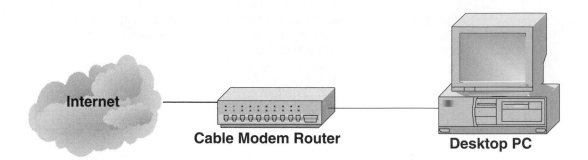

EXPERIMENT

While capturing a trace, we generated some typical network activity. Specifically, we opened and used several SSH sessions, downloaded a large file from the Internet, and visited a number of web pages.

CAPTURE FILTERS

Even though this is still a relatively small capture, we set the capture options as we might for a larger capture. Specifically, we limited the number of bytes captured from each packet, specified a simple capture filter, disabled name resolution of all kinds, and directed the capture to be saved directly to the file, **busyNetwork.cap**.

Figure 1.3.2: Adding a Capture Filter

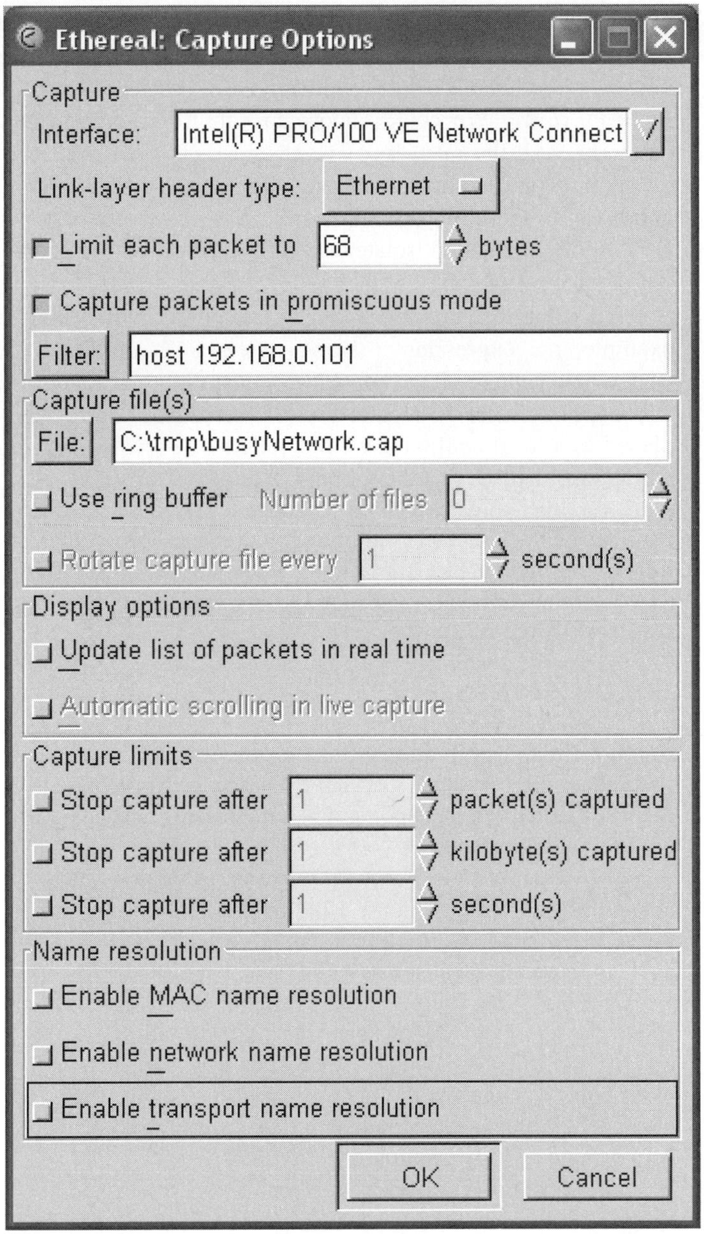

The capture filter we specified was `host 192.168.0.101`. This filter limits the capture to those packets sent to or from IP address 192.168.0.101.

We could have further limited the capture to packets sent to the address with the key words `dst host` or to the packets sent from the address with the key words `src host`. Similarly, we could have filtered based on Ethernet address rather than IP address with keywords `ether host`, `ether src`, and `ether dst`. We could choose to capture packets sent to or from entire networks with the `net`, `src net`, and `dst net`. We could isolate packets involving specific port numbers with `src port` and `dst port`. This is a good way to focus on particular applications. For example, port 80 is usually an HTTP port. We could isolate only TCP packets with the keyword `tcp` or UDP with the keyword `udp`.

Individual capture filters can be combined with `and`, `or`, and `not`. For example, the expression `((host 192.168.0.101) and not port 80)` would capture all the non-HTTP traffic sent to or from 192.168.0.101.

Capture filters you enter can be saved for future use. Saved filters are placed in a local configuration file called `cfilters`. If you open it in a text editor, you will see that the format is straightforward.

The Ethereal capture filter language is based on the one used by tcpdump, a command line based network protocol analyzer written by Van Jacobson, Craig Leres, and Steven McCanne from Lawrence Berkeley National Laboratory. To explore other options for capture filters, consult the manpage for tcpdump at **http://www.tcpdump.org**.

COLOR FILTERS

Capture filters help reduce the size of the trace itself by focusing on packets of particular interest. Once you have a trace in front of you, however, you may need some help understanding and categorizing what you see. Color filters can help you do just that.

For example, in the file **busyNetwork.cap** (available on the accompanying CD), there are 1392 packets. Certainly, this is too many to look through by hand. Color filters can give us a quick way to categorize these packets into individual streams of data.

The Coloring Rules Dialog available from the View menu allows you to specify a set of expressions and their corresponding display properties. At first no coloring rules will appear. To create a new rule, choose the New button. You must enter a name for the new rule and a display filter expression. You must also specify how packets matching these rules are to be displayed by choosing a background and foreground (or font) color.

For example, enter a filter `((tcp.dstport == 80) || (tcp.srcport == 80))` and call it "HTTPcolor." Change the background color and the foreground or font color (see Figure 1.3.3).

Figure 1.3.3: Adding a Color Filter

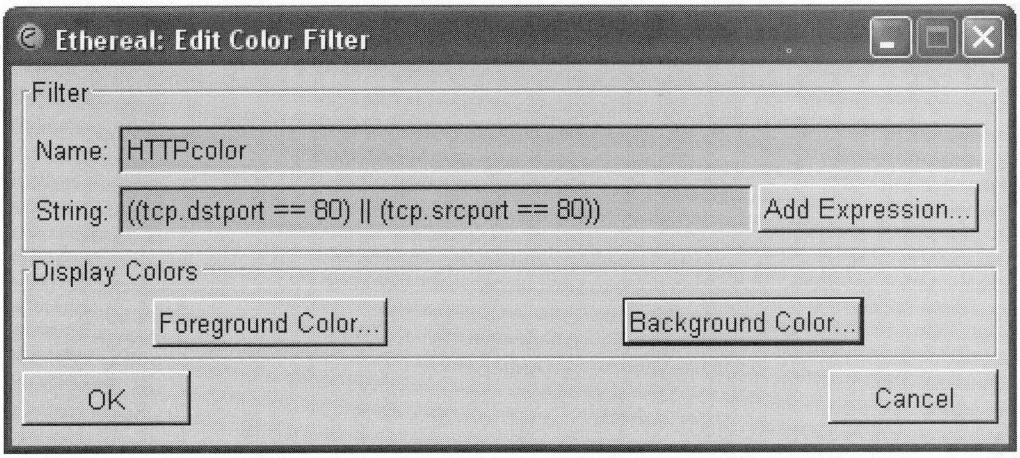

When this filter is applied, all the IITTP data is highlighted in the list pane. We could have captured only this data with the capture filter (tcp and src port 80 and dst port 80), but then we would have lost the information that this data was interleaved with other traffic on the network.

Figure 1.3.4: Colorized Display

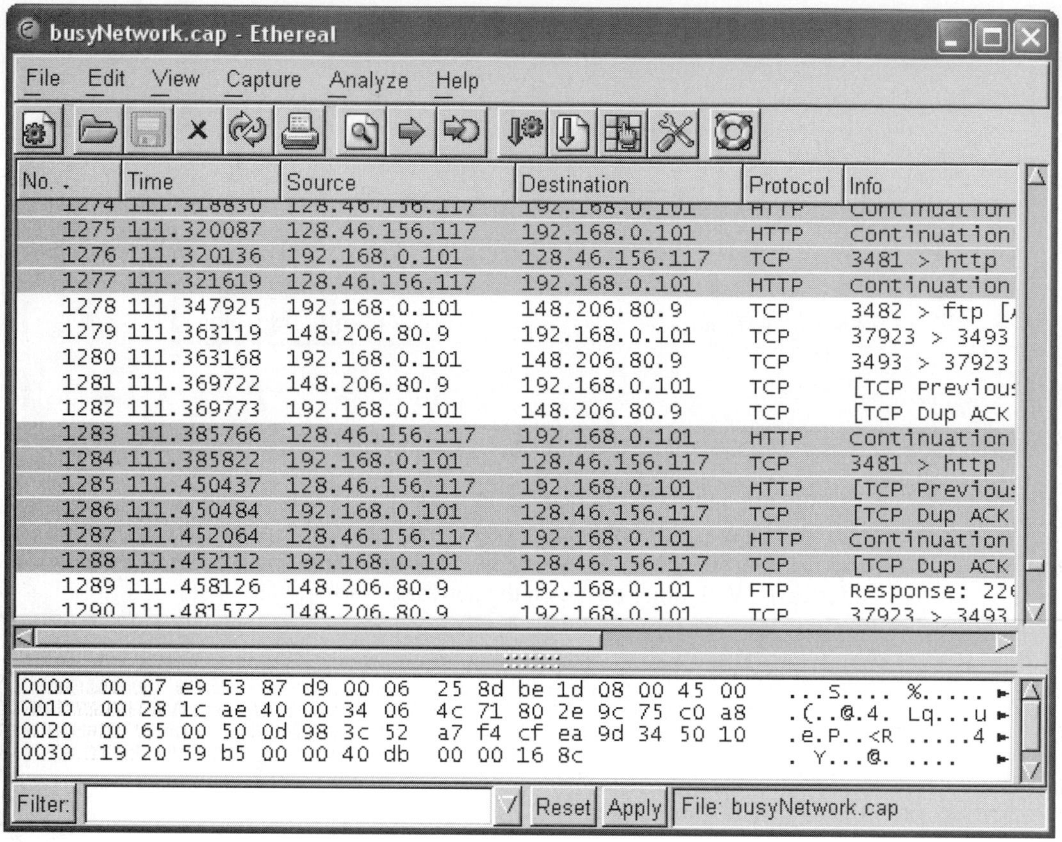

We entered this filter manually under String in the Edit Color Filter dialog, but Ethereal also provides a convenient Add Expression button that can help you build an expression from a menu of choices. It is a good place to start when you are new to writing color or display filters because it can show you the variety of expressions that are available. Many protocols appear in the expression list, including link, network, transport, and application layer protocols. Under each protocol, filter options exist based on various protocol elements. Writing effective color filters requires knowledge of the protocols used. There is also a special set of filters related the to frame itself. These can be used to filter based on the time the frame arrived or even the packet's number in this trace.

Figure 1.3.5: Filter Expressions

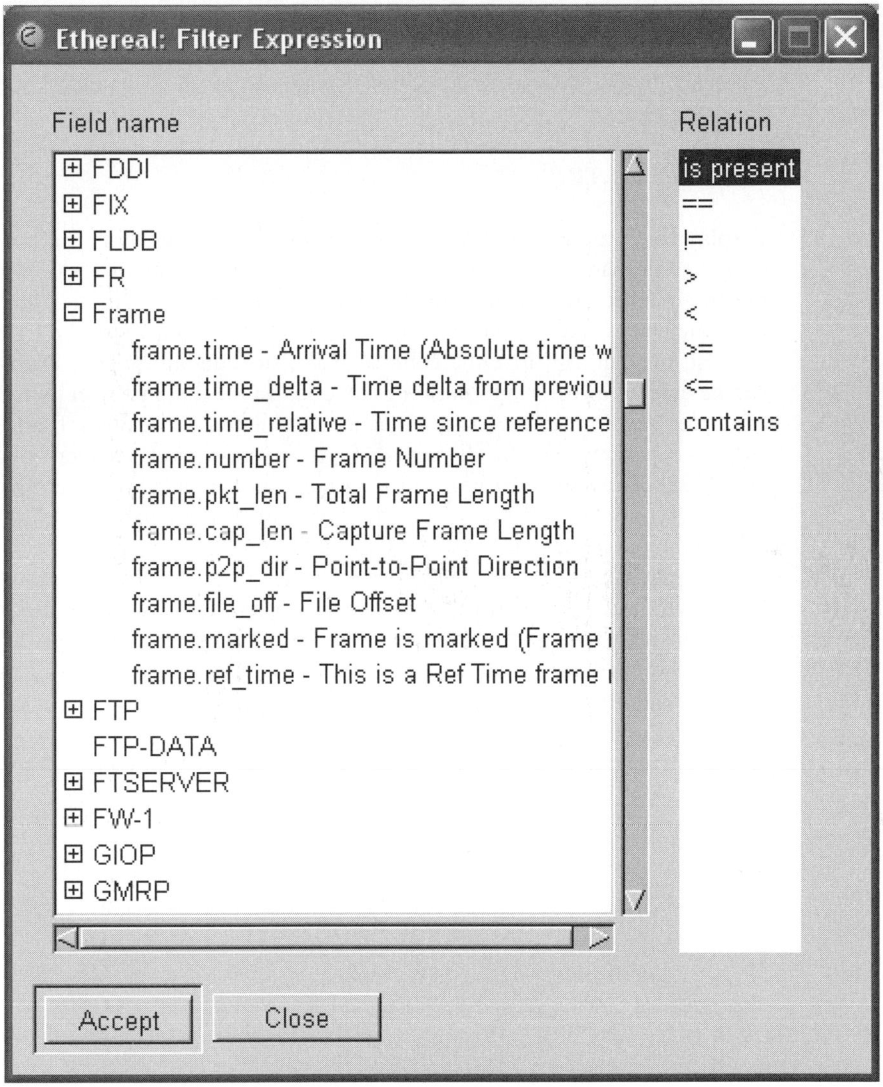

Once a color filter is defined, you can return to the Coloring Rules Dialog to edit it at any time. You can also add multiple filters. These filters are evaluated in the order that they appear in the Coloring Rules Dialog. Once a given packet matched a rule, no additional rules are evaluated. If a packet matches multiple rules, only the first matching rule will be used so when entering multiple rules it is good to put the most specific ones first. You can export color filters to a file and then import them when analyzing other traces. We recommend that over time you develop a personal color filter file that will help you quickly analyze traces. For this trace, we created a color filter, **generic.col** to get you started. You will be asked to experiment with this file in the Questions section of this exercise. For more information on Ethereal filters, you can consult the ethereal-filter manpage. It is included when Ethereal is installed and is also available on-line.

DISPLAY FILTERS

Display filters are in many ways a cross between capture filters and color filters. They use the same language as color filters and like color filters do not omit or remove packets from the trace. However, like capture filters, they remove nonmatching packets from consideration. This can help zero in on traffic of interest, but can also lose the context of the surrounding traffic. Display filters can be entered directly into the Filter text box in the main Ethereal window. For example, if we enter the same filter as we entered for a color filter, only the colorized packets will be displayed. Gaps in the packet number column (e.g. 1289-1293) are the only indication that additional packets appear in the full trace. To apply a new filter, enter it in the Filter text box and chose "Apply." To restore the full trace to the display, choose "Reset."

Display filters can also be entered under the Analyze Menu. As with color filters, you must give the filter a name and you can use the Add Expression button to help you form the expression. You can save the display filters you enter. They will be written to a configuration file called `dfilters` and restored each time you run Ethereal. If you open `dfilters` in a text editor, you will see that the format is straightforward.

Figure 1.3.6: Entering Display Filters

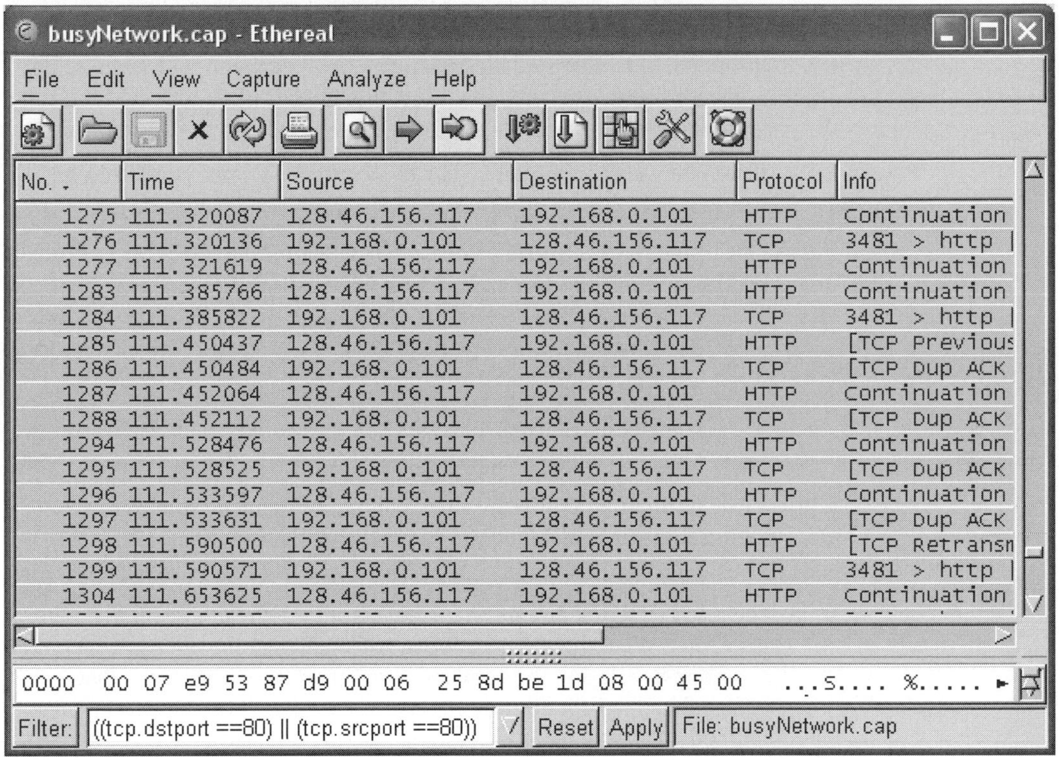

SEARCHING FOR PACKETS

Display filters can also be used to search for packets using Find Packet from the Edit menu. When you click on the Filter button in that dialog it will allow you to choose any saved display filter as the basis for the search. You can subsequently use Find Next and Find Previous to search for additional matching packets.

QUESTIONS

Answer the following questions about the file **busyNetwork.cap**.

1. Import the color filter **generic.col** and apply the rules. What series of steps starting from the View menu are required?

2. How many rules are specified in generic.col? How many rules involve TCP ports and how many rules involve UDP ports?

3. Each rule has the same basic format. What is it?

4. After applying the generic.col rules, how many packets remain uncolored? Write a single display filter that will display only the uncolored packets. Once the filter is applied, choose Summary or Protocol Hierarchy Statistics from the Analyze menu to determine the number of packets remaining. Give the number of packets and the filter you used.

5. If we had wanted a capture filter to isolate these same packets, what would it be?

6. One of the rules in **generic.col** is never used to color any of the packets. Which one is it and explain why it is never used?

DISCUSSION AND INVESTIGATION

1. Write some new coloring rules that categorize the rest of the traffic in some way. Give the rules you added and explain why you chose them.

2. Write a filter that will ensure you capture only traffic sent to or from the machine on which you are running the tracer.

3. Try launching a network intensive operation (e.g. downloading a large file via HTTP or FTP) and trace the activity. How large is the resulting trace file? Were there any dropped packets? Did the computer become unresponsive during the capture? Were there any other signs that Ethereal had a difficult time capturing the traffic? If so, experiment with other tracing methods (filters, limiting the size of data, tethereal). If possible, repeat this experiment with computers of varying CPU speed, memory capacity, or network interface speed.

4. Investigate other applications, both commercial and open source, that produce network traces in PCAP format.

5. Investigate libraries of functions that make it easy to program applications that write and read traces in PCAP format. Download and examine the code to Ethereal and tetheral.

RESOURCES

- Ethereal man page: **http://www.ethereal.com/ethereal.1.html**

- Ethereal Filters man page: **http://www.ethereal.com/ethereal-filter.4.html**

- Tethereal man page: **http://www.ethereal.com/tethereal.1.html**

- tcpdump man page, **http://www.tcpdump.org/tcpdump_man.html** (See especially the section on allowable primitives.)
- Web search: PCAP format

Section 2: Application Layer Protocols

Introduction

In this section, we focus on the highest level of the network protocol stack, the application layer. Application layer protocols directly support the features of network applications like web browsers and e-mail readers.

Application layer protocols define the language that network applications speak to fulfill user requests. For example, an application layer protocol defines what message a web browser sends to a remote server to retrieve a web page. Application layer protocols define all valid requests that a client may send to a server and how the server should respond to each one. They define the format of any data exchanged. They specify how clients and servers should react if they receive invalid or unexpected information.

Application programmers typically use high-level objects called sockets to read or write data over the network. Sockets behave much like a file—data written into the file is sent over the network and data read from the file comes from another application running somewhere else in the network. Sockets hide most of the complexity of actually sending the data over the network. Allowing application programmers and application layer protocol writers to concentrate on developing a simple and natural means of exchanging the data required for supporting the functionality of the application. Application layer protocols define what application programmers write into these sockets.

Many application layer protocols are written in human-readable ASCII text. For example, HTTP includes commands to GET and POST data. Much like a programming language, application layer protocols often consist of a highly specified and exact subset of human language. This makes them relatively easy to understand.

We focus on the application layer protocols used by some of the most common network applications. We will begin with the Hypertext Transfer Protocol (HTTP) that is used to support web browsing. We will examine the File Transfer Protocol (FTP), one of the oldest application layer protocols in the Internet. We will conclude with an investigation of protocols used to support the transfer of e-mail including the Simple Mail Transfer Protocol (SMTP) and the Post Office Protocol (POP).

The exercises in this section will allow you to look under the hood of network applications you use every day.

Application Layer Protocols:
Exercise **2.1**

Under the Hood of HTTP

INTRODUCTION

You are probably familiar with HTTP if only because it is the beginning of most URLs like `http://www.foo.com`. HTTP stands for the Hypertext Transfer Protocol and it is an application layer protocol responsible for the majority of the traffic traversing Internet backbone links.

Application layer protocols are used for communication between computer programs or applications. Typically, the client application sends request messages to a server application and the server application sends back response messages. Application layer protocols rely on the lower layers of the network protocol stack to handle the details of delivering the message over the network. In the case of HTTP, a web browser is typically the client and a web server is typically the server.

Figure 2.1.1: HTTP Request and Response

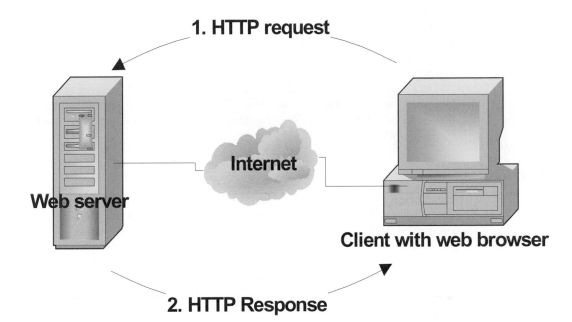

When you enter a URL in your web browser or click on a hyperlink, your web browser sends an HTTP request over the network to the web server specified in the URL. For example, if you enter the URL **http://www.ethereal.com/introduction.html**, your web browser will send a message to the machine **www.ethereal.com** requesting the file introduction.html. In this example, your web browser program is an HTTP client and the web server program running on the machine www.ethereal.com is the HTTP server.

Hypertext Transfer Protocol as its name suggests was defined as a means to transfer hypertext. Most web pages are written in the Hypertext Markup Language (HTML). However, HTTP can be used to transfer more than HTML pages. HTTP can be used to transfer everything from pictures to songs to movies to e-mail.

HTTP is defined in a set of RFC or Request for Comments documents.   For example, RFC 2616, Hypertext Transfer Protocol – HTTP 1.1, contains the main

HTTP 1.1 specification. It consists of approximately 200 pages of text that describe the format of all legal HTTP requests and responses. It also describes the format of URLs, the controls that exist for the caching of web pages at the client and many other details.

RFCs, like RFC 2616, are written to allow independent programmers to implement clients and servers that communicate using the protocol. This is harder than it might sound. Humans are able to extract the meaning of a request despite many unexpected variations in language, but computer programs require each detail to be specified.

Given the necessity for precision in the protocol definition, it may surprise you to learn that HTTP looks quite a bit like English text. The client literally sends the ASCII text "GET" to the server in order to request a page or "POST" to send data to the server.

In this exercise, we will see some examples of the HTTP protocol in action. You may want to explore the full HTTP specification yourself both to understand the messages we see in greater detail and to get an appreciation for the full protocol.

CONFIGURATION

This trace was taken on a private home network. A single PC running Windows was connected to a Linksys cable modem router. A Mozilla web browser was running on the PC. All other applications using the network were closed.

Before taking any traces, we cleared the web browser's cache to ensure that web pages would be fetched over the network rather than satisfied from the cache. (Most web browsers provide a way to do this. In Mozilla, we choose Preferences from the Edit menu and then chose Cache under the Advanced Category. This displays a Clear Cache button that can be used to flush all cached web pages.) We also flushed the DNS cache on the client to ensure that the name to IP address mapping for the web server name had to be requested over the network. On our Windows XP machine, we did this with the command `ipconfig /flushdns` at a command prompt.

Figure 2.1.2: Exercise Configuration

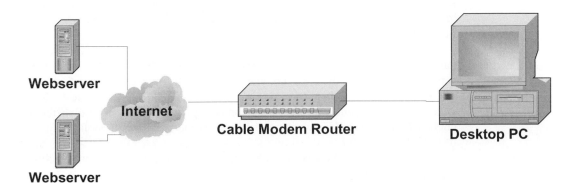

EXPERIMENT

We started Ethereal on the PC and began capturing a trace. In the web browser, we entered the URL **http://www.google.com** and then the URL **http://www.gnu.org**. These URLs both point to relatively simple web pages.

We saved the traffic captured in the file **httpWebBrowsing.cap**. You can open this file from the accompanying CD and follow along.

In the URL **http://www.google.com**, **www.google.com** is the name of a specific web server machine. Look first at packets 1 and 2. Packet 1 is a request to translate the name **www.google.com** into its corresponding IP address and packet 2 contains the translation to 216.239.37.99. These two packets are using an application level protocol called DNS or the Domain Name System.

This translation is necessary because the network layer protocol, IP, uses numeric addresses like 216.239.37.99 to refer to machines on the Internet rather than names like **www.google.com**. When we entered the URL **http://www.google.com**, we were asking the web browser to request data from the machine **www.google.com**. In order to send that request, the web browser must first determine the IP address of the machine.

With the translation complete, our web browser establishes a TCP connection to the web server machine. This connection establishment is shown in packets 3 through 5.

Finally, the established TCP connection is used by the web browser to send the request "GET / HTTP/1.1" as shown in packet 6. This specifies the action desired ("GET"), the file desired (simply "/" since we did not specify an additional file name) and the protocol version to be used ("HTTP/1.1").

HTTP GET REQUEST

This basic request is followed by a series of additional request headers. If you select the HTTP layer for packet 6 in the protocol pane, you can see these headers. The "\r\n" after each header indicates that it is a carriage return and line feed that separate one header from the next.

The "Host" header is required in HTTP version 1.1. It specifies the machine name from the URL, in this case, **www.google.com**. This allows a single web server to host many different domains at the same time (e.g. **www.foo.com**, **www.bar.com**). With this header, the web server can tell from the request which web server the client was trying to contact and can respond with different content for each one. This was one of the major changes from version 1.0 to 1.1 of the HTTP protocol.

The User-Agent header describes the web browser and client machine making the request.

There are a series of Accept headers including Accept, Accept-Language, Accept-Encoding and Accept-Charset. Each of these tells the web server the types of data that this web browser is prepared to process. A web server may be able to transfer data in multiple languages and formats. These headers indicate the abilities and preferences of this particular client.

The Keep-Alive and Connection headers specify information about the TCP connection over which the HTTP requests and responses are sent. It indicates if the connection should be kept active following a request and for how long. Most HTTP 1.1 connections are *persistent* meaning that they do not terminate after each request but rather stay open to allow multiple requests from the same server. This was another major change from HTTP 1.0 and greatly improves the performance when you fetch multiple objects from the same server.

Figure 2.1.3: HTTP Get Request

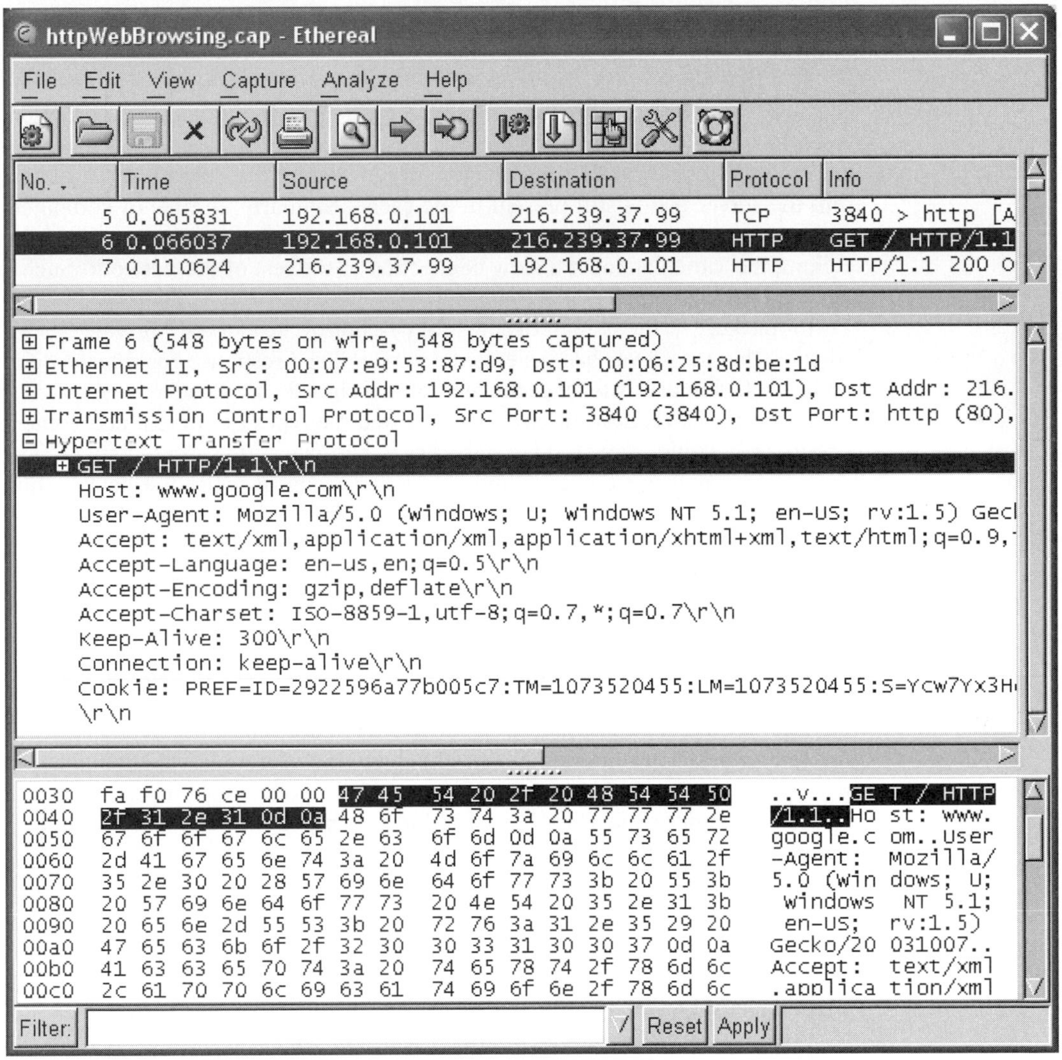

```
 httpWebBrowsing.cap - Ethereal                                    _ □ X

 File   Edit   View   Capture   Analyze   Help

 [icons]

 No. .    Time        Source              Destination        Protocol  Info
       5 0.065831    192.168.0.101       216.239.37.99      TCP       3840 > http [A
       6 0.066037    192.168.0.101       216.239.37.99      HTTP      GET / HTTP/1.1
       7 0.110624    216.239.37.99       192.168.0.101      HTTP      HTTP/1.1 200 O

 ⊞ Frame 6 (548 bytes on wire, 548 bytes captured)
 ⊞ Ethernet II, Src: 00:07:e9:53:87:d9, Dst: 00:06:25:8d:be:1d
 ⊞ Internet Protocol, Src Addr: 192.168.0.101 (192.168.0.101), Dst Addr: 216.
 ⊞ Transmission Control Protocol, Src Port: 3840 (3840), Dst Port: http (80),
 ⊟ Hypertext Transfer Protocol
     ⊞ GET / HTTP/1.1\r\n
       Host: www.google.com\r\n
       User-Agent: Mozilla/5.0 (windows; U; windows NT 5.1; en-US; rv:1.5) Gec
       Accept: text/xml,application/xml,application/xhtml+xml,text/html;q=0.9,
       Accept-Language: en-us,en;q=0.5\r\n
       Accept-Encoding: gzip,deflate\r\n
       Accept-Charset: ISO-8859-1,utf-8;q=0.7,*;q=0.7\r\n
       Keep-Alive: 300\r\n
       Connection: keep-alive\r\n
       Cookie: PREF=ID=2922596a77b005c7:TM=1073520455:LM=1073520455:S=Ycw7Yx3H
       \r\n

 0030   fa f0 76 ce 00 00 47 45  54 20 2f 20 48 54 54 50   ..v...GE T / HTTP
 0040   2f 31 2e 31 0d 0a 48 6f  73 74 3a 20 77 77 77 2e   /1.1..Ho st: www.
 0050   67 6f 6f 67 6c 65 2e 63  6f 6d 0d 0a 55 73 65 72   google.c om..User
 0060   2d 41 67 65 6e 74 3a 20  4d 6f 7a 69 6c 6c 61 2f   -Agent:  Mozilla/
 0070   35 2e 30 20 28 57 69 6e  64 6f 77 73 3b 20 55 3b   5.0 (win dows; U;
 0080   20 57 69 6e 64 6f 77 73  20 4e 54 20 35 2e 31 3b    windows  NT 5.1;
 0090   20 65 6e 2d 55 53 3b 20  72 76 3a 31 2e 35 29 20    en-US;  rv:1.5)
 00a0   47 65 63 6b 6f 2f 32 30  30 33 31 30 30 37 0d 0a   Gecko/20 031007..
 00b0   41 63 63 65 70 74 3a 20  74 65 78 74 2f 78 6d 6c   Accept:  text/xml
 00c0   2c 61 70 70 6c 69 63 61  74 69 6f 6e 2f 78 6d 6c   .applica tion/xml

 Filter:                                              /   Reset  Apply
```

HTTP RESPONSE

We have examined the request sent by the web browser. Now, we will examine the web server's answer in packet 7.

The response begins by indicating that it is OK for it to send the page using HTTP version 1.1 ("HTTP/1.1 200 OK"). As in the response packet, this is followed by a number of headers. Finally, the actual data requested is sent.

The first header, "Cache-control," is used to specify whether copies of the data may be stored or cached for future reference. Individual web browsers typically store a cache of recently accessed pages on the local machine. Subsequent accesses to the same page will not require the data to be sent again from the server if it is still present in the cache. Similarly, groups of computers on the same network may share a cache of pages to prevent multiple users from fetching the same data over a slow connection to the rest of the network. Such a cache is typically called a *proxy cache*.

In packet 7, the value of the Cache-control header is "private." This indicates that the server has generated a personalized response for this user and can be cached in user's local cache but not in a shared proxy cache.

In the HTTP request, the web server listed the types of content and content encodings it could accept. The web server has chosen to send content type `text/html` and content encoding `gzip`. This means that the data section itself is compressed HTML.

The server specifies some information about itself. In this case, the web server software is Google's own web server, GWS version 2.1. The response also specifies the length of the data with the Content-length header. Notice that the value of this header, 1216, matches the number of bytes in the data section as reported by Ethereal in the protocol pane. Finally, the server supplies the Date header listing the date and time the data was sent.

You can examine the data itself in Ethereal, but because it is compressed it will not appear meaningful. When the web browser receives this data, it uncompresses and displays it an HTML page. In your web browser, you can view the uncompressed HTML source for a web page by choosing Source or Page Source from the View menu.

MULTIPLE GET REQUESTS PER URL

Although we entered only 1 URL, there is a second request to **www.google.com** shown in packet 8. Do you know what causes this second request?

We have already seen that the first request to **www.google.com** fetched the main HTML page. The second request is "GET /images/logo.gif HTTP/1.1" and it requests the picture of the Google logo that is displayed on the page. This picture is a not stored in the same file as the HTML source, but rather the HTML source refers to this file with an image tag.

It is likely you can see this tag if you go to **www.google.com** in your web browser and view the page source.

```
<img src="/images/logo.gif" width=276 height=110 alt="Google">.
```

This second request is equivalent to the URL **http://www.google/images/logo.gif**. It is requested not by the user but by the web browser itself. After the web browser receives the web server's response and uncompresses the HTML, it must process the HTML file in order to know how to display it to the user. As it does this, it finds the image tag containing `src="images/logo.gif."` This tells the web browser that in order to display this web page it should also fetch the image or picture from the server. It does so and displays the page and the image together.

The main Google web page is relatively simple (a good idea since it is fetched so often). Some web pages refer to many images, style sheets, and other objects.

PLAIN TEXT DATA

The exchange between our web browser and the web server running on **www.gnu.org** follows a similar pattern. In packet 26, our web browser sends the same request 'GET / HTTP/1.1" that it sent to www.google.com. All the headers are the same except the Host header, which in this case is set to **www.gnu.org**. There are some interesting differences in the response however.

The response, found in packet 28, begins the same as the response from **www.google.com** with "HTTP/1.1 200 OK." The Content-type is also the same (`text/html`), but there is no Content-Encoding header. In this response, the data is sent in plain text. If you select the Data section of the HTTP layer in the protocol pane, you can read some of the page source directly from Ethereal.

Figure 2.1.4: HTTP OK Response

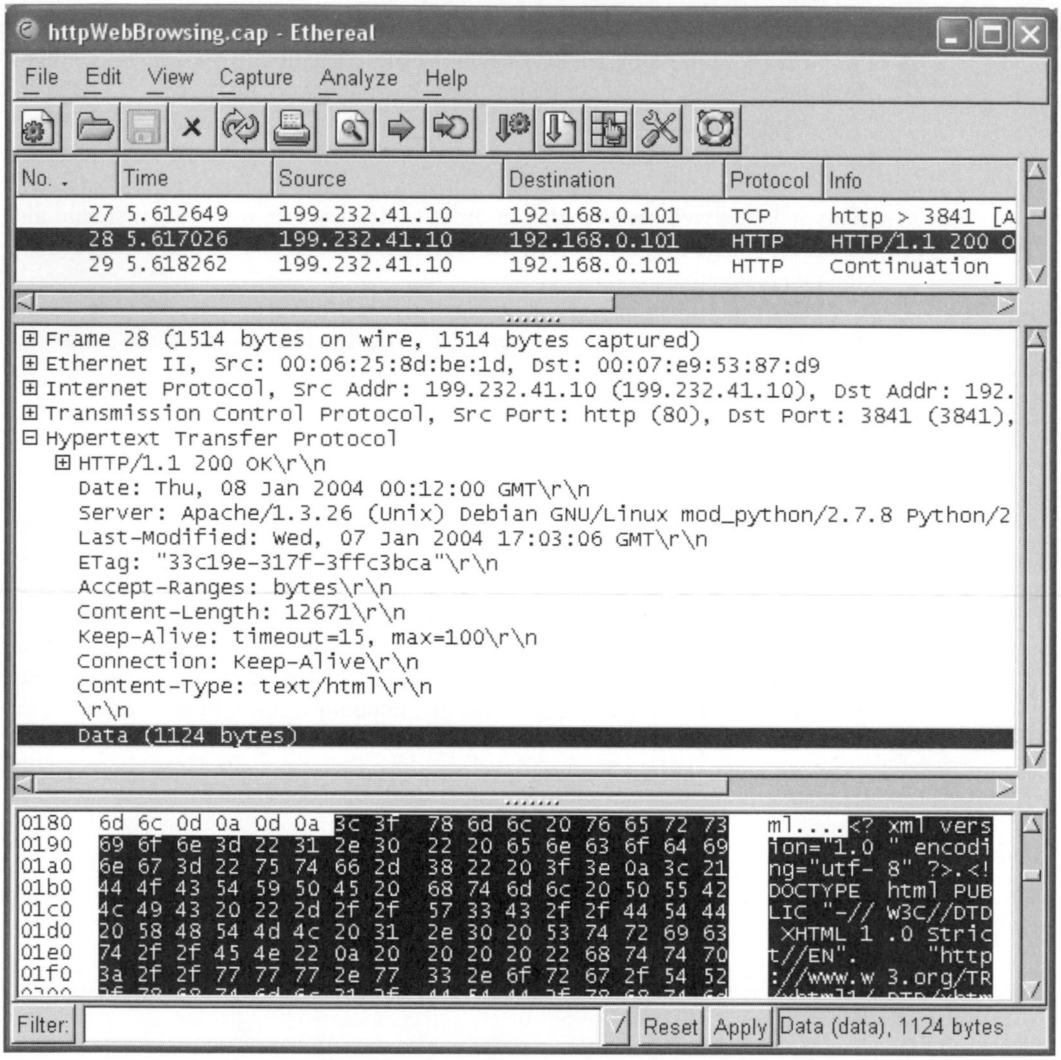

Another interesting thing to notice is that in this case the value of the Content-Length header (12671) does not match the size of the data region in bytes (1124). This is because the page is too big to fit into a single packet. The rest of the page is sent in packets 29, 31, 32, 34, 36, 38, 39, and 44. Each of these packets is labeled HTTP Continuation in the list panes and contains only HTTP data.

You can browse through each of these packets reading the HTML page source. However, Ethereal provides an easy way to see the entire conversation between the web browser and the web server.

Select one of the packets in the stream for example packet 29, then from the Analyze menu choose "Follow TCP Stream." The entire data stream is displayed in a separate window. All the data sent by the web browser is shown in one color and all the data sent by the web server is shown in another. You can also isolate one half of the conversation by choosing the appropriate item in the drop down menu in the lower left that is initially labeled "Entire conversation."

Figure 2.1.5: Follow HTTP Stream

```
Contents of TCP stream                                              _ □ X
GET / HTTP/1.1
Host: www.gnu.org
User-Agent: Mozilla/5.0 (windows; U; windows NT 5.1; en-US; rv:1.5) Gecko/20031007
Accept: text/xml,application/xml,application/xhtml+xml,text/html;q=0.9,text/plain;q=0.8,i
mage/png,image/jpeg,image/gif;q=0.2,*/*;q=0.1
Accept-Language: en-us,en;q=0.5
Accept-Encoding: gzip,deflate
Accept-Charset: ISO-8859-1,utf-8;q=0.7,*;q=0.7
Keep-Alive: 300
Connection: keep-alive

HTTP/1.1 200 OK
Date: Thu, 08 Jan 2004 00:12:00 GMT
Server: Apache/1.3.26 (Unix) Debian GNU/Linux mod_python/2.7.8 Python/2.1.3
Last-Modified: wed, 07 Jan 2004 17:03:06 GMT
ETag: "33c19e-317f-3ffc3bca"
Accept-Ranges: bytes
Content-Length: 12671
Keep-Alive: timeout=15, max=100
Connection: Keep-Alive
Content-Type: text/html

<?xml version="1.0" encoding="utf-8" ?>
<!DOCTYPE html PUBLIC "-//W3C//DTD XHTML 1.0 strict//EN"
    "http://www.w3.org/TR/xhtml1/DTD/xhtml1-strict.dtd">
<html xmlns="http://www.w3.org/1999/xhtml" xml:lang="en">

<head>
<title>GNU's Not Unix! - the GNU Project and the Free Software Foundation (FSF)</title>
<meta http-equiv="Content-Type" content="text/html; charset=utf-8" />
<meta http-equiv="Keywords" content="GNU, FSF, Free Software Foundation, Linux, Emacs, GC
C, Unix, Free Software, Operating System, GNU Kernel, HURD, GNU HURD" />
<meta http-equiv="Description" content="Since 1983, developing the free Unix-like operati
ng system GNU, so that computer users can have the freedom to share and improve the softw
are they use." />
<link rev="made" href="mailto:webmasters@gnu.org" />
<link rel="stylesheet" type="text/css" href="gnu.css" />
<link rel="icon" type="image/png" href="/graphics/gnu-head-mini.png" />
</head>
Entire conversation (14544 bytes)    □   ◆ ASCII ◇ EBCDI Print Save As Filter out this stream Close
```

Close this window and return the main list pane. Notice that a filter has been entered in the Filter box in the lower left. This filter (ip.addr eq 199.232.41.10 and ip.addr eq 192.168.0.101 and `tcp.port eq 80 and tcp.port eq 3841`) defines the TCP stream over which the HTTP conversation was transmitted. 199.232.41.10 is the IP address of the machine **www.gnu.org** and 80 is the HTTP port. Recall from Exercise 1.2 that the port number identifies an application end point. In this case, port 80 is the endpoint used by the web server. 192.168.0.101 is the IP address of our local machine, and 3841 is the application end point used by the web browser.

The filter was used to support the "Follow TCP Stream" option we just used. Even though we closed the TCP stream window, the filter is still active. If you look in the list pane, you will see that only packets matching this filter are currently displayed. For example packets 1 to 22 are missing. To restore the full trace in the list pane, you must choose "Reset" at the bottom of the screen. This Reset button will clear the filter box and restore the full trace. Be careful—it is easy to forget to reset the display filter!

MULTIPLE TCP STREAMS

After resetting the display filter, locate packet 35, 41, and 42. These packets open a second TCP connection from our web browser to the www.gnu.org web server. This connection is defined by the same IP addresses as the first connection. It even uses the same port 80 on the web server, but the port on the local machine is different (3842 instead of 3841).

Notice that the other TCP connection to port 3841 has not failed and in fact is actively being used to transfer data. Why then is this second connection opened? It is done purely for performance reasons. It is quicker to use multiple TCP connections in parallel.

QUESTIONS

Answer the following questions about the file **httpWebBrowsing.cap**

1. Follow the TCP stream between our web browser and the web server at **www.google.org**. Isolate only the requests sent by the web browser and copy the text.

2. Follow the first TCP stream between our web browser and **www.gnu.org**. Copy the HTML source from the server's first response and paste in into a text file using your favorite editor. Save it to a file called foo.html and open this file in a web browser. In what ways does it look like the main page from **www.gnu.org**? What is missing? Why?

3. Write a color filter to highlight all of the HTTP requests in the trace and another to highlight all the HTTP responses. What string is used for each filter?

4. How many HTTP requests are sent to **www.gnu.org**? Which objects are requested? How big is each object? How can you tell?

5. Which of these requests go over the connection from port 3841 and how many over the connection from port 3842?

6. Are all the objects we see transferred HTML pages? How does the web browser know if data sent should be interpreted as HTML or as some other type of file?

7. Make a list of all unique header types found in all of the requests. Do you see any header types other than the ones we examined in the exercise? If so which ones?

8. Make a list of all the unique header types found in all of the responses. Do you see any header types other than the ones we examined in the exercise? If so which ones?

9. Compute the average response time for **www.google.com** and **www.gnu.org**. Which server had the fastest response time? Describe how you calculated your answer.

10. Which packets contain the DNS request to translate **www.gnu.org** and the reply? What is the IP address of www.gnu.org?

DISCUSSION AND INVESTIGATION

1. What happens when your web browser first starts up? Trace it and find out.

2. In our trace, the web servers answered "200 OK" to all of our requests. What would be the answer if we had asked for a page that did not exist like **http://www.google.com/foobar**? You can determine this by tracing with Ethereal or by examining the HTTP specification. Give the contents of the server response shown by Ethereal and give a relevant excerpt from the HTTP specification.

3. RFC 2616 defines HTTP/1.1, but many other RFCs document aspects of HTTP. Search for HTTP using the RFC Editor's search engine (**http://www.rfc-editor.org/rfcsearch.html**). How many documents match your query? What is the most recent publication date?

4. Summarize some of the proposals for next generation HTTP made by the HTTP-NG group within W3C. What is the status of this HTTP-NG effort? Have its goals been achieved?
    (**http://www.w3.org/Protocols/HTTP-NG/,
    http://www.w3.org/TR/1998/WD-HTTP-NG-goals**)

RESOURCES

- RFC 2616, Hypertext Transfer Protocol – HTTP/1.1, **ftp://ftp.rfc-editor.org/in-notes/rfc2616.txt**

- RFC 1945, Hypertext Transfer Protocol – HTTP/1.0, **ftp://ftp.rfc-editor.org/in-notes/rfc1945.txt**

- RFC 2854, The text/html Media Type, **ftp://ftp.rfc-editor.org/in-notes/rfc2854.txt**

- W3C's HTTP page, **http://www.w3.org/Protocols**

- W3C's HTTP-NG page, **http://www.w3.org/Protocols/HTTP-NG**

- Web search: HTTP/1.1 Criticism

Application Layer Protocols:
Exercise 2.2

HTTP Caching, Authorization, and Cookies

INTRODUCTION

HTTP is a *stateless* protocol. This means that as far as HTTP is concerned each request is independent of any previous requests. HTTP itself provides no way for servers to associate one request from a client with the next request from the same client. It maintains no "state" or information about the previous requests.

You may have noticed that many web sites do remember information about your previous visits—your name, things you have purchased or looked at, etc. Similarly, web sites that ask for login information do not require this information for each individual request. If you examine traces of HTTP traffic, you will also discover that servers often do not return a web page if the client already has an up-to-date copy.

In this exercise, we will explore how HTTP clients and servers are able to use information about previous requests despite the stateless nature of HTTP itself. In particular, we will examine how special headers control caching, authorization, and "cookies."

CONFIGURATION

This trace was taken on a private home network. A single PC running Windows was connected to a Linksys cable modem router. A Mozilla web browser was running on the PC. All other applications using the network were closed.

Before taking any traces, we cleared the web browser's cache to ensure that web pages would be fetched over the network rather than satisfied from the cache. Most web browsers provide a way to do this. In Mozilla, we choose Preferences from the Edit menu and then chose Cache under the Advanced Category. This displays a Clear Cache button that can be used to flush all cached web pages. Similarly, we also removed all cached cookies.

Figure 2.2.1: Exercise Configuration

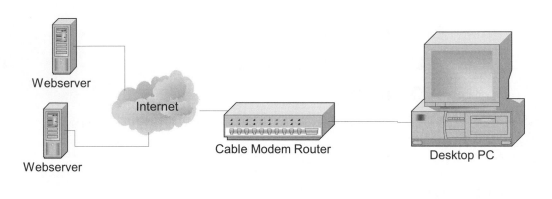

EXPERIMENT

In this exercise, we trace a series of HTTP connections: one which illustrates the use of cookies, one which illustrates the use of authorization headers, and one which illustrates the use of caching headers.

COOKIES

One of the ways in which HTTP clients and servers simulate a stateful protocol is with the use of cookies. Cookies are pieces of information that web servers ask clients to store on their behalf. The HTTP protocol does not specify their format or contents and even the clients themselves cannot interpret what they are storing.

A server can send a "Set-Cookie" header along with their response. The client can then store this value on the local machine and send it back as a "Cookie" header along with any subsequent requests to the same server.

Servers can use a cookie to store any information they want. For example, if the client issues a request for page X, the server could record this fact in the cookie. If the client then asked for a page Y, the server could send a new cookie recording that the client visited page X and then Y. Similarly, any input given by the client (e.g. when filling out a form) could be recorded.

All the information a server might want to store about each client could get pretty big. Therefore, servers often ask clients to store a cookie containing only a key that will allow them to retrieve the proper state from their own database.

In the file **http_cookie.cap**, we saved a trace of fetching the URL http://www.google.com. Immediately before this trace was taken, we removed all stored cookies.

Using Follow TCP Stream from the Analyze menu, examine the contents of the TCP stream beginning with packet 3. The first GET request (packet 6) has no "Cookie" header. However, the server's response (packet 7) contains a "Set Cookie" header. This header specifies the cookie itself and the date at which the cookie will expire.

```
Set-Cookie:
PREF=ID=2ecb9e2538c958fe:TM=1079200263:LM=1079200263:S=VMss9fWvgLAtllSq;
expires=Sun, 17-Jan-2038 19:14:07 GMT; path=/; domain=.google.com
```

The next request (packet 10) includes a "Cookie" header that returns this exact cookie to the server.

```
Cookie:
PREF=ID=2ecb9e2538c958fe:TM=1079200263:LM=1079200263:S=VMss9fWvgLAtllSq
```

Storing a cookie is a bit like allowing a web server to use some space on your machine to store information it would like to remember. You may not like web servers using your machine in this way or you may not like servers accumulating information about your web browsing habits over time. Some companies make money by using cookies to track your web surfing behavior across many servers. For this reason, most web browsers allow you to control whether cookies are saved and returned including disabling cookies altogether. If you disable cookies, however, many popular web sites will not behave as expected.

AUTHORIZATION HEADERS

Web server administrators can protect certain pages by requiring that clients provide a username and password to access them. One simple way to do this is placing a .htaccess file in the directory with the protected files. The .htaccess file can specify a set of allowable usernames and passwords as well as deny access based on the client's IP address or hostname.

I placed such a file on a directory containing an early draft of this book. I captured the network traffic generated as I fetched the index page from this directory.

The web browser popped up a dialog box asking that I enter the proper username and password. The first time I deliberately entered the wrong

password. The browser once again displayed the dialog and this time I entered the correct username and password. Once I did so, the page loaded properly. I proceeded to reload the same page and fetch other data from the same directory and the web browser did not require me to reenter this information. I saved the trace to the file **http_auth.cap**.

To understand how this works with the stateless HTTP protocol, we follow the TCP stream beginning with packet 4. The first request (packet 6) is "GET /~jnm/networks/book." This request contains no Authorization headers.

```
GET /~jnm/networks/book/ HTTP/1.1
```

The server responds (packet 8) with an error code 401which specifies that authorization be required to access this page. This response contains a "WWW-Authenticate" header that specifies that the authorization should be done by password. The relevant headers are shown below.

```
HTTP/1.1 401 Authorization Required
WWW-Authenticate: Basic realm="ByPassword"
```

This is the point at which the browser popped up a dialog box asking that I enter a username and password. The first time I entered the wrong password. The browser repeated the "GET /~jnm/networks/book" request; this time adding an Authorization header.

```
GET /~jnm/networks/book/ HTTP/1.1
Authorization: Basic bmV0bGFiOnNwMjAwNQ==
```

Because the password supplied was incorrect, the server again answered with error code 401. The browser tries the request again with a different Authorization header based on the new username and password.

```
GET /~jnm/networks/book/ HTTP/1.1
Authorization: Basic bmV0bGFiOnNwMjAwNA==
```

This time the server responds with a 200 OK message and returns the requested data.

There are two other requests shown in the trace, a reload of the same page and a GET request for /~jnm/networks/book/PrefaceMaterials/HowToUse.doc. However, the browser does not request that a username and password be entered. This is because the browser has stored a copy of the correct username and password. By sending the Authorization header along with each request, it appears as if we have a stateful HTTP session.

Unlike cookies, username and password information is typically only cached in the browser's memory. If you exit your browser and restart it, you would typically be asked to renter the information.

```
GET /~jnm/networks/book/PrefaceMaterials/HowToUse.doc HTTP/1.1
Authorization: Basic bmV0bGFiOnNwMjAwNA==
```

The Authorization headers do not contain the username and password in plain text. However, it is important to realize that they are not encrypted using a secret key. Instead, they are only obscured using a well-known encoding algorithm. Using this algorithm, it is straightforward to decode the obscured username (netlab) and password (sp2004) from the Authorization header. Also, the data being protected (index.html and HowToUse.doc) are both clearly visible in the trace as well. Web browsers and servers often use the Secure Socket Layer (SSL) for more secure interaction. This is covered later in this book in an exercise on encryption.

Figure 2.2.2: Authorization Header

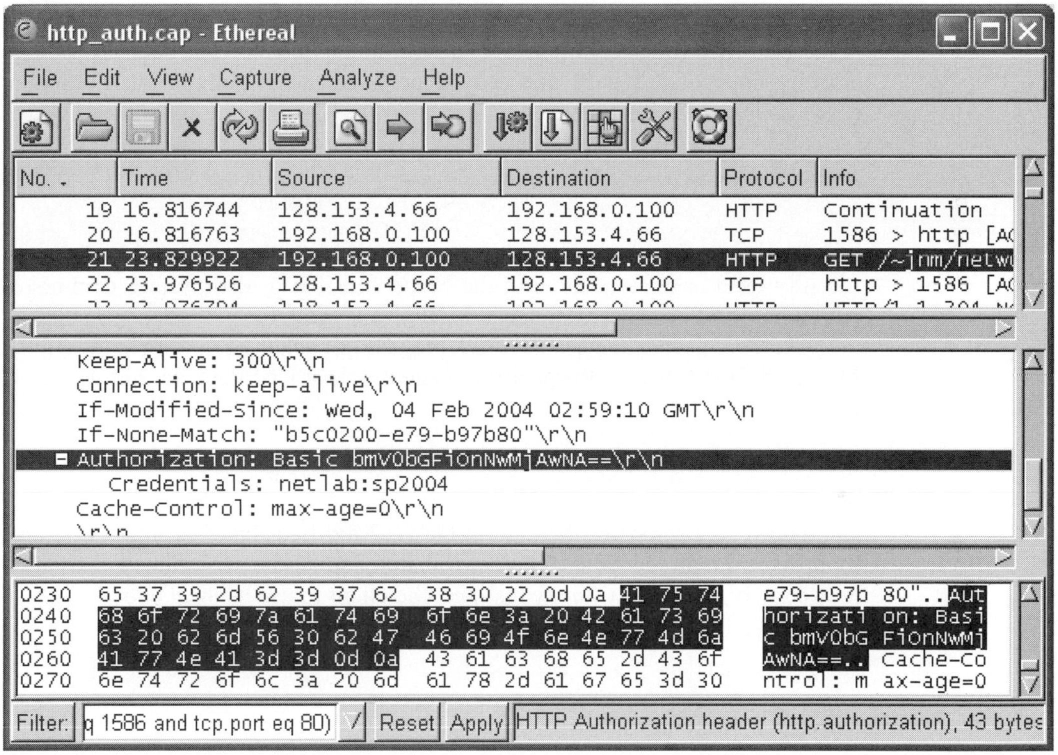

CACHING HEADERS

Web servers do not always return the web page data with each successful response. Data is often cached on the client's local machine and sometimes at intermediate machines called web proxies. Web proxies are typically shared by a community of users on a local area network and are designed to conserve outgoing bandwidth by fetching only one copy of each page and then allowing it to be shared.

There are a variety of headers that allow the client to check whether a cached copy matches the current data available on the server. This is another way in which HTTP clients and servers are able to use data from previous requests despite the stateless nature of the protocol.

To illustrate the use of the caching related headers, we fetched RFC 1149 via the URL **http://www.rfc-editor.org/rfc/rfc1149.txt**. (This classic RFC presents a standard for the transmission of IP datagrams on avian carriers ☺.) After loading the page for the first time, we used our browser's Reload button to reload the newest copy of the page. We saved the resulting network traffic in the file **http_uselocal.cap**.

The client sends the first GET request in packet 6 and the server responds by sending a full copy of the page beginning in packet 7. The server includes a "Last-Modified" header to specify the age or version of the data. The client stores a copy of this page in the local browser cache along with information about its last modified time.

```
HTTP/1.1 200 OK
Last-modified: Thu, 29 Mar 1990 14:31:04 GMT
```

Browsers allow users to limit the size of the local browser cache. The most recently used pages are stored in the cache and if it is already full, then pages which have not been accessed for some time are evicted.

The client sends the second GET request in packet 12 and includes an "If-Modified-Since" header to specify the age or version of the data that it already has.

```
GET /rfc/rfc1149.txt HTTP/1.1
If-Modified-Since: Thu, 29 Mar 1990 14:31:04 GMT
```

The server compares the date in the "If-Modified-Since" header to the last modified time on the page. The dates match and so the server need not send a new copy of the data. It simply instructs the client to use its local copy.

```
HTTP/1.0 304 Use local copy
Cache-Control: max-age=0
```

The client also sends a "Cache-Control" header. Cache-Control headers are used by both clients and servers. Clients use them to specify the types of cached data they are willing to accept. In this case, the Cache-Control header specifies that the client would be willing to accept a cached copy that is no greater than 0 seconds old. In other words, they are unwilling to accept a cached answer from any intermediate proxy server.

Servers use the Cache-Control header to specify what data is cacheable. For example, the keyword "public" specifies that the data can be cached by both local and shared caches. The keyword "private" indicates that the response is intended for a specific user and therefore should not be cached on a shared proxy server. The keyword "no-cache" specifies that the data is not to be cached. Even though a web browser or proxy server could cache a copy of anything it handles, they are expected to honor the caching directives of the server.

In **http_auth.cap**, there is another example of a conditional GET request. When the server returns /~jnm/networks/book/index.html it specified an entity tag with the Etag header.

```
HTTP/1.1 200 OK
Last-Modified: Wed, 04 Feb 2004 02:59:10 GMT
ETag: "b5c0200-e79-b97b80"
```

When the page is reloaded, the client sends a GET request that species both the modification time and the ETag. In particular, the "If-None-Match" tag specifies that the client would like a new copy if the copy of the server no longer matches the specified ETag.

```
GET /~jnm/networks/book/ HTTP/1.1
If-Modified-Since: Wed, 04 Feb 2004 02:59:10 GMT
If-None-Match: "b5c0200-e79-b97b80"
Cache-Control: max-age=0
```

QUESTIONS

Answer the following questions. Refer to the files **http_cookie.cap**, **http_auth.cap**, and **http_uselocal.cap** as necessary.

1. Explore the options for controlling cookies in your own browser. (For Mozilla, you can open the Preferences dialog from the Edit menu. There is a section on Cookies in the Privacy and Security section.) Does your browser allow you to disable cookies completely? Only for certain sites? Prompt you before accepting or returning a cookie? Delete cookies already stored? How?

2. Web browsers typically store cached web pages and cookies in the local file system. Identify the directory where they are stored. Can you view web objects directly by opening the files in this directory? Can you determine where your browser stores information such as the last modified time associated with each file?

3. What limit have you set on the amount of cached data? Compare this to the size of the directory that contains the cached web pages.

4. Cookies and cached data are typically stored in the local file system. Authorization information such as username and password are typically stored only for the current session. Why do you think this is?

5. In the file **http_auth.cap**, the server twice responded with a 401 authorization required. How were the circumstances of each different? Are the responses the same or different?

6. In the file **http_auth.cap**, the first password entered was incorrect. What was it? How do you know?

7. In the file **http_uselocal.cap**, how much data is not transferred because the client can use its cached copy? How do you know?

DISCUSSION AND INVESTIGATION

1. Discuss the type of web page for which a server might specify "Cache-Control: private."

2. Search the web for information on the privacy issues involved in using cookies. Describe an example of how cookies could be used to disclose information about you to third parties. Are you comfortable with your browser's current settings for handling cookies? Why or why not?

3. Try disabling cookies completely in your browser. Visit five to ten popular web sites. Describe any differences with cookies disabled.

RESOURCES

- RFC 2616, Hypertext Transfer Protocol – HTTP/1.1, **ftp://ftp.rfc-editor.org/in-notes/rfc2616.txt**

- RFC 2617, HTTP Authentication: Basic and Digest Access Authentication, **ftp://ftp.rfc-editor.org/in-notes/rfc2617.txt**

- Netscape, Cookie Specification, **http://home.netscape.com/newsref/std/cookie_spec.html**

- Electronic Privacy Information Center, Cookies, **http://www.epic.org/privacy/internet/cookies**

- Web search: Cookie Privacy

Application Layer Protocols:
Exercise **2.3**

File Transfer Protocol

INTRODUCTION

The File Transfer Protocol or FTP is one of the earliest protocols in the Internet. The first RFC describing FTP was released in 1972 (RFC 959) and it was standardized in 1982 (STD 9). For comparison, the HTTP/1.0 RFC was not released until 1996.

HTTP and FTP can both be used to transfer objects or files over the network, but they do so in very different ways. HTTP focuses on the transfer of files for immediate viewing and short-term caching on clients. Recall the different headers that specify caching behavior. HTTP also focuses on the presentation of information including headers that specify file formats so that the web browser can correctly interpret the contents. FTP, on the other hand, focuses more exclusively on the transfer of the data. Leaving it the user to decide how long the file will remain on the local machine or what to do with the data.

FTP is a *stateful* protocol (unlike HTTP which is a stateless protocol). FTP clients establish an on-going session with a server and can use this session to issue multiple requests. A username and password are specified to initiate the session. However, many FTP servers allow public access through connections in which clients specify the username "anonymous" and then set the password value to anything they want.

Once connected, an FTP session behaves much like a command shell. Users are provided with a prompt and can browse through a set of files and directories. As users move through the directories, the FTP server keeps track of their position. Users can issue requests to retrieve files from or store files to the server and these requests are interpreted relative to the current working directory.

FTP typically maintains one TCP connection for the ongoing control channel and then establishes separate TCP connections over which data is transferred. The control channel is usually established from the client machine to port 21 on the FTP server. The control channel is then used to specify the attributes of each data channel used including whether client or server will initiate the transfer and which IP address and port to use for the connection.

The full FTP protocol offers great flexibility in specifying the type of data channel to use including who will initiate the data connection, what IP address and port should be used to establish the connection and what character encoding to use. By default, the client will listen on a local port for an incoming connection from the FTP server. Interestingly, this means that the FTP client plays the role of a server for the data connection. However, this configuration will not work for most clients behind firewalls or network address translation (NAT) machines. These clients can establish outgoing TCP connections but the firewall blocks incoming TCP connections. However, the FTP control channel can be used to request passive mode in which the server opens a port for an incoming data connection from the client.

The FTP protocol was specified long before firewalls and network address translation became popular, but the flexibility built into the protocol allowed it to accommodate these new requirements. However, malicious clients can also abuse this flexibility. FTP allows the client to request that a data channel be established with a machine that is unrelated to either the client or the server. In one exploit, this feature was used was to ask the server to establish a data connection to a mail server and then write a file containing the SMTP commands necessary to transfer SPAM e-mail. Because the mail appeared to be coming from the FTP server, the identity of real culprit was harder to trace. Many FTP servers no longer support this full flexibility and many SMTP servers limit the machines from which they are willing to accept mail.

CONFIGURATION

This trace was taken on a private home network. A single PC running Windows was connected to a Linksys cable modem router. An FTP client was started on the PC.

Prior to the experiment, we used the RFC-Editor search feature to identify the RFC for the FTP protocol (RFC 959). This search indicated that this RFC was available at the following URL, **ftp://ftp.rfc-editor.org/in-notes/rfc959.txt**. This URL indicates that the file rfc959.txt can be retrieved from the machine **ftp.rfc-editor.org** via FTP. It also indicates the file will be located in a directory called in-notes.

If you enter a URL beginning with **ftp://** in most browsers, they will act as an FTP client to retrieve the file indicated. There are also many stand-alone FTP clients available. We chose to use a stand-alone FTP client for this experiment.

Figure 2.3.1: Exercise Configuration

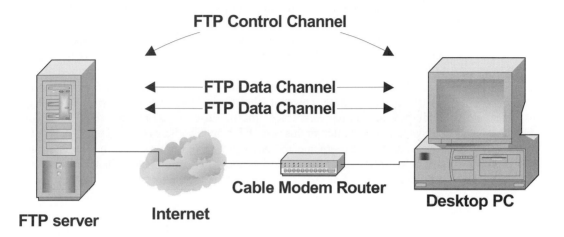

EXPERIMENT

Using our FTP client, we connected to the FTP server, ftp.rfc-editor.org via anonymous FTP, opened the directory in-notes and retrieved the file rfc959.txt. We captured the resulting network traffic and saved it to the file **ftpRFC959.cap**. You can open this file from the accompanying CD and follow along.

CONTROL CHANNEL

In packets 1 through 5, we see the local client initiate the TCP connection for the control channel to the FTP port (port 21) on the machine 128.9.176.20. This is the IP address of the machine, **ftp.rfc-editor.org**. Interestingly, the client tries three times to initiate the connection (packets 1 through 3). You can learn more about TCP connection establishment in Exercise 3.1.

Once the control channel is established, the server is the first one to send information over the channel. Specifically, the server reports in packet 6 that it is **ftp.isi.edu** and that it is ready to service requests. Interestingly, the machine with IP address 128.9.176.20 has several names including **ftp.rfc-editor.org**, **ftp.isi.edu**, and even **www.isi.edu**.

Before retrieving data, the FTP client must send a username to the server (packet 7). This is done with the FTP command USER. In this case, we send USER anonymous because we are doing anonymous FTP. The FTP server responds with a message that indicates that guest login is ok and instructs the client to send their complete e-mail address as a password.

Although, the server requests a complete e-mail address, many FTP clients will instead send a string identifying the client software in the password field. Some FTP servers check that the password is in the form of an e-mail address, but many do not. We chose to send the password "netlab" and this is accepted by the server.

Interestingly, the FTP client we used obscured the password as we typed it on the screen. Notice, however, that the username and password are clearly displayed in the network trace. In the case of anonymous FTP, no secret passwords are revealed in this way. FTP can also be used to connect to a system with your private username and password. Even in this case, the information is sent in plain text over the network. Other applications like telnet have the same problem.

Figure 2.3.2: FTP Username and Password

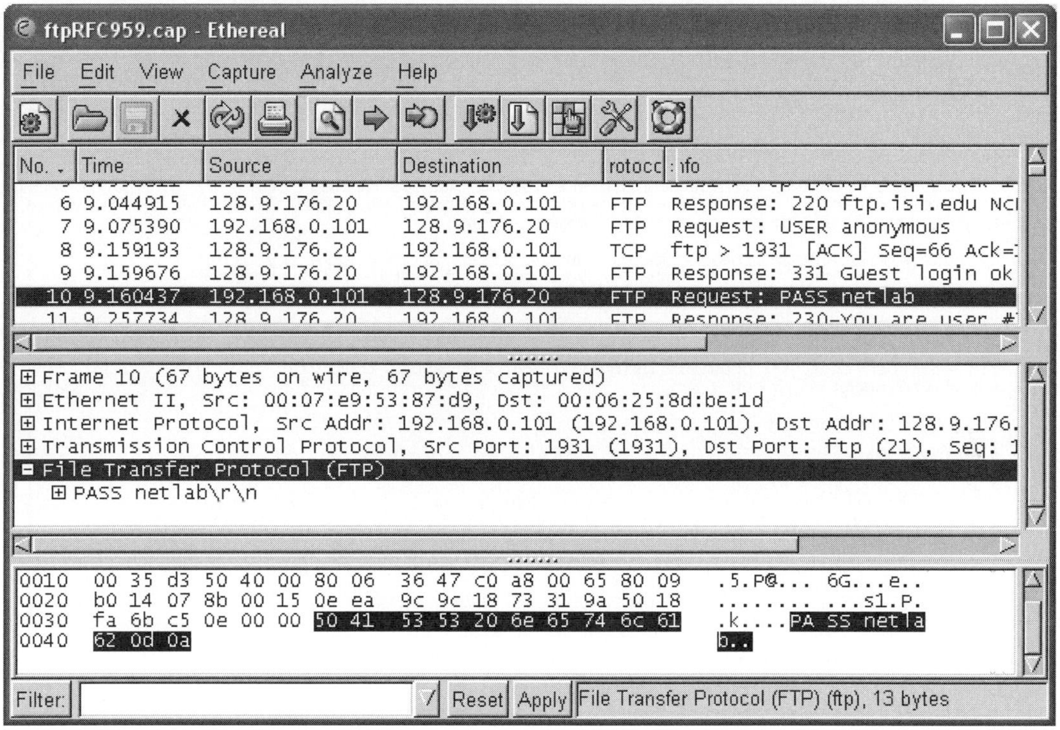

This problem with plain text passwords is one reason that many system administrators do not permit users to run protocol analyzer software like Ethereal on their networks. In response to this problem, more secure application protocols like secure copy (scp) and secure shell (ssh) have been designed to replace FTP and telnet. These applications encrypt messages on the sending machine and decrypt them on the receiving machine. These applications typically encrypt not only the username and password, but also the data being transferred. This protects both user's passwords and the privacy of the information they are exchanging.

You can view the full contents of the control channel by selecting one of the packets in the stream (e.g. packet 10) and then choosing "Follow TCP Stream" from the Analyze menu. Notice that the client commands are highlighted with a darker background than the server responses.

Figure 2.3.3: Transcript of FTP Control Channel

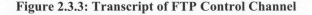

```
Contents of TCP stream

USER anonymous
331 Guest login ok, send your complete e-mail address as password.
PASS netlab
230-You are user #28 of 550 simultaneous users allowed.
230-
230-If you have problems downloading and are seeing "Access denied" or
230-"Permission denied", please make sure that you started your FTP client in
230-a directory to which you have write permission.
230-
230-If your FTP client crashes or hangs shortly after login please try using
230-a dash (-) as the first character of your password.  This will turn off
230-the informational messages that may be confusing your FTP client.
230-
230-All transfers and commands to and from this host are logged.
230-
230-If you experience any problems using ftp, please report them via
230-e-mail to Action@isi.edu.
230-
230 Logged in anonymously.
PWD
257 "/" is cwd.
SYST
215 UNIX Type: L8
PASV
227 Entering Passive Mode (128,9,176,20,133,130)
LIST
150 Data connection accepted from 24.95.16.111:1932; transfer starting.
226 Listing completed.
CWD in-notes
250-"/in-notes" is new cwd.
250-
250-*==================================================================*
250-*                                                                  *
250-* This directory is maintained by the RFC Editor.  If you experience *
250-* any problems, please report them to rfc-editor@rfc-editor.org.   *
250-*                                                                  *
250-*==================================================================*
250 
PWD
257 "/in-notes" is cwd.
PASV
227 Entering Passive Mode (128,9,176,20,133,140)
LIST
150 Data connection accepted from 24.95.16.111:1933; transfer starting.
226 Listing completed.
TYPE I
200 Type okay.
PASV
227 Entering Passive Mode (128,9,176,20,133,199)
RETR rfc959.txt
```

Entire conversation (2005 bytes)　　▲ ASCII ◇ EBCDIC Print Save As Filter out this stream Close

Once the username and password exchange is complete, the FTP client issues the command "PWD" to identify the current working directory. The server responds that the current working directory is the root directory "/". The client also requests information about the FTP server itself with the command "SYST."

The next command "PASV" asks the server to prepare for the first incoming data connection. The server responds in packet 19 "227 Entering

Passive Mode." This indicates its willingness to open a socket on which it will accept an incoming data connection from the client.

The server sends 6 numbers (128, 9, 176, 20, 133, 130) to indicate the IP address and port number to which the client should connect. The first four should look familiar; they represent the four components of the server's IP address 128.9.176.20. The second two numbers together represent the port number; the first indicates the high order 8 bits of the port number, and the second indicates the low order bits of the port number. The decimal number 133 corresponds to the binary number 10000101 (high order bits) and similarly the decimal number 130 corresponds to the binary number 10000010 (low order bits). Concatenating these two numbers together (high then low), we get 1000010110000010 or decimal, 34178. Sure enough, in the next packet (20), the client initiates a connection to IP address 128.9.176.20 port 34178. (To see this you will need to rest the display filter to show the entire trace and not simply the control channel.)

DATA CHANNELS

This data channel is used to list the contents of the current working directory (the root directory in this case). This client requests this by sending the LIST command over the control channel once the data channel is established. When the directory listing is complete, the data channel is closed.

After the directory information is transferred, the FTP client displayed it to us. Some clients display the information as a set of folders in a GUI window while others display the information in a text based listing. Regardless of the display format, the user uses the information to navigate through the directory structure. For example, we chose to enter the in-notes directory. This choice was then translated into the "CWD in-notes" command sent over FTP control channel.

Once in the directory in-notes, the contents of the directory is listed over a second data channel using the same procedure we described from the root directory. Finally, we choose to retrieve the file rfc959.txt using the RETR command.

Before the file transfer, there is one additional command "TYPE I." FTP supports various data representations for files including I for Image, A for ASCII and E for EBCDIC. Although the file being transferred is a plain text ASCII file, it is still transferred as an Image type by our FTP client. Image is designed to transfer binary files efficiently but can also be used to transfer text files as illustrated in this example.

The file, rfc959.txt, is sent over a third data channel in much the same way as the directory listings. In each case, the FTP client requests a passive channel, connects to the server and then requests the data to be transferred over this channel. Although the process is the same, the FTP client handles the data transferred in different ways. The directory contents are displayed to the user while the file contents are written into a file on the local machine.

In total, there are four TCP connections established in this trace between our local machine and the FTP server – one control channel, two data channels for directory listings, and one data channel for file transfer. We can view some summary information about each of these connections using a tool in the Analyze Menu. Choose Analyze...Statistics…Conversation List...TCP (IPv4 IPv6).

Figure 2.3.4: TCP Conversations List

EP1 Address	Port	EP2 Address	Port	Frames *	Bytes	-> Frames	-> Bytes	<- Frames	<- Bytes
128.9.176.20	34188	192.168.0.101	1933	293	272481	192	267019	101	5462
128.9.176.20	34247	192.168.0.101	1934	168	156408	110	153268	58	3140
192.168.0.101	1931	128.9.176.20	21	46	4525	25	1488	21	3037
128.9.176.20	34178	192.168.0.101	1932	10	4879	5	4601	5	278

Note that in TCP conversation display, the connections are not listed in the order in which they occur. The first connection established is actually listed third. It is the connection from port 1931 of the local machine (192.168.0.1) to port 21 of the server machine (128.9.176.20).

The following table lists the connections in the order they occur along with the port numbers used on either end. Notice that the port numbers on the local machine are increasing order from 1931 through 1934. It is common for operating systems to assign ports in increasing order to new connections that do not request a particular port number.

On the server machine, the control connection uses port 21. FTP servers typically listen on the well-known port number 21 much like HTTP servers typically listen on the well-known port number 80. These conventions are set by an organization called the Internet Assigned Numbers Authority (**www.iana.org**). In the earlier days of the Internet, this information was published in a series of RFC called "Assigned Numbers." RFC 1700 was the last one in this series and RFC 3232 officially noted the transition of this information to the IANA.

The data channels do not use a well-known port number on the server machine. They are instead assigned increasing numbers 34178, 34188, 34247. Unlike on the local machine, there are gaps in this increasing set. This is due to other incoming connections being serviced simultaneously by the same FTP server. If we were using Ethereal to capture traffic on the FTP server, we would be able to see all of these simultaneous connections.

	Port on local machine 192.168.0.1	Port on server machine 128.9.176.20
Control channel	1931	21
Data channel 1 Directory listing for /	1932	34178
Data channel 2 Directory listing for in-notes	1933	34188
Data channel 3 Retrieve file	1934	34247

Notice that for each data connection, the server reports an incoming data connection from IP address 24.95.16.111 instead of 192.168.0.1. This is because the Linksys cable modem router on our local network is performing network address translation (NAT). NAT takes a private set of IP addresses and maps them on to one or more globally routable IP addresses.

Using Follow TCP Stream, we can view the contents of the data channels as we did for the control channel. Notice that the directory listings and file data are also sent in plain text. This illustrates that usernames and passwords are not the only pieces of information that can be compromised using protocols like FTP. If you retrieve a private file using FTP, its contents are clearly visible on the network.

QUESTIONS

Answer the following questions about the file **ftpRFC959.cap**.

1. Record the packet number for the first packet (i.e. TCP SYN packets) for each of the four connections in the trace. How can you make it easier to find these packets using a display filter?

2. Draw a time line showing when the control channel and each of the data channels begin and end. How can you use display filters to make this easier?

3. How long did it take to transfer the file? What if we consider the entire FTP session? What if we consider just the data connection that transmitted the file itself? Compute the bandwidth (MB/sec) for each? How can you determine the size of the file?

4. Use Follow TCP Stream to examine the control channel. How much data is sent from server to client? From client to server?

5. Use Follow TCP Stream to examine each of the data channels. In each case, how much data is sent from server to client? How much data is sent from client to server? Which required the most data, the text of the RFC or the directory listings?

6. We discussed how the gaps in the sequence of port numbers on the server indicate simultaneous requests. Besides these gaps, find some other evidence of other simultaneous connections. (Hint: Examine the contents of the control channel.)

7. For the second data channel, how does the server respond to the client's request for a passive connection? What 6 numbers accompany this response? How does the client use these 6 numbers to identify the IP address and port number? For the port number, give the 16 digit binary number that indicated the port number and describe how it is computed? (Hint: The Calculator in the Start menu of most Windows machines under Accessories can be used in Scientific Mode (View.Scientific Mode) for this purpose. There are also decimal to binary conversion calculators available on-line.)

DISCUSSION AND INVESTIGATION

1. What should happen if the user of an FTP client attempts to CD into a directory that does not exist? How could the FTP client prevent this error locally? How should the server respond if the FTP client issued a CWD for a directory that does not exist? Give the response code and specify the sections of RFC 959 that specify this behavior.

2. In this example, data was always transferred over a separate channel. Could data be transferred over the control channel? Propose the syntax for such a transfer. Does such a facility exist in FTP?

3. When using PASV, the client instructs the server to wait for an incoming data connection. What would happen if a third party connected before the real client? Is there anything in the FTP specification to prevent this? Could such an attack be automated?

4. From what you've learned in this exercise, do you see any other weaknesses in FTP that could be exploited by an attacker? First, attempt to analyze the protocol yourself and then search the web for information on vulnerabilities in FTP.

RESOURCES

- RFC 959, File Transfer Protocol (FTP), **ftp://ftp.rfc-editor.org/in-notes/rfc959.txt**

- RFC 3232, Assigned Numbers: RFC 1700 is Replaced by an On-line Database, **ftp://ftp.rfc-editor.org/in-notes/rfc3232.txt**

- RFC 1700, Assigned Numbers, **ftp://ftp.rfc-editor.org/in-notes/rfc1700.txt**

- Internet Assigned Numbers Authority, **http://www.iana.org**

- Port Numbers, **http://www.iana.org/assignments/port-numbers**

- Web search: FTP Attacks

Application Layer Protocols:
Exercise 2.4

Sending and Receiving E-mail with SMTP and POP

INTRODUCTION

E-mail was one of the first "killer" applications in the Internet and after web browsing; it is probably still the most popular.

Most e-mail clients (Outlook, Eudora, Netscape mail, etc.) allow users to compose e-mail messages and place them in an outgoing mailbox, send all messages in the outgoing mailbox and retrieve new mail messages into an incoming mailbox. Most users are aware that they must be connected to the Internet to send and receive messages, but they may not know the details of the network traffic required. This exercise will help you explore these details.

The process of sending mail is quite different than the process of receiving mail; they even use different application level protocols. E-mail clients typically use Simple Mail Transfer Protocol (SMTP) to transfer outgoing mail and the Post Office Protocol (POP) for retrieving incoming mail. However, there is a good deal of variation. Internet Message Access Protocol or IMAP is another popular protocol for retrieving messages. Some e-mail clients retrieve mail through a file system shared with the mail server. Some e-mail clients can also use proprietary protocols in addition to open Internet standards when transferring mail. Some e-mail clients even send and receive e-mail using HTTP.

When sending mail, an e-mail client typically connects to a single local mail server. It sends all the outgoing mail to this server regardless of the address of the intended recipient. This local mail server places the messages in an outgoing mail queue. At this point, the e-mail client that sent the mail is no longer involved in the transfer. Instead, the local mail server takes responsibility for transferring the message to a local mail server for each recipient. SMTP is often used both for the original transfer between the e-mail client and the local mail server as well as the transfers from the local mail server to each recipient's mail server.

Once an e-mail message reaches the recipient's incoming mail server, it is placed in a queue with all the other incoming messages for that same user. The user can then retrieve all their incoming mail from the server with a protocol like POP.

Figure 2.4.1: Role of SMTP and POP in E-mail Delivery

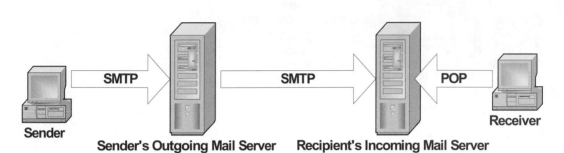

Before using an e-mail client to send and receive mail, you must specify your e-mail address, a password for the account, and the names of the outgoing and incoming mail servers. Users must present a password in order to retrieve their mail, but typically they can send mail without a password.

CONFIGURATION

This trace was taken on a private network. A server machine and a laptop both running Linux were connected to a cable modem router.

The server machine was set to run a DNS server, an SMTP server and a POP3 server. These servers were configured to use the domain testingsmtp.org. This domain was only set up locally for the purpose of this experiment and is not registered in the global Internet.

On the mail servers, we created two accounts: sendmemail@testing smtp.org and netwatcher@testingsmtp.org. We configured a mail client on the laptop with these two accounts. For both accounts, we directed the mail client to use mail.testingsmtp.org for outgoing mail and pop3.testingsmtp.org for incoming mail.

The machine names mail.testingsmtp.org and pop3.testingsmtp.org both refer to the same machine, 192.168.32.206. The SMTP server listens on port number 25 and the POP3 server listens on port 110. This machine also happens to run the DNS server that is configured to translate names in the testingsmtp.org domain. It is actually not uncommon for small ISPs to run many server processes on the same machine.

In this configuration, we will see only the transfers between the e-mail clients and the mail servers. The mail servers take advantage of the fact that they are on the same machine to communicate directly rather than over the network.

Figure 2.4.2: Exercise Configuration

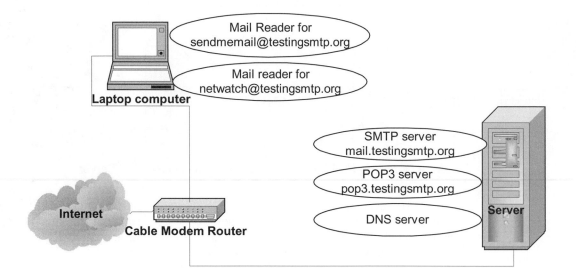

EXPERIMENT

OUTGOING MAIL

Using an e-mail client on the laptop, we sent a simple message from netwatch@testingsmtp.org to sendmemail@testingsmtp.org. We captured the resulting network traffic in the file **plain_smtp.cap.** You can open this file from the accompanying CD and follow along.

The first traffic we see is several DNS request and replies. The first three DNS requests (packets 1, 3, and 5) ask for the IP address of the outgoing mail server, mail.testingsmtp.org. The first two of these are AAAA records and the third is an A record. These all request machine name to IP address translation, but the AAAA records are used for Ipv6 compatibility. The DNS server responds to the A request with the IP address, 192.168.32.206. To double check the identify of this machine, a PTR request is sent in packet 7 to translate the IP address 192.168.32.206 back to its corresponding machine name. The DNS server responds with the name, mail.testingsmtp.org.

Notice that the PTR query specifies the IP address 192.168.32.206 as 206.32.168.192.in-addr.arpa. DNS or the Domain Name Service is most often used to translate domain names into IP addresses. The in-addr.arpa domain is a special domain used to enable these reverse lookups.

In packet 9, a TCP connection is initiated from e-mail client on the laptop to the port 25 of 192.168.32.206. This is the well known port on which the SMTP server listens.

The server is the first to send data over the newly established connection. In packet 12, it says "220 Welcome! Please send your message! ESMTP." This indicates that it is ready to receive the outgoing mail and that it is capable of speaking Extended SMTP. The e-mail client responds in packet 16 with "EHLO laptop.testingsmtp.org." In original SMTP, the client answers "HELO," but in extended SMTP the client answers "EHLO." It also identifies itself as the machine "laptop.testingsmtp.org."

In packets 14 and 15, we see that the mail server issues a DNS request so that it will be able to validate the identity of the client. It knows the IP address of the client from the TCP connection itself (192.168.32.208). It issues a DNS PTR request asking for the machine name corresponding to that IP address. The DNS server responds with "laptop.testingsmtp.org." Thus, when the client claims to have that machine name in packet 16, the mail server responds with "250-Welcome! Please send your message." Notice that even though the response message is similar, the response code has changed from 220 to 250.

Most SMTP servers today are configured to check the identity of e-mail clients and to accept outgoing mail only from machines in their local network. This makes it harder to use the resources of third party mail servers to send large numbers of SPAM messages or to hide the true source of the forged mail.

You can view the full contents of the control channel by selecting one of the packets in the stream (e.g. packet 9) and then choosing "Follow TCP Stream" from the Analyze menu. Notice that the client commands are shown in red and the server responses in blue.

Transferring an e-mail message over SMTP involves three primary commands: "MAIL FROM," "RCPT TO," and "DATA," as described in RFC 2821. The MAIL FROM line specifies the e-mail address of the sender. The "RCPT TO" line specifies the e-mail address of one recipient. Multiple "RCPT TO" commands are used to specify multiple recipients. Finally the DATA command instructs the server to treat the lines that follow as the body of the e-mail message. The DATA section is terminated by a single "."on a line by itself (CRLF.CRLF).

Figure 2.4.3: Sending mail with SMTP

Notice the DATA section contains a series of headers (Subject, From, To, Content-Type, etc.) as well as the actual text of the message. These headers are simply part of the DATA section as far as SMTP is concerned. Only SMTP commands, MAIL FROM and RCPT TO, affect how the mail is delivered. Headers in the DATA section affect what is displayed to recipients.

An excellent example of this is the "Bcc" or Blind Carbon Copy line provided by most e-mail clients. When a user is composing a message, they list the recipients of the message in the To field, the Cc field and the Bcc field. The e-mail client will translate an e-mail address in each of these fields into a "RCPT TO" command line. However, only the To and Cc fields are translated into headers within the DATA section. It is the RCPT TO lines that control the actual delivery of data so recipients on the Bcc line will get a copy of the e-mail.

However, the headers within the DATA section determine what is displayed to recipients. Since the Bcc addresses are not listed in the headers, there will be no indication that they received a copy.

Notice that there is one blank line between the last header (Content-Transfer-Encoding) and the first line of the e-mail message (Hi!). This division between the mail headers and the mail body is defined by RFC 2822.

Once the DATA section is terminated with CRLF.CRLF, the e-mail client could use the same SMTP connection to transfer additional mail messages. It would simply send another set of MAIL FROM, RCPT TO, and DATA commands. In this case, the e-mail client had only one message to transfer, and so it terminates the connection with a RSET and a QUIT.

The recipient of this message is another user in the same domain testingsmtp.org. If the recipient of the message were in another domain, we would expect to see mail.testingsmtp.org initiate an SMTP connection to the recipient's incoming mail server. This SMTP session would look similar. In particular, the MAIL FROM and RCPT TO commands would be the same. The DATA section would also be the same with the exception of some additional header lines that are added by each mail server that handles the message.

Before such an SMTP connection could be established, the local name server would first need to learn the name and IP address of the recipient's local name server. (It is not always mail.DOMAINNAME like mail.testingsmtp.org nor it is usually the name following the @ in their e-mail address like testingsmtp.org.) This can be accomplished with a special DNS query of type MX for mail exchange.

INCOMING MAIL

Using an e-mail client on the laptop, we retrieved messages sent to sendmemail@testingsmtp.org, including the message we saw sent in the previous trace. We captured the resulting network traffic in the file `pop3_initial.cap`. You can open this file from the accompanying CD and follow along.

The first 8 packets contain a set of DNS requests to determine the IP address for the incoming mail server, pop3.testingsmtp.org. These are similar to the DNS requests in the file `plain_smtp.cap`.

The POP connection begins with packet 11. Using Follow TCP Stream, we can view the entire exchange. The protocol used is version 3 of the Post Office Protocol, which is defined in RFC 1939. As in SMTP, the server speaks first (+OK <24906.1074667309@pop3.testingsmtp.org>).

The first command issued by the client is CAPA. This is actually defined in RFC 2449, "POP3 Extension Mechanism." It requests that the server return a list of the capabilities including authorization mechanisms that it supports. This server does not implement this feature and answers "-ERR authorization first."

Lacking information on other possible authorization mechanisms, the client sends the username and password in the plain text with the USER and PASS commands. The server responds that the username and password are both acceptable.

The client once again tries the CAPA command and the server now answers "-ERR unimplemented." It appears that authorization was required to find out that the CAPA command was unimplemented.

The next three commands: "UIDL 1," "LIST," and "UIDL," are used to gather information about the messages waiting in the incoming queue for the user, sendmemail. They indicate that there are two messages. The LIST command returns a list of messages with their size in octets. The UIDL command returns a list of messages with an identification number. The POP RFC does not specify how the server should assign these identification numbers. It simply requires that the same number be used to identify a message across sessions, and that it be unique in that user's mailbox.

The LIST and UIDL commands provide information to the e-mail client, which can allow it to decide whether to download the messages in the queue. For example, it can look at the identification number to decide if it already has a copy of a given message or it can look at the size to determine if it is willing to download a message of that size. This can be especially important on slow network links where it is important to avoid downloading large or unnecessary messages.

The e-mail client next issues the command "RETR 1" to request that message 1 is sent over the channel. It turns out that message 1 is the mail message that we saw transferred over SMTP in the file **plain_smtp.cap**.

E-MAIL HEADERS

If you compare the mail message that we saw transferred over SMTP to the message we see being retrieved here, you will see that it is the same except that four additional header lines have been added. The first header line in the SMTP transfer was "Subject: The network racks need to be organized." The four lines above it were added by the mail servers as they processed the message.

If we read the headers in order, starting with the header immediately above the Subject header, we can follow the processing steps in order. The first line added is "Received: from laptop.testingsmtp.org (192.168.32.208) by mail.testingsmtp.org with SMTP; 21 Jan 2004 06:40:40 –0000." This is a record of the SMTP transfer we observed.

The second line added is "Received: (qmail 24897 invoked from network); 21 Jan 2004 06:40:40 –0000." This line indicates that just as soon as the SMTP server received it from the e-mail client on the laptop, it transferred the message to the qmail server we were running. Then qmail placed it in the mailbox for user sendmemail and added the header "Delivered-To: sendmemail@testing smtp.org." Finally, qmail added a Return-Path header to reflect the contents of the MAIL FROM field used in transferring the message.

The full set of headers are delivered to the recipient. Although e-mail clients generally do not display the full headers by default, most can be used to export the message along with all its headers. These headers can be extremely useful in tracking the origin of unwanted or abusive messages. However, these headers can be forged. If you trust your local mail server, then the header they add should be legitimate as well as the IP Address information they report as the source of the message. Any headers before that may or may not have been added by legitimate mail servers.

On-line services like Spamcop (**www.spamcop.net**) allow you to enter an e-mail with full headers and it will extract from it the likely source of the message. They do this by consulting domain registration information, IP address allocation information, and lists of known spammers.

After retrieving message one, the client issues a request to retrieve message two. This message is also from netwatch@testingsmtp.org and was sent from laptop.testingsmtp.org. We did not trace the sending of this message however.

This second message contains both a text message and a picture. Pictures, like many other things we transfer over e-mail these days, are stored as binary data and not as plain text. However, SMTP and POP are designed to transfer only ASCII characters.

A standard called Multipurpose Internet Mail Extensions or MIME was introduced both to allow binary data to be encoded in ASCII text and to allow multiple separate objects to be combined into a single e-mail message. It also allows the sender to specify the type of each object in the message so that the recipient's e-mail client will know how best to display it.

Both the first and second message use Mime1.0 as specified by the Mime-Version Header. The first message is of type plain text (Content-Type: text/plain) and is represented in 7-bit ASCII (Content-Transfer-Encoding: 7bit). The second message, however, contains multiple objects of different types, and so the type of the overall messages is multipart/mixed. The Content-Type header for the second message also specifies a string that will be used to separate the two objects (=-WXX8AgJUfvZdvWKypDE8). This string occurs before the first object, which is a plain text message, and again before the second object, which is a picture of type image/png. The picture file, MessyRack.png, which contains binary data is encoded in base64 encoding so that it can be sent through SMTP and POP.

The POP3 connection shows what this message looks when it traverses the network and the following screenshot shows what it looked like when it was displayed in the recipient's mailbox.

Figure 2.4.4: E-mail Message

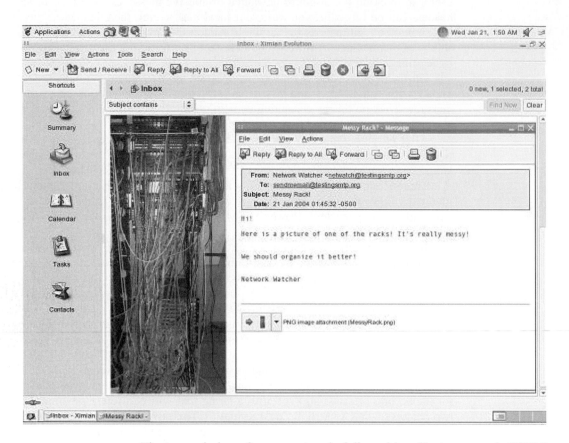

The transmission of message two is followed by client commands "DELE 1" and "DELE 2." This deletes the messages from sendmemail's mailbox on the mail server. If the client does not issue a DELE command for a message, it will remain on the server and will appear in the list of available messages in subsequent sessions. Many e-mail clients allow users to choose whether they will leave all messages on the server, delete them all, or delete them after a specified amount of time.

Finally, the client ends the session with the QUIT command.

NO MAIL

After terminating the previous POP connection to the server, we established another one to illustrate what the POP session looks like when there is no mail on the server. We captured the resulting network traffic in the file `pop3.nonewmessages.cap`. You can open this file from the accompanying CD and follow along.

The POP3 session begins in packet 15. You can use Follow TCP Stream to display the full conversation. It begins identically with a failed CAPA command, a successful set of USER and PASS commands, and a second failed CAPA command.

This time, the command "UIDL 1" returns "-ERR not that many messages," and the LIST command returns an empty list.

If you configure your e-mail client to check for new mail every few minutes, then a session like this would traverse the network every few minutes. This is equivalent to announcing your username and password over and over again. If you use POP with plain text passwords, you greatly reduce the window of opportunity for capturing your password if you check mail manually.

QUESTIONS

Answer the following questions about the files `plain_smtp.cap`, `pop3.initial.cap`, and `pop3.nonewmessages.cap`.

1. What is the password for user sendmemail? How did you know?

2. Examine the headers of the first e-mail in the `pop3.initial.cap` trace. Which headers are added by the sending machine and which by the mail server machine? How do you know?

3. What time does the Received header indicate that the first e-mail message (Subject "The network racks need to be organized") was received? What time does the Date header indicate that the message was sent by the user? What time does the Ethereal trace indicate that the e-mail message was sent? Suggest an explanation for the differences.

4. How much time elapsed between the SMTP session we captured in `plain_smtp.cap` and the SMTP session that transferred Messy Rack.png? How did you know?

5. We saw the transfer of the first e-mail message via SMTP, but not the second. Give the SMTP commands that would be required to transfer the second message. Give the headers that would have been transferred with the e-mail message originally, but do not repeat the entire DATA section of the transfer. Describe how you determined your answer.

6. Is it safe to use the Date stamp on an e-mail message as proof of when an e-mail was sent? For example, should an instructor accept the date stamp on an e-mail as iron clad proof that an assignment was completed on time? Why or why not?

7. From the perspective of SMTP, is there any distinction between recipients on the To line and the Cc (or carbon copy) line of an e-mail message? Why or why not? How about recipients on the Bcc (or blind carbon copy) line?

8. How might an e-mail client implement a policy to leave messages on the POP server for one week before deleting them? What would happen if you did not retrieve your mail for over a week? Would this policy delete mail you had never seen?

DISCUSSION AND INVESTIGATION

1. Many web sites offer e-mail accounts for which mail is both sent and received via HTTP. Briefly describe how mail might be sent over SMTP and how it might be retrieved. If you have access to a web-based e-mail account, you may want to watch what they really do.

2. Spammers often add forged e-mail headers to the e-mail they send. Describe how e-mail headers could be forged? What advantage might they gain from doing this? What safe guards are in place to detect such a forgery?

3. HTTP specifies the length of objects being transferred. Rather than specify a length, SMTP has a special sequence of characters that indicates the end. Compare and contrast these methods. Would it be easy to specify a length in SMTP? Why or why not?

4. See if you can extract the data for the picture from the second e-mail in the **pop3.initial.cap** trace. To display the picture, you will need to decode it (recall it is encoded in ASCII for transmission over SMTP), save it to a PNG file (ex. foo.png), and then open it with an application that displays images in that format.

5. Spam mail is an epidemic in the Internet. Research the state-of-the-art in Spam prevention. Historically, new tactics for fighting spam have been countered by increasing sophisticated spamming techniques. Do any of the proposed techniques seem promising for ending spam or will they simply require a corresponding response from spammers?

RESOURCES

- RFC 2821, Simple Mail Transfer Protocol, **ftp://ftp.rfc-editor.org/in-notes/rfc2821.txt**

- RFC 2822, Internet Message Format, **ftp://ftp.rfc-editor.org/in-notes/rfc2822.txt**

- RFC 821, Simple Mail Transfer Protocol, **ftp://ftp.rfc-editor.org/in-notes/rfc821.txt**

- RFC 2505, Anti-Spam Recommendations for SMTP MTAs, **ftp://ftp.rfc-editor.org/in-notes/rfc2505.txt**

- RFC 1939, Post Office Protocol – Version 3, **ftp://ftp.rfc-editor.org/in-notes/rfc1939.txt**

- RFC3501, Internet Message Access Protocol – Version 4rev1, **ftp://ftp.rfc-editor.org/in-notes/rfc3501.txt**

- RFC 2449, POP3 Extension Mechanism, **ftp://ftp.rfc-editor.org/in-notes/rfc2449.txt**

- RFC 2045, Multipurpose Internet Mail Extensions (MIME) Part One: Format of Internet Message Bodies, **ftp://ftp.rfc-editor.org/in-notes/rfc2045.txt**

- Spamcop, **http://www.spamcop.net**

- Spam Conference, **http://www.spamconference.org**

- Web search: Spam legislation

Section 3: Transport Layer Protocols

Introduction

Transport Layer protocols deliver data from one application running in the Internet to another. They are not concerned with the actual data being transferred nor are they concerned with identifying the correct destination host.

There are two main transport layer protocols in use in the Internet today, the Transmission Control Protocol (TCP) and the User Datagram Protocol (UDP).

Transport protocols specify source and destination port numbers that are used in locating the correct application end point for both the sender and the receiver. This process is called *multiplexing* and *demultiplexing*. Multiple streams of data generated by applications on the same Internet host are multiplexed over a single outgoing connection. Multiple streams of data destined for different applications on the same Internet host may arrive on a single incoming connection, but they are demultiplexed and delivered to the correct application endpoint. For example, a web browser and an e-mail client may be running on the same machine, but their traffic is separated correctly by the source and destination port numbers.

Both TCP and UDP provide multiplexing and demulitplexing, but TCP provides many other features that UDP does not including reliable, in-order message delivery, flow control and congestion control. We will discuss each of these features in detail in the exercises in this section.

In Exercise 1, we begin by examining simple TCP streams. We look at the TCP segment header and discuss how TCP accomplishes reliable, in-order message delivery.

In Exercise 2, we look in detail at retransmission in TCP. We consider the various events that cause TCP to send another copy of data previously transmitted. We look at variants of TCP including TCP with selective acknowledgements.

In Exercise 3, we introduce UDP and the UDP datagram header. We compare a TCP stream and UDP stream that transmit the exact same data. We also analyze how TCP and UDP transmitters handle the case when there is no receiver listening for incoming data.

Finally, in Exercise 4, we examine the flow control and congestion control properties of TCP. Flow control means that TCP senders avoid overwhelming receivers with more data than they can handle. Congestion control means that TCP senders avoid overwhelming the network with too much data. We compare this to UDP, which has neither flow control nor congestion control. We examine traces of concurrent streams, two TCP streams running in parallel, a TCP stream running in parallel with a UDP stream, and two UDP streams running in parallel. We show that TCP senders adapt to share the network fairly with each other, while UDP senders make no attempt to limit their sending rate.

Transport Layer Protocols:
Exercise **3.1**

Introduction to TCP

INTRODUCTION

TCP or the Transmission Control Protocol is the dominant transport layer protocol in the Internet. It provides a reliable, in-order stream of data between two applications, even if the applications are running on different machines and separated by a network that can drop, reorder, or corrupt the packets. TCP provides this reliable data stream by detecting if packets are lost, delayed, or changed in transit and retransmitting them.

A good way to understand how TCP accomplishes this is to think how you might handle sending a very large document over a fax machine that skips pages. You would most likely number the pages so that the receiver could tell what portions were missing. You might send a special cover page that tells how many pages there are so that the receiver would know how many pages to expect. You would need feedback from the receiver to know what was missing so that you could resend them. TCP records much of this same information in the header that it adds to each segment.

Every TCP segment consists of a header followed by an optional data portion. The format of the header is defined in RFC 793 and is shown below. The header always begins with 32 bits for the port used on the sending machine and is followed by 32 bits for the port used on the destination machine.

The next 32 bits are used for a sequence number. In our example of faxing pages with a machine that skips pages, this is the equivalent of numbering the pages. The sequence number indicates the number of the first byte of data in this packet.

The next 32 bits are used for an acknowledgement number. In our fax machine example, this is the equivalent of feedback from the receiver indicating which pages have been successfully received. A TCP receiver always sets this field to the number of the next byte it is expecting in the stream. An acknowledgment number of 10 would indicate that bytes 0 through 9 have been successfully received. Any data that arrives out of order is not acknowledged until all the previous data can be acknowledged. In other words, if bytes 0 through 9 have been received correctly, and then byte 11 arrives, the TCP receiver cannot indicate that 11 has arrived until 10 arrives.

Figure 3.1.1: TCP Segment Header

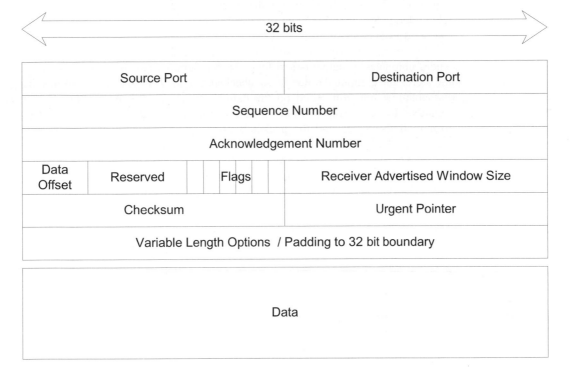

The next field of the header is the "Data Offset" field, it indicates where the data portion of segment begins. This is necessary because the TCP header can vary in length depending on whether the variable length option field is used.

The flag section contains six different bits: the URGENT bit, the ACKNOWLEDGEMENT bit, the PUSH bit, the RESET bit, the SYN bit, and the FIN bit. The ACKNOWLEDGEMENT bit simply indicates whether the acknowledgment field is valid. The PUSH bit is used to indicate the sending application specifically requested that the data be sent immediately. The SYN, FIN, and RESET bits are all used in opening or closing the connection. We will discuss these later in this exercise. The URGENT bit and the Urgent pointer field are less commonly used and will not be discussed.

The next field is the "Receiver Advertised Window" field. It indicates how much data the receiver can handle receiving. There is no point sending data when a receiver is overwhelmed. Resources both on the sender and in the network are wasted when they are used to send data that the receiver drops as soon as it arrives.

It is important to realize that a TCP connection is a *full duplex* connection. This means that both end points can both send and receive data simultaneously. A TCP segment sent from end point A to B can contain data sent from A to B as well as acknowledgements of data previously sent from B to A. In particular, the sequence number field refers to the data being sent from A to B and the acknowledgement number field and the receiver's advertised window refer to data send from B to A.

The checksum field is used to detect corruption of data in transit. The sender computes a mathematical function that summarizes the header and data and stores the computed value in the checksum field. The receiver computes the mathematical function based on the data received and compares the value it computed to the checksum field. If there is a mismatch, then there has been an error in transmission and the packet is discarded. Eventually, the sender will detect this as a loss and resend.

In this exercise, we will explore some of the basics of how TCP streams work. We will start by looking at a synthetically generated TCP stream on a local network. Then we will look at a TCP stream carrying interactive data.

CONFIGURATION

The traces used in this exercise were taken on a private network. A desktop PC and a laptop were connected to the Internet via a cable modem router.

On both machines, we installed a tool for generating TCP streams with specific characteristics called **ttcp**. (We actually used **pcattcp**, a version of **ttcp** for Windows.) To use **ttcp**, you start a receiver on one machine and then start a transmitter on the other machine. The transmitter establishes a TCP connection with the waiting receiver and then sends data over the opened channel.

Figure 3.1.2: Exercise Configuration

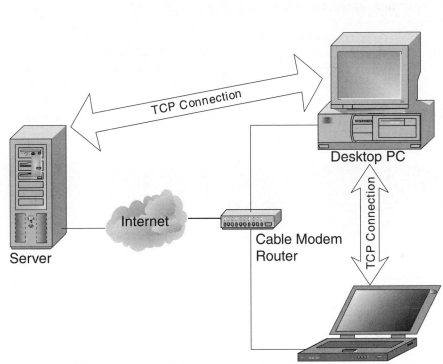

EXPERIMENT

LOCAL TTCP CONNECTION

We started our experiment with a quiet network. On the laptop, we ran the receiver for our **ttcp** stream. It began listening on TCP port 5001. Here is the entire command line output for the receiver:

```
C:\Downloads\ttcp>pcattcp -r
PCAUSA Test TCP Utility V2.01.01.07
TCP Receive Test
Local Host  : cs-00065be34d1d
***************
Listening...: On port 5001

    Accept      : TCP <- 192.168.0.100:2440
```

```
Buffer Size : 8192; Alignment: 16384/0
      Receive Mode: Sinking (discarding) Data
      Statistics  : TCP <- 192.168.0.100:2440
8192 bytes in 0.02 real seconds = 400.00 KB/sec ***
numCalls: 2; msec/call: 10.24; calls/sec: 100.00
```

We started a network capture using Ethereal. On the desktop machine, we started the transmitter for our **ttcp** stream. On the command line, we specified the IP address of the laptop, 192.168.0.102. By default, **ttcp** will send 2048 buffers of size 8192 bytes for a total of 16 MB of data. Both the size of the buffers and the number of sends can be controlled from the command line. We choose to send just one buffer of size 8192 bytes. Here is the entire command line output from the transmitter:

```
C:\Downloads\ttcp>pcattcp -t -n 192.168.0.102
PCAUSA Test TCP Utility V2.01.01.07
TCP Transmit Test
    Transmit    : TCP <- 192.168.0.102:5001
    Buffer Size : 8192; Alignment: 16384/0
    TCP_NODELAY : DISABLED (0)
    Connect     : Connected to 192.168.0.102:5001
    Send Mode   : Send Pattern; Number of Buffers: 1
    Statistics  : TCP <- 192.168.0.102:5001
8192 bytes in 0.00 real seconds = 1.#J KB/sec ***
numCalls: 1; msec/call: 0.0; calls/sec: 1.#J
```

We waited for both the transmitter and the receiver to exit and then we stopped the capture. We saved the resulting trace in the file **tcp_pcattcp_n1.cap**. You can open this file from the accompanying CD and follow along.

CONNECTION ESTABLISHMENT

TCP connections are established with a set of three messages called the *three-way handshake.* The three-way handshake is found in packets 3 through 5 of **tcp_pcattcp_n1.cap.**

The first message in this handshake is a TCP segment with no data and the SYN bit in the header set to one. This first message is often called the SYN packet. The sequence number in this segment may be set to any value. Regardless of its value, it indicates the first number the client will use to number subsequent messages.   It may seem odd that connections do not automatically start counting at one. Choosing a random number to begin counting helps avoid misinterpreting packets from old connections as part of the existing connection.

Notice that in packet 3, Ethereal displays the sequence number as zero. However, if you select the sequence number field in the header, the data "94 f2 2e be" is highlighted in the raw pane. Ethereal's display reflects the logical sequence number, but the real initial sequence number is not zero.

Figure 3.1.3: Logical vs. Actual Initial Sequence Number

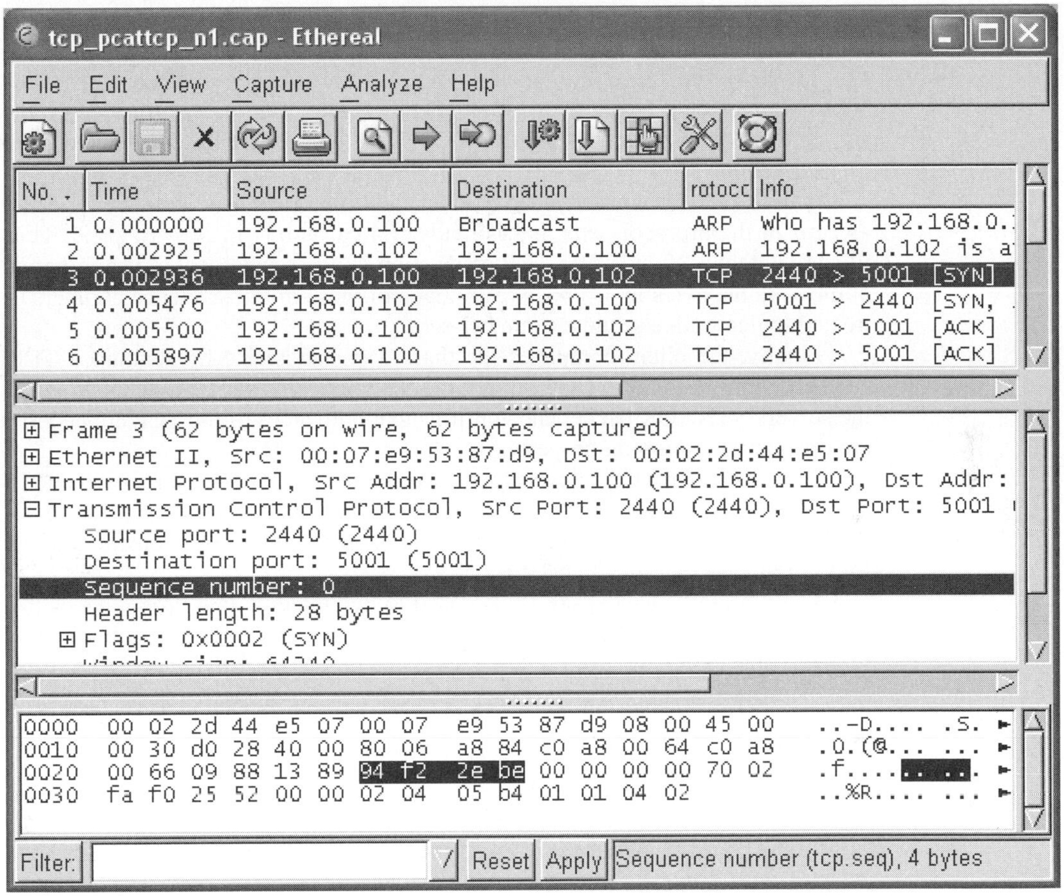

```
tcp_pcattcp_n1.cap - Ethereal                                    _ □ X

File   Edit   View   Capture   Analyze   Help

⚙  📂  💾  ✕  ⟳  🖨  🔍  ➡  ⏩  ⏬  ⏬  ▦  ✂  ◎

No. .  Time        Source            Destination       rotocc  Info
    1  0.000000    192.168.0.100     Broadcast         ARP     who has 192.168.0.:
    2  0.002925    192.168.0.102     192.168.0.100     ARP     192.168.0.102 is a
    3  0.002936    192.168.0.100     192.168.0.102     TCP     2440 > 5001 [SYN]
    4  0.005476    192.168.0.102     192.168.0.100     TCP     5001 > 2440 [SYN,
    5  0.005500    192.168.0.100     192.168.0.102     TCP     2440 > 5001 [ACK]
    6  0.005897    192.168.0.100     192.168.0.102     TCP     2440 > 5001 [ACK]

⊞ Frame 3 (62 bytes on wire, 62 bytes captured)
⊞ Ethernet II, Src: 00:07:e9:53:87:d9, Dst: 00:02:2d:44:e5:07
⊞ Internet Protocol, Src Addr: 192.168.0.100 (192.168.0.100), Dst Addr:
⊟ Transmission Control Protocol, Src Port: 2440 (2440), Dst Port: 5001
     Source port: 2440 (2440)
     Destination port: 5001 (5001)
     Sequence number: 0
     Header length: 28 bytes
  ⊞ Flags: 0x0002 (SYN)
     Window size: 64240

0000  00 02 2d 44 e5 07 00 07  e9 53 87 d9 08 00 45 00    ..-D.....S....
0010  00 30 d0 28 40 00 80 06  a8 84 c0 a8 00 64 c0 a8    .0.(@........
0020  00 66 09 88 13 89 94 f2  2e be 00 00 00 00 70 02    .f............
0030  fa f0 25 52 00 00 02 04  05 b4 01 01 04 02          ..%R........

Filter:                              / Reset Apply Sequence number (tcp.seq), 4 bytes
```

The SYN packet is always sent from client to server. This segment requests the establishment of the connection. For the connection to be successfully established, a server process must already be listening at the IP address and port number to which the SYN packet is addressed. If not, the SYN packet will go unanswered. The client will typically send several SYN packets in case the first one is lost, but then will stop and report an error to the application.

If the server process is listening and accepts the incoming connection, then it responds with a segment in which the SYN bit and ACK bits are both set to one. This segment is typically called the SYNACK packet. This SYNACK packet both acknowledges that the server received the SYN packet and sends the initial sequence number for the data stream from server to client. This sequence number need not match the initial sequence number for the data stream from client to server.

Notice that the acknowledgement number field of packet 4 is listed by Ethereal as one in the protocol pane and as "94 f2 2e bf" (or one more than "94 f2 2e be") in the raw pane. This illustrates the pattern of TCP acknowledgements. A TCP receiver acknowledges the receipt of byte X by setting the acknowledgment number to X+1 indicating that this is the next byte it is expecting.

Notice also that the sequence number field of packet 4 is listed by Ethereal as zero in the protocol pane, but is really "84 ca be b3" in the raw pane. This illustrates that each side of a TCP connection chooses what it will use to begin numbering the bytes in its data stream. Each of these initial sequence numbers is treated logically like sequence number zero.

Finally, the client completes the three-way handshake by sending a TCP segment with the ACK bit set, but not the SYN bit. This segment acknowledges the servers SYNACK packet and confirms that both sides of the TCP connection are open and functioning properly.

All subsequent TCP segments will have the ACK bit set because each end is always able to report the next expected byte in the data stream. If one side sends no data, then the other side will simply send the same acknowledgement number for the remainder of the connection.

The three-way handshake is also used to negotiate certain properties of the connection. For example, the client and server in our trace agree on a maximum segment size (MSS) or 1460 bytes. This is the largest TCP segment that can be sent over the local network.

ONE-WAY DATA FLOW

Once the connection is established, the **ttcp** transmitter (i.e. the client) writes 8192 bytes into the data stream. From the application's perspective, this is sent as one unit. However, the underlying network cannot support packets large enough to hold all 8192 bytes of data and so TCP breaks this single logical transmission into multiple segments.

In our trace, the first segment to contain data is shown in packet 6. It contains the first 1460 bytes. Along with 20 bytes for the TCP header and another 20 bytes for the IP header, this adds up to 1500 bytes or the maximum size allowed over the Ethernet. The total frame size including the 14 bytes of the Ethernet frame header is 1514 bytes.

Packets 7, 9, 10, and 11 also send 1460 bytes. This gives a total of 1460*5 or 7300 bytes. The remaining 8192-7300 or 892 bytes are sent in packet 13.

Notice that the sequence number of packet 6 is one. Packet 6 contains 1460 bytes numbered 1 to 1460. Similarly, the sequence number of packet 7 is 1461. It contains 1460 bytes numbered 1461 to 2920. These sequence numbers allow the server to detect if any packets in the stream are missing or reordered. For example, if packet 9 had been lost, the server would not mistakenly deliver the data in packet 10 in its place.

In our example, the server is not sending any data back to the client. Therefore, all the packets sent from port 5001 to port 2440 contain only the TCP header and no data. Even though it has no data of its own to send, it responds with TCP segments in order to provide feedback to the client about what data has been successfully received. For example, in packet 8, the server sends a segment with the acknowledgement number 2921. This single packet actually acknowledges the receipt of both packet 6 and 7 by declaring that the next byte it is expecting is byte 2921.

CLOSING A CONNECTION

The TCP connection is closed when the two end points exchange TCP segments with the FIN bit set and each side acknowledges the FIN packet sent by the other side. The FIN bit literally means that no additional new data will be sent on that side of the connection. Retransmitted data may however still be sent until the receiver acknowledges all the data.

The closing of a TCP connection can be seen in packets 13 through 16 `tcp_pcattcp_n1.cap`. Once the `ttcp` transmitter wrote the 8192 bytes of data, it was ready to close the connection. Packet 13 contains the last 892 bytes of data and has the FIN bit set indicating that no additional data will be sent.

In packet 14, the server acknowledges that it has received all the data sent. Notice that the acknowledgement number is 8194 and not 8193. This is because the FIN itself is treated as byte 8193.

In packet 15, the server also sends a FIN indicating that it will not be sending any additional data. The client acknowledges this FIN by sending a final segment with acknowledgement 2. Once again, the acknowledgment number is 2 rather than 1 because the FIN itself is treated as the final byte.

This sequence of two FINs and their corresponding ACKs is the preferred way to terminate a TCP connection. TCP connections can also be terminated by setting the RESET bit. Although the RESET was designed to be used for unrecoverable errors, it is often used in practice for fast termination that avoids the formalities of the FIN-ACK exchanges.

CONNECTION STATISTICS

Ethereal has a set of tools to analyze TCP streams (TCP Stream Analysis under the Analyze menu). These tools display graphs of various aspects of the TCP connection including the pattern of sequence numbers over time and how the throughput or round-trip times vary over the life of the connection.

It is important to realize that each of these tools works on only one side of the TCP connection at a time. To illustrate this point, first choose a packet sent from client to server like the SYN packet #1. Next, choose "Time-Sequence Graph (tcptrace)" from the TCP Stream Analysis menu. A graph will appear showing how the sequence numbers varies from 1 through 8194 over the life of the connection. If however, you choose a packet sent from server to client and then viewed the same graph, you would see that the sequence number varied only from 0 to 2 over the life of the connection.

You can also isolate each side of the connection using the "Follow TCP Stream" option from the Analyze menu. It allows you to view all data sent over both connections or just the data sent from client to server or just the data sent from server to client. In this case, it shows 8192 bytes sent from client to server and 0 bytes sent in the other direction.

Another useful tool to be aware of is the Protocol Hierarchy Statistics option of the Analyze menu. It breaks down the trace by protocol. In this case, it reports that there is a total of 9090 bytes of data in the entire trace, 8988 bytes of TCP traffic and 8516 bytes of data. The Data category is a bit misleading as we know that the total amount of data sent over this connection was 8192 bytes. This Data category includes the total size of any frame that contains TCP data. In the trace, there are 6 packets containing TCP data (packets 6, 7, 9, 10, 11, and 13). They each contain 54 bytes of headers (20 bytes of TCP header, 20 bytes of IP header, and 14 bytes of Ethernet header). The 8516 bytes include the 8192 bytes of actual data and the 54*6 = 324 bytes of headers in these packets.

REMOTE SSH CONNECTION

In addition to a TCP connection generated by **ttcp** on a local network, we traced an SSH connection using TCP between a local machine and remote server. We captured the resulting network traffic in the file **tcp_ssh.cap**. You can open this file from the accompanying CD and follow along.

There are many similarities between this TCP connection and one generated by **ttcp**, including the three-way handshake to open the connection and the FIN segments to close the connection. They are also similar in that there is no packet loss or retransmission in either case.

One important way in which they are different, however, is that in the SSH trace, both client and server are sending data. You can see this quickly by using Follow TCP Stream to isolate each side of the data channel. You can also view the Time Sequence Graph for each side independently.

Another important way in which they are different is that the SSH client is sending many segments with only a small amount of data. This is because it represents an interactive data stream rather than the **ttcp** stream that was sending 8192 bytes in bulk.

Notice that many TCP headers have the PUSH flag set. The TCP layer normally attempts to collect enough data to fill a maximize segment before sending data across the network. The PUSH flag is set when the application requests that a segment be sent immediately without waiting for a full segment to be filled.

In the SSH stream, even though the maximum segment size is still 1460 bytes, there are no segments this large. In fact, most of the segments contain less than 100 bytes of data. The entire conversation is 8606 bytes. This is not much more than the 8192 bytes of the ttcp stream, but in this case there are 118 segments containing data instead of 6.

One important consequence is that the TCP headers consume a significantly larger percentage of the total stream. In this case, the TCP stream contains 8606 bytes of data and 18508 bytes total (46% data). The **ttcp** stream on the other hand contained 8192 bytes of data and 8988 bytes total (91% data).

QUESTIONS

Answer the following questions about the files **tcp_pcattcp_n1.cap** and **tcp_ssh.cap**.

1. Which packets contain the three-way handshake in **tcp_ssh.cap**?

2. What is the actual initial sequence number in each direction in **tcp_ssh.cap**? How did you determine this?

3. Use the SYN and SYNACK packets in both traces to compute the round trip time for each connection. How does the round trip time for a machine in the local network compare to the round trip time to a remote server?

4. In **tcp_pcattcp_n1.cap**, which of the packets contain only a header and no data? Write a display filter to isolate these packets. How many packets match this filter in **tcp_ssh.cap**?

5. What is the only segment in a TCP stream without the ACK bit set? Why?

6. In **tcp_pcattcp_n1.cap**, do all of the packets from server to client contain the same acknowledgement number? Why or why not? Do all the packets from client to server have the same acknowledgement number? (Note: In this case, the server is the receiver because it listens for the incoming connection.)

7. In **tcp_pcattcp_n1.cap**, how many packets does packet 12 acknowledge? Packet 14?

DISCUSSION AND INVESTIGATION

1. Is there data sent in the SYN, SYNACK, and ACK packets? Does RFC 793 prohibit data in these packets?

2. In RFC 793 on page 22, there is a state diagram illustrating the phases of TCP connection setup and tear down. Both client and server begin in the CLOSED state. The server does a passive open when it opens a

socket to accept incoming connections from clients. This state is called the LISTEN state. The client does an active open when it initiates a connection to a server. After sending the first SYN, the client enters the SYN SENT phase. Once a connection is successfully established on both ends, both client and server will be in the ESTABLISHED state until they are ready to terminate the connection. Trace the path through this state diagram from CLOSED to ESTABLISED for the client and then for the server.

3. You can use a tool called netstat, available on many UNIX and Windows machines to view the state of all TCP connections involving your local machine. For example, at the Windows command prompt on my local machine, I typed netstat. It shows several ssh connections, several AIM connections and one HTTP connection. All but one of the connections are in the ESTABLISHED state. I was able to capture the SYN_SENT state by attempting to ssh to a random IP address (in this case 100.100.0.100) at which I did not expect to find an SSH server. Experiment with netstat on your own machine. How many states can you capture? Explain what you had to do to capture each state and for those you cannot capture, explain why it was difficult to capture them. You may also want to investigate other uses of the netstat tool.

```
C:\Documents and Settings\Jeanna>netstat

Active Connections

  Proto  Local Address          Foreign Address        State
  TCP    MATTHEWS:1052          205.188.7.146:5190     ESTABLISHED
  TCP    MATTHEWS:1060          64.12.27.238:5190      ESTABLISHED
  TCP    MATTHEWS:2796          crux.clarkson.edu:22   ESTABLISHED
  TCP    MATTHEWS:4253          ausoladsds2web1.us.dell.com:http  ESTABLISHED
  TCP    MATTHEWS:4293          100.100.0.100:22       SYN_SENT
  TCP    MATTHEWS:4323          herakles.cs.cornell.edu:22  ESTABLISHED
```

4. TCP connections can be opened by both ends simultaneously sending a SYN (i.e. two clients doing an active connect at the same time rather then client/server). Find this path through the TCP state diagram on page 22 of RFC 793.

5. Start 5 to 10 TCP connections between the same client and server rapidly one after another. Note the local port number assigned to each connection and also the initial sequence number assigned by client and server to each connection. Do you see a pattern?

6. In the preface of RFC 793, Jon Postel writes that there were nine earlier editions of the ARPA TCP specification on which RFC 793 is based. Investigate these earlier documents and earlier versions of TCP. Originally TCP stood for Transmission Control Program (rather than Protocol) and incorporated functionality found in both TCP and IP

today. One place to start is RFC 675, Specification of the Internet Transmission Control Program written in 1974.

7. What happened on January 1, 1983?

8. Investigate the role of Vint Cerf and Robert Kahn in defining TCP and IP.

RESOURCES

- RFC 793, Transmission Control Protocol, **ftp://ftp.rfc-editor.org/in-notes/rfc793.txt**

- RFC 675, Specification of the Internet Transmission Control Program, **ftp://ftp.rfc-editor.org/in-notes/rfc675.txt**

- Test TCP (TTCP) Benchmarking Tool for Measuring TCP and UDP Performance, **http://www.pcausa.com/Utilities/pcattcp.htm**

- The Story of the TTCP Program, **http://ftp.arl.mil/~mike/ttcp.html**

- Web search: netstat

- Web search: TCP History

Transport Layer Protocols:
Exercise **3.2**

Retransmission in TCP

INTRODUCTION

In the last exercise, we examined the basics of the Transmission Control Protocol (TCP). We discussed how TCP provides reliable data transmission over an unreliable network by relying on feedback from the receiver to detect loss. We said that TCP responds to indications of packet loss by retransmitting. However, in the traces we looked at, all the packets were received correctly the first time and thus there was no retransmission. In this exercise, we are going to examine traces of TCP connections in which retransmission does occur.

When a TCP sender transmits a segment, it also sets a timer called a *retransmission timer*. When an acknowledgment arrives, the timer is cancelled. If the timer expires before an acknowledgement of the data arrives, the data will be retransmitted.

The retransmission timer is set adaptively. Initially, TCP bases the retransmission timer on the time between the initial SYN and the SYN ACK. It actually sets the retransmission timer to several times this value to prevent unnecessary retransmission. Throughout the connection, TCP notes the time between each segment sent and its corresponding acknowledgement. A running average of these times is computed in which more weight is given to the accumulated average than the most recent sample.

TCP does not always wait for a retransmission timer to expire before retransmitting data. TCP will also interpret a series of duplicate acknowledgements as an early sign of packet loss. To understand why, consider what a receiver must do for each out-of-order packet that follows a lost packet. Receivers must set their acknowledgement number to the next in-order byte that they are expecting. If they are expecting byte 1000, but receive bytes 2000 through 3000, they must continue to set their acknowledgement number to 1000. If the segment containing bytes 1000 through 1099 is lost, they will continue to send an acknowledgment number of 1000 for each new segment received. When the sender sees a series of segments with the same acknowledgement number, it can assume that although data is reaching the other end and prompting that acknowledgements be sent, the segment containing byte 1000 has been lost.

Later versions of TCP even provide a way for receivers to indicate which data they have received out of order. This is referred to as selective acknowledgements and TCP with this feature is often called TCP SACK. Senders and receivers negotiate whether to use additional features such as SACK during the three-way handshake that establishes the connection.

CONFIGURATION

The traces used in this exercise were taken on a private network. A desktop PC and a laptop were connected to the Internet via a cable modem router. The laptop is connected via a wireless interface and we specifically placed the laptop so as to interfere with a strong signal.

As in the previous exercise, we use **ttcp** to generate a TCP stream with specified properties. We also download a file from a remote server over a TCP connection.

Figure 3.2.1: Exercise Configuration

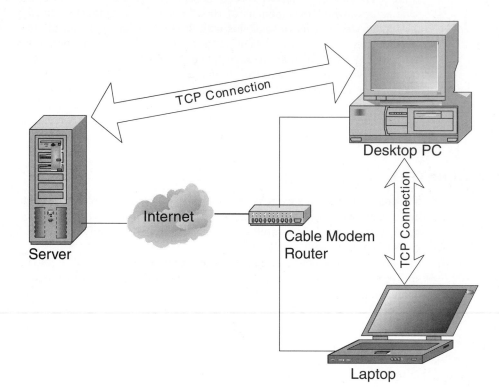

EXPERIMENT

LOCAL TTCP CONNECTION

We started our experiment with a quiet network. On the laptop, we ran the receiver for our **ttcp** stream. It began listening on TCP port 5001. Here is the entire command line output for the receiver:

```
C:\Downloads\ttcp>pcattcp -r -l 1000
PCAUSA Test TCP Utility V2.01.01.07
TCP Receive Test
Local Host  : cs-00065be34d1d
***************
Listening...: On port 5001

   Accept      : TCP <- 192.168.0.100:4480
   Buffer Size : 1000; Alignment: 16384/0
```

```
        Receive Mode: Sinking (discarding) Data
        Statistics  : TCP <- 192.168.0.100:4480
50000 bytes in 4.03 real seconds = 12.13 KB/sec ***
numCalls: 63; msec/call: 65.44; calls/sec: 15.65
```

We started a network capture using Ethereal on both the desktop and the laptop so that we would have two views of the lost packets. For both traces, we limited the portion of each packet captured to 68 bytes.

On the desktop machine, we started the transmitter for our **ttcp** stream. On the command line, we specified the IP address of the laptop, 192.168.0.102. By default, **ttcp** will send 2048 buffers of size 8192 bytes for a total of 16 MB of data. Both the size of the buffers and the number of sends can be controlled from the command line. We choose to send 50 buffers of size 1000 bytes. Here is the entire command line output from the transmitter:

```
C:\Downloads\ttcp>pcattcp -t -l 1000 -n 50  192.168.0.102
PCAUSA Test TCP Utility V2.01.01.07
TCP Transmit Test
    Transmit    : TCP <- 192.168.0.102:5001
    Buffer Size : 1000; Alignment: 16384/0
    TCP_NODELAY : DISABLED (0)
    Connect     : Connected to 192.168.0.102:5001
    Send Mode   : Send Pattern; Number of Buffers: 50
    Statistics  : TCP <- 192.168.0.102:5001
50000 bytes in 3.16 real seconds = 15.47 KB/sec ***
numCalls: 50; msec/call: 64.63; calls/sec: 15.84
```

We waited for both the transmitter and the receiver to exit and then we stopped the captures. We saved the trace from the transmitter (i.e. the desktop) in the file **pcattcp_retrans_t.cap** and the trace from the receiver (i.e. the laptop) in the file **pcattcp_retrans_r.cap**. You may want to start two instances of Ethereal so that you can open both traces simultaneously.

SACK OPTION NEGOTIATED

In either trace, we can examine the three-way handshake that establishes the connection. In the SYN packet (packet 1 in both traces), the desktop machine indicated its willingness to use TCP SACK by including the "SACK permitted" option in the options section of the TCP header. In the SYN ACK packet (packet 2 in both traces), the laptop also indicated that SACK is permitted. Thus, both sides agree to receive selective acknowledgement information.

Figure 3.2.2: SACK Option

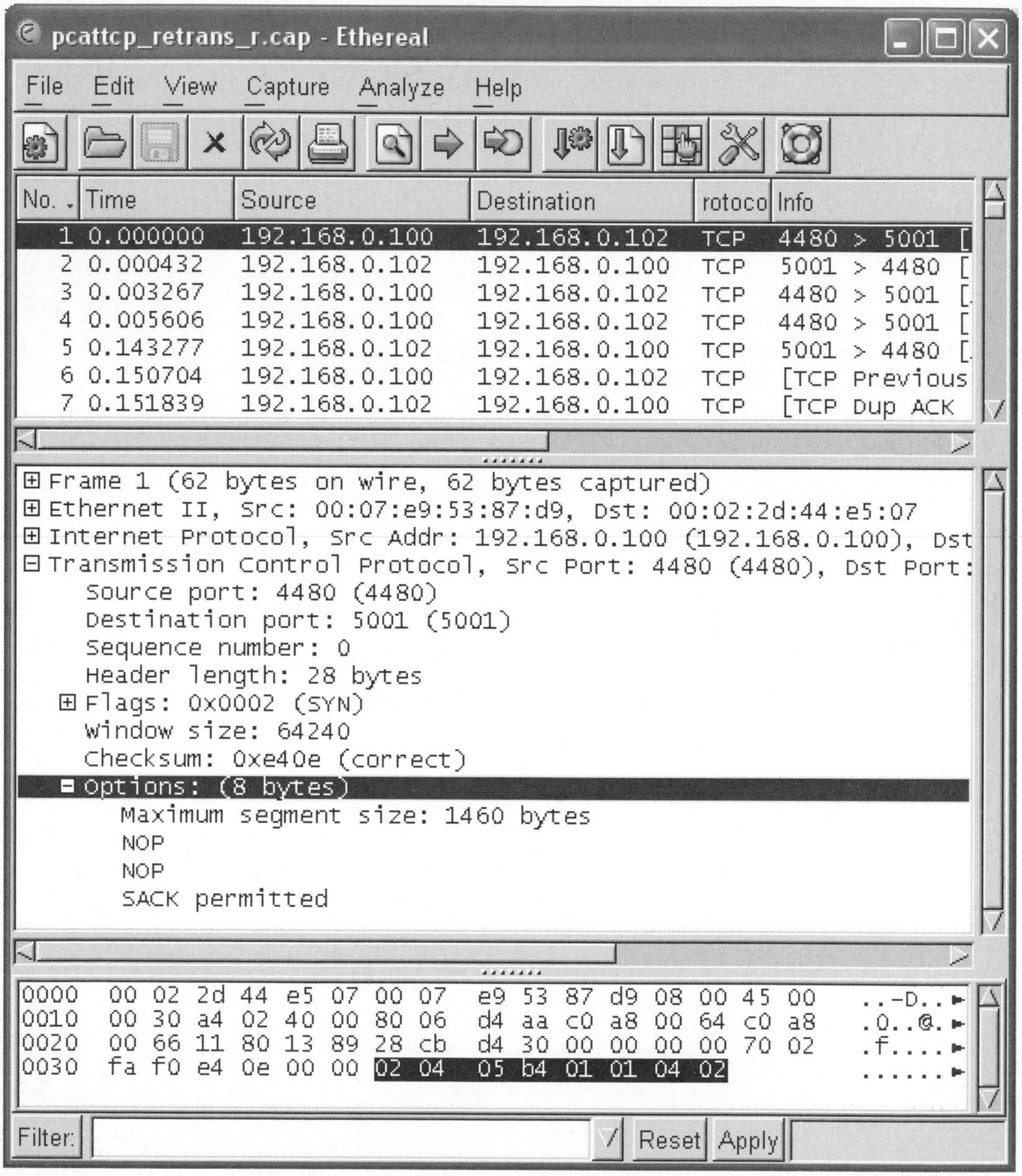

In TCP SACK, if one end of the connection receives out-of-order data, it uses the option area to send information about the start and the end of this out of order data. This allows the sender to retransmit only the exact data that is missing. This is particularly useful in cases where several packets are dropped because duplicate acknowledgements already serve as a hint of one dropped packet.

This additional selective acknowledgement information is used only as a hint. In particular, it does not change the meaning of the acknowledgement number in the TCP header nor does it change the receiver's obligations concerning the out of order data. TCP receivers cannot deliver data that they receive out of order up to the waiting application because it always delivers data in-order. Therefore, any data received out of order must either be discarded (forcing the sender to retransmit) or stored.

The amount of such storage space on the receiver is limited and TCP receivers are free to discard data until they acknowledge the data using the acknowledgment number in the header. TCP senders must maintain a copy of the data they send in case they must retransmit. Senders must store the data until they receive an acknowledgment. The SACK options do not change these requirements.

Receivers typically allocate a fixed amount of buffer space to store both out-of-order data and data waiting for an application to read it. If they run out of buffer space to hold incoming data, then they have no choice but to drop data even if it arrives successfully. The receiver's advertised window field is used to inform the sender how much room is left for incoming data. If data is sent faster than it is consumed by the application, then the receiver will typically send a series of acknowledgements with decreasing receiver's advertised window size.

In this trace, the receiver's advertised window sent by the laptop varies somewhat from a low of 16520 bytes to a high of 17520 bytes. This is easiest to see if you isolate the responses from the laptop with a display filter such as `tcp.srcport == 5001`.

TCP senders also have a limited amount of space available to hold data before transmission. However, unlike receivers, senders can limit the sending rate on their own. If the buffer space is full, an application that attempts to write additional data will simply be blocked until additional space becomes available.

MISSING PACKETS AND RETRANSMISSION

Now, let's look at an example of retransmission in TCP. You can search for retransmissions with the display filter `tcp.analysis.retransmission`. Applying this filter to **pcattcp_retrans_t.cap**, we see that packet 12 is the first of 9 suspected retransmissions in the trace.

Figure 3.2.3: TCP Retransmission Filter

No.	Time	Source	Destination	rotoc	Info
12	0.157773	192.168.0.100	192.168.0.102	TCP	[TCP Retransmission]
20	0.177570	192.168.0.100	192.168.0.102	TCP	[TCP Retransmission]
28	0.190427	192.168.0.100	192.168.0.102	TCP	[TCP Retransmission]
42	0.224101	192.168.0.100	192.168.0.102	TCP	[TCP Retransmission]
44	1.825971	192.168.0.100	192.168.0.102	TCP	[TCP Retransmission]
57	1.863323	192.168.0.100	192.168.0.102	TCP	[TCP Retransmission]
59	3.138411	192.168.0.100	192.168.0.102	TCP	[TCP Retransmission]
72	3.175543	192.168.0.100	192.168.0.102	TCP	[TCP Retransmission]
74	4.013368	192.168.0.100	192.168.0.102	TCP	[TCP Retransmission]

Filter: tcp.analysis.retransmission ✓ Reset Apply File: pcattcp_retrans_t.cap

Examining packet 12 in more detail, we can see that the sequence number is 1001. Using the filter `tcp.seq == 1001`, we can see that packet 5 also had this same sequence number. Interestingly, packet 5 is a transmission of bytes 1001 through 2460, but packet 12 is a retransmission of only 1001 through 2000. Packet 20 is actually the retransmission of bytes 2001 through 2460.

For a little context, let's look at the packets surrounding packet 5 in the trace. Packet 4 is the transmission of bytes 1 through 1000, packet 5 is the transmission of bytes 1001 through 2460, and packet 7 is the transmission of bytes 2461 through 3920.

We have been examining the trace taken at the transmitter. If we now look at the same connection from the receiver's perspective, we see a somewhat different story. In **pcattcp_retrans_r.cap**, we find the transmission of bytes 1 through 1000 is also in packet 4 and the transmission of bytes 2461 through 3920 is in packet 6 (not packet 7). In this trace, packet 5 is the receiver's acknowledgement of bytes 1 though 1000. We see no transmission of bytes 1001 through 2460. They were sent, but somewhere between the sender and the receiver they were lost.

Now, let's examine how the receiver handles this loss. After packet 4 arrived, the receiver responded with acknowledgement number 1001 (packet 5). After packet 6 arrives with bytes 2461 through 3920, it once again responds with acknowledgement number 1001 (packet 7). Even though it has received additional data, the acknowledgment number must still reflect the next in-order byte that it is expecting.

Packet 7 also contains some selective acknowledgement information in the option field of the header. In particular, the SACK option specifies that it has received out of order data with a left edge of 684449229 and a right edge of 684450689. To understand this SACK option, recall that although Ethereal displays the sequence numbers starting at 0, initial sequence numbers are really chosen somewhat randomly. Bytes 68449229 through 684450689 are really the 1460 bytes contained in the out-of-order packet 7. (You can see this clearly by comparing the raw data for the left edge in the SACK option to the sequence number for packet 7. They are both "28 cb dd cd.")

Similarly, after packet 8 arrives with bytes 3921 through 5381, the receiver once again responds with acknowledgement number 1001. However, the right edge of the SACK option in packet 9 is increased to 684452149 to reflect the additional out-or-order data received. If there had been an additional skip in the data received, it would have been possible to specify multiple left and right edge pairs to describe the data that did arrive. In this case, we simply extended the right edge of the existing out-of-order region so one left and right edge pair was sufficient.

Finally, bytes 1001 through 2000 are retransmitted. This can be seen in packet 12 of both traces. This allows the receiver to increase its acknowledgment number to 2001 (packet 14 in **pcattcp_retrans_r.cap**). Oddly, the left edge of the SACK information is not updated in packet 14. This causes no harm as updating the SACK information would only provide the same information as the updated acknowledgement number.

The loss of bytes 1000-2460 is finally completely repaired with bytes 2001 through 2460 are retransmitted (packet 20 in **pcattcp_retrans_t.cap** and packet 19 in **pcattcp_retrans_r.cap**). Following this retransmission, the receiver is able to jump from acknowledging byte 2001 to acknowledging byte 11221 immediately because it saved the out-of-order data it received (packet 20 in **pcattcp_retrans_r.cap**). Notice that in packet 20 there is no SACK option because no additional out-of-order data has been received. Unfortunately, the very next packet received (packet 21) is another piece of out of order data.

IMPACT ON SENDING RATE

Now, let's consider the impact of losses on the overall sending rate. After selecting one packet in the stream from the desktop to the laptop (4480-> 5001), we chose Time Sequence Graphs (Steven's) from the TCP Stream Analysis

Tools in the Analyze menu. This graph plots time on the *x*-axis and the sequence number on the *y*-axis.

Figure 3.2.4: Time Sequence Graph for pcattp

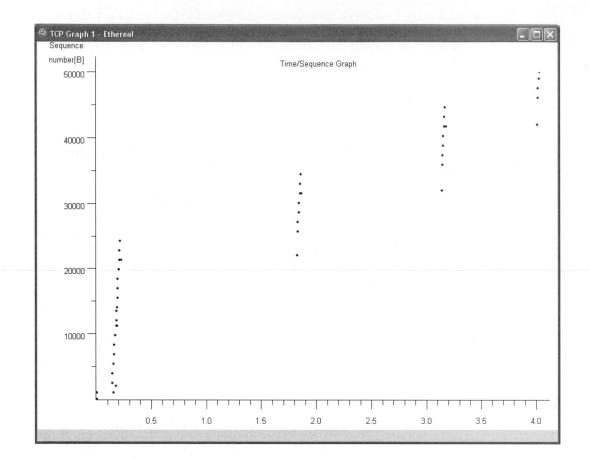

We see four vertical groupings of points at approximately 0.15 seconds, 1.8 seconds, 3.1 seconds, and 4.0 seconds respectively. The grouping at 1.8 seconds includes a single point just above sequence number 20000 followed by a set of closely grouped points above 25000. The lowest point is the retransmission of a sequence number sent around 0.15 seconds. It is separated from the other points in the same vertical stripe because the SACK information allows the sender to retransmit only the one missing segment. The loss and retransmission of this packet causes a significant delay in the sending of data.

REMOTE TTCP CONNECTION

In addition, to a TCP connection generated by **ttcp** on a local network, we traced an HTTP connection using TCP between a local machine and remote server. We captured the resulting network traffic in the file **tcp_http.cap**. In this case, we have the trace only from the perspective of the receiver. You can open this file from the accompanying CD and follow along.

The three-way handshake for this connection occurs in packets 1 through 3. Our local machine sends the SYN packet and includes the "SACK permitted" option in the option field of the TCP header. However, in this case, the remote server does not include the "SACK permitted" option in the SYNACK packet and so selective acknowledgements will not be sent for this connection.

By looking at the receiver's trace only, it is difficult to definitively identify retransmitted segments. Most likely, they are dropped before they reach the local network and therefore do not appear in the trace. However, we can identify suspected retransmissions when we see duplicate acknowledgements.

For example, packet 17 is marked as a suspected retransmission. The sequence number in this packet is 8761. It is marked as a suspected retransmission because packet 14 and 16 both contain the acknowledgement number, 8761. Packet 16 is produced immediately after receiving an out-of-order segment containing bytes 10221 through 11680. We know that the remote server sent the segment with sequence number 8761 before packet 15. Therefore, packet 17 is either a retransmission or the packets were reordered in the network (e.g. by taking different paths from the remote server).

Displaying the Steven's Time/Sequence Graph as we did for the pcattcp trace, we can see a similar pattern of packet loss causing delays in transmission.

Figure 3.2.5: Time Sequence Graph for Remote TCP Connection

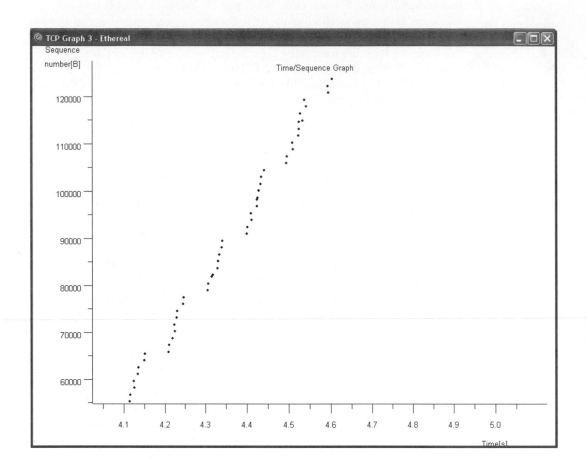

QUESTIONS

Answer the following questions about the files **pcattcp_retrans_t.cap**, **pcattcp_retrans_r.cap**, and **tcp_http.cap**.

1. How many TCP segments are sent from port 4480 on the desktop machine to port 5001 on the laptop machine? Write a display filter to isolate this side of the connection and use it to answer the question for both **pcattcp_retrans_r.cap** and **pcattcp_retrans_t.cap**. (Hint: Use the Summary option in the Analyze menu to get the packet count of the data in the filtered packets.)

2. The answers found in question 1 should not match. Why? We noted 9 retransmissions in this trace. Does this account for the difference? If not, explain the discrepancy.

3. Examine the suspected retransmissions that are identified by Ethereal in both **pcattcp_retrans_r.cap** and **pcattcp_retrans_t.cap**. (Hint: Use the filter `tcp.analysis.retransmission`). Are the same packets identified in both traces? If yes, how do you know they are the same exact packets? If no, which are different?

4. Identify all of the packets in **pcattcp_retrans_t.cap** that are lost before reaching the receiver. For each segment that is lost, identify the retransmitted packet(s). (Shorter Option: Find the first bytes lost and the packets that retransmit them.)

5. When the receiver sends a TCP segment to acknowledge data received (even if it is only a TCP header), this segment can also be lost. Are there any such losses in **pcattcp_retrans_t.cap** or **pcattcp_retrans_r.cap**? How did you determine your answer?

6. In this **tcp_http.cap**, we saw a trace of the client side of the TCP connection. What would we need to do in order to get a trace of the other side of the connection? What else would you expect to see in such a trace?

7. In this exercise, we examined packet 17 in the trace **tcp_http.cap**, and determined that it was either a retransmission or that packets were reordered in the network. Which do you think it is? (Hint: Determine the round-trip time between the local client and remote server and compare this to the time between packets 15, 17, and 19.)

DISCUSSION AND INVESTIGATION

1. If the receiver's advertised window never exceeded one TCP segment, then only one segment could be outstanding (i.e. sent but not yet acknowledged) at any one time. This would lead to very poor performance especially if the latency between sender and receiver is high. Protocols that allow only one outstanding segment are sometimes called "Stop and Wait" protocols because the sender sends one segment and then stops and waits until the receiver acknowledges that segment. Protocols that allow multiple outstanding segments are sometimes called "Pipelined" protocols because they allow multiple outstanding segments to fill the pipeline between the sender and the receiver. If you were using a 1 MB/sec link and the latency between sender and receiver was 5 ms, what percentage of the total link bandwidth could be

used when sending only a single 8KB packet at a time (stop and wait)? How many 8 KB packets would have to be in the "pipeline" to fully utilize the link bandwidth?

2. What is the maximum receiver's advertised window in TCP? With a 1 MB/sec link, what is the largest latency between sender and receiver that will still allow TCP to fill the pipeline?

3. Investigate the window scaling options to TCP that allow a larger receiver's advertised window to be used.

RESOURCES

- RFC 793, Transmission Control Protocol, **ftp://ftp.rfc-editor.org/in-notes/rfc793.txt**

- RFC 2018, TCP Selective Acknowledgement Options, **ftp://ftp.rfc-editor.org/in-notes/rfc2018.txt**

- RFC 1323, TCP Extensions for High Performance, **ftp://ftp.rfc-editor.org/in-notes/rfc1323.txt**

- Web search: TCP window scaling option

Transport Layer Protocols:
Exercise **3.3**

Comparing TCP to UDP

INTRODUCTION

The Transmission Control Protocol (TCP) and the User Datagram Protocol (UDP) are the two main transport protocols used in the Internet. In Exercises 3.1 and 3.2, we have examined the characteristics of TCP in detail. In this exercise, we will introduce UDP and illustrate major differences between the two.

TCP turns a sequence of application writes into a reliable, in-order stream of bytes across the network. It also provides flow control or the ability for a receiver to slow down the sending rate. It provides congestion control or the ability to limit the sending rate in response to signs of network congestion. It is fundamentally a point-to-point protocol meaning that every TCP connection has two and only two endpoints. A TCP connection is also full-duplex meaning that each endpoint can be both a sender and a receiver simultaneously. TCP uses port numbers to clearly identify the application end point at each end of the connection. It also has a checksum to detect errors in transmission.

In contrast to this laundry list of features provided by TCP, UDP is a much simpler protocol. It provides only a thin layer of additional functionality over the network layer protocol, IP. The UDP header provides a good clue to the functionality it offers. Like the TCP header, it begins with source and destination port numbers. These are used as in TCP for demultiplexing or in other words for identifying the correct recipient process for each incoming datagram. It also contains a checksum like in the TCP header to detect any corruption of the packet that may have occurred. It also indicates the total length of the UDP datagram. In the UDP case, the header size is fixed at 8 bytes.

Figure 3.3.1: UDP Datagram Header

UDP does not provide reliable, in-order message delivery. In particular, any UDP datagrams sent over the network can be lost or reordered and UDP provides no support for detecting or correcting this. For those applications that can tolerate loss or reordering of transmissions, UDP can be a good choice because they are not forced to incur the overhead of retransmission.

UDP does not provide a point-to-point connection between one sender and one receiver. This has both advantages and disadvantages. UDP can avoid the overhead of the three-way handshake to set up the connection and begin immediately sending data. Also, UDP can be used to send to multiple recipients via a broadcast or multicast address while TCP cannot. However, as we will see in this exercise, it can be difficult to program an application in which there is no awareness of the beginning or end of an incoming data stream.

Much of TCP functionality relies on feedback from the receiver. In Exercises 3.1 and 3.2, we saw that the sender uses the acknowledgement numbers sent by the receiver to determine what messages must be retransmitted. In UDP, there is no explicit support for feedback from the receiver. However, a receiver is always free to send a UDP datagram back to the sender. In this case, however, it is under explicit application control rather than handled by the transport layer itself.

Throughout this exercise, as we highlight the differences between TCP and UDP, we will point out that all the functionality of TCP can be implemented by an application over UDP. A good way to think of the comparison is that TCP provides an efficient implementation of features commonly used by applications. Using TCP makes network programming simple for the application programmer because it hides much of the complexity within the transport layer. We will also see in this exercise that this functionality comes at a price. TCP can have significant overhead relative to UDP for transferring the same data. For some applications that do not require all the functionality of TCP, this cost is too high. Applications like this can choose to implement only the aspects of TCP functionality that they require on their own.

CONFIGURATION

The traces used in this exercise were taken on a private network. A desktop PC and a laptop were connected via a hub. No traffic is exchanged with the global Internet. We will use **ttcp** to generate both TCP and UDP streams with specified properties.

Figure 3.3.2: Exercise Configuration

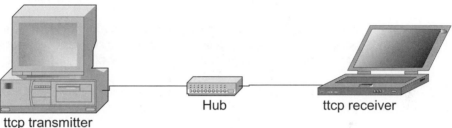

ttcp transmitter   Hub   ttcp receiver

EXPERIMENT

In this experiment, we use **ttcp** first to generate two TCP streams and then to generate two UDP streams. The first TCP and UDP streams attempt to send the same amount of data to a waiting receiver. This allows us to compare TCP and UDP as a means of transferring a stream of similar properties. The second TCP and UDP streams attempt to send data but with no waiting receiver. This allows us to compare how TCP and UDP react to failure.

 We saved the trace from the TCP streams in the file **tcp_2transmit.cap** and the trace from the UDP streams in the file **udp_2transmit.cap**. You can open these files from the accompanying CD. You may want to start two instances of Ethereal so that you can view both traces simultaneously.

USING TTCP TO GENERATE TCP AND UDP TRAFFIC

For the first TCP stream, we began by running the receiver on the laptop. It began listening on TCP port 5001. Then we started the transmitter on the desktop requesting that it send 5 buffers of 1000 bytes each or a total of 5000 bytes of data.

The output from both the transmitter and receiver are shown below. Notice that the receiver reports receiving all 5000 bytes. This is not surprising given that TCP provides reliable message delivery. It is interesting to note that the receiver reports that the transfer took 2.48 seconds while the transmitter reports 0 seconds. From the sending application's perspective, as soon as the channel was successfully opened, it immediately wrote all the data into the channel. However, in reality the data was simply transferred down to the TCP layer in the operating system for delivery to the other side. From the receiving applications perspective, it was 2.48 seconds from when the channel was successfully opened until all the data was transferred over the network.

Here is the entire command line output for the receiver:

```
C:\Downloads\ttcp>pcattcp -r -l 1000
PCAUSA Test TCP Utility V2.01.01.07
TCP Receive Test
  Local Host  : cs-00065be34d1d
***************
  Listening...: On port 5001

  Accept      : TCP <- 192.168.0.100:4957
  Buffer Size : 1000; Alignment: 16384/0
  Receive Mode: Sinking (discarding) Data
  Statistics  : TCP <- 192.168.0.100:4957
5000 bytes in 2.48 real seconds = 1.97 KB/sec ***
numCalls: 8; msec/call: 317.82; calls/sec: 3.22
```

Here is the entire command line output from the transmitter:

```
C:\Downloads\ttcp>pcattcp -t -l 1000 -n 5 192.168.0.102
PCAUSA Test TCP Utility V2.01.01.07
TCP Transmit Test
  Transmit    : TCP <- 192.168.0.102:5001
  Buffer Size : 1000; Alignment: 16384/0
  TCP_NODELAY : DISABLED (0)
  Connect     : Connected to 192.168.0.102:5001
  Send Mode   : Send Pattern; Number of Buffers: 5
  Statistics  : TCP <- 192.168.0.102:5001
5000 bytes in 0.0 real seconds = 1.#J KB/sec ***
numCalls: 5; msec/call: 0.00; calls/sec: 1.#J
```

For the first UDP stream, we again began by running the receiver on the laptop. It began listening on UDP port 5001. Then we started the transmitter on the desktop requesting that it send 5 buffers of 1000 bytes each or a total of 5000 bytes of data. Notice that we add a "-u" flag to **ttcp** to request a UDP stream.

The output from both the transmitter and receiver are shown below. Notice that the receiver reports receiving all 5000 bytes. In this case, UDP was able to reliably deliver all the data sent. However, as we will see in the second UDP stream, this is not always the case. This time the receiver reports receiving all 5000 bytes in 0.01 seconds – a significant time savings over the 2.48 seconds reported by the sender in the TCP case.

Here is the entire command line output for the receiver:

```
C:\Downloads\ttcp>pcattcp -r -l 1000 -u
PCAUSA Test TCP Utility V2.01.01.07
UDP Receive Test
   Protocol   : UDP
   Port       : 5001
   Buffer Size : 1000; Alignment: 16384/0
   recvfrom    : UDP <- 192.168.0.100:4961
   Statistics  : UDP <- 192.168.0.100:4961
5000 bytes in 0.01 real seconds = 488.28 KB/sec ***
numCalls: 6; msec/call: 1.71; calls/sec: 600.00
```

Here is the entire command line output from the transmitter:

```
C:\Downloads\ttcp>pcattcp -t -l 1000 -n 5 -u 192.168.0.102
PCAUSA Test TCP Utility V2.01.01.07
UDP Transmit Test
   Transmit    : UDP <- 192.168.0.102:5001
   Buffer Size : 1000; Alignment: 16384/0
   Send Mode   : Send Pattern; Number of Buffers: 5
   Statistics  : UDP <- 192.168.0.102:5001
5000 bytes in 0.00 real seconds = 1.#J KB/sec ***
numCalls: 7; msec/call: 0.00; calls/sec: 1.#J
```

NORMAL DATA TRANSFER IN TCP

Now, let's examine the traces we captured of this activity. The TCP connection is shown in **tcp_2transmit.cap** in packets 1 through 13. Most of the elements of this stream should be familiar from previous exercises. We see the three-way handshake (packets 1-3) that opens the connection. Packets 10-13 show the termination of the connection. Interestingly, packet 10 is both a FIN packet that requests termination of the connection and the retransmission of the last 1080 bytes of data (sequence numbers 3921 through 5000). Due to this retransmission, the total amount of data sent over the TCP channel is actually 6080.

TCP merges application writes into a stream of bytes. It does not attempt to maintain the boundaries of the original application writes. Notice also that TCP does not transfer each application write of 1000 bytes in a single packet. The first 1000 bytes is sent in packet 4, but then packet 5 contains 1460 bytes of data – some from the second buffer write and some from the third buffer write. Packet 7 contains 1460 bytes of data and packet 8 contains the remaining 1080 (5000-1000-1460-1460 = 1080).

Notice that Ethereal does indeed report 2.48 seconds from packet 1 that initiates the connection to packet 10 that signals the close of the connection. Packets 11-13 would not necessarily contribute to the receiving application's time calculation because the TCP layer could signal the close of the connection as soon as the first FIN was received. Packets 11-13 would then be sent in the background by the TCP layer in the operating system of each machine.

If we note the time between the first packet containing data (packet 4) and the last (packet 8), we see approximately 0.01 seconds just like is reported by the UDP receiver. In this case, the main factor in the increased time for TCP is the retransmission in packet 10. To be fair, UDP was lucky in that all its packets were received the first time.

Another thing worth noting in this trace is the number of packets that contain no data. All the packets from the receiver and several packets from the sender contain only the TCP segment header. In total (including the retransmission), 6822 bytes of traffic are sent to support the transmission of 5000 bytes of data. This is an overhead of 36 percent!

NORMAL DATA TRANSFER IN UDP

Now, let's examine the UDP stream. It is shown in packets 1 through 11 of **udp_2transmit.cap**. Although the exact same data is transferred as in the TCP stream we just examined, there are many differences in this trace.

Unlike TCP, UDP is a connectionless transport protocol. Where TCP explicitly opens the connection with SYN and SYNACK packets, UDP starts directly sending packets containing data. Similarly, where TCP explicitly closes the connection with FIN and FINACK packets, UDP simply stops sending packets containing data. In fact all eleven UDP packets sent contain some data.

The connectionless nature of UDP causes some troubles for the **ttcp** application. In particular, the receiver is supposed to record statistics including how much time is required for the transfer and the total amount of data received. However, it does not know how much data is sent or which packet is the *last* one. Combined with the fact that UDP does not provide reliable delivery, it is difficult for the receiver to determine when it should declare the stream completed.

To address this problem, **ttcp** transmitter itself actually simulates connection establishment and termination by sending special UDP datagrams containing only 4 bytes. Before sending any data, the transmitter sends one of these special datagrams containing 4 bytes of data (packet 1) and after sending all the data, the transmitter sends five more (packets 7-11).

The receiver uses the first special datagram to start the timer for the data transmission. If this special datagram is dropped, it could also use the first packet of real data to start the timer. However, if the receiver does not see the special datagram, it cannot be sure that it has seen the beginning of the data transmission and may time the transmission inaccurately. Unlike TCP, UDP does not place sequence numbers on the data transmitted so it is impossible for the receiver to identify missing or reordered transmissions.

Similarly, the receiver uses the final special datagrams to stop the timer for data transmission. The receiver will stop the timer when it receives any one of these, but five are sent to allow for the possibility that some may be lost. If all five are lost, the receiver will wait indefinitely for more data to arrive.

The actual data is sent in packets 2 through 6. Each packet contains 1000 bytes of data. The application writes of 1000 bytes are translated directly into UDP datagrams. TCP, on the other hand, does not attempt to preserve the boundaries of the application writes but instead merges them into a single byte stream.

Unlike TCP, UDP provides no feedback from receiver to sender. In the TCP case, the receiver sends back segments containing only the TCP segment header and no data. The header itself carries information about what data has been successfully received and how much data the receiver is able to accept. We have already seen that UDP does not provide reliable message delivery and therefore does not require information about what data has been successfully received. It also provides no information to tell a sender to slow down because either the receiver or the network is being overwhelmed.

Although UDP itself provides no feedback from receiver to sender, we do see several ICMP packets (packets 12-14) sent from receiver to sender. ICMP is a companion protocol to the network layer protocol, IP and provides certain control and error reporting functionality. (ICMP is discussed in greater detail in Section 4.) In this case, the ICMP packets indicate that some of the UDP datagrams sent were undeliverable because the port was unreachable. This means that there was no receiver listening on that port when the datagrams arrived. Notice that he ICMP packets carry a portion of the undeliverable UDP datagram.

When the **ttcp** receiver saw one of the special datagrams with 4 bytes of data, it knew that the data transmission was complete and therefore closed the port on which it was listening. We saw that the **ttcp** transmitter actually sent five of these packets and when the later ones arrived they found that the receiver was no longer listening. We will see similar behavior when the transmitter sends all the data without a corresponding receiver present.

It is interesting to note the functionality provided by TCP can also be implemented by an application itself using UDP. We have already seen how **ttcp** attempts to indicate the beginning and ending of the connection. It would also be possible for **ttcp** to mark each packet with sequence numbers or for the receiver to send back datagrams describing the data successfully received. Implementing reliable message delivery over UDP is actually an excellent exercise.

One other difference between TCP and UDP is that the TCP connection is fundamentally point-to-point. In other words, TCP is used between one sender and one receiver. With UDP, a single sender can send to multiple receivers (e.g.

broadcast or multicast traffic) or multiple senders can send to a single receiver. One hint of this can be seen in the output of the UDP receiver:

recvfrom : UDP <- 192.168.0.100:4961
Statistics : UDP <- 192.168.0.100:4961

If multiple senders had sent to this receiver, then it was prepared to report statistics for each one of them.

One last important difference between TCP and UDP is in the size of the headers. The UDP header is always 8 bytes. The TCP header varies in size, but it is never smaller than 20 bytes. This contributes to the 36 percent overhead for TCP to transmit the 5000 bytes of actual data.

NO RECEIVER PRESENT FOR TCP AND UDP

In addition to examining the differences between TCP and UDP for normal data transfer, we also examined the differences during failed data transfer. In particular, we ran **ttcp** transmitters with the same parameters in the previous experiment, but this time we did not start a **ttcp** receiver.

The output from the TCP transmitter is shown below. Notice that the transmitter is aware of the failure to connect and send data.

```
C:\Downloads\ttcp>pcattcp -t -l 1000 -n 5 192.168.0.102
PCAUSA Test TCP Utility V2.01.01.07
TCP Transmit Test
   Transmit    : TCP <- 192.168.0.102:5001
   Buffer Size : 1000; Alignment: 16384/0
   TCP_NODELAY : DISABLED (0)
*** Winsock Error: connect Failed; Error: 10061 (0x0000274D)
```

The output from the UDP transmitter is show below. In this case, the output is identical to the successful transmission case. The UDP transmitter has no idea that the transmission has completely failed!

```
C:\Downloads\ttcp>pcattcp -t -l 1000 -n 5 -u 192.168.0.102
PCAUSA Test TCP Utility V2.01.01.07
UDP Transmit Test
   Transmit    : UDP <- 192.168.0.102:5001
   Buffer Size : 1000; Alignment: 16384/0
   Send Mode   : Send Pattern; Number of Buffers: 5
   Statistics  : UDP <- 192.168.0.102:5001
5000 bytes in 0.00 real seconds = 1.#J KB/sec ***
numCalls: 7; msec/call: 0.00; calls/sec: 1.#J
```

Now, let's examine the traces we captured of this activity. The TCP connection is shown in **tcp_2transmit.cap** in packets 14 through 19. In packet 14, the transmitter attempts to open a TCP connection by sending a SYN packet to the receiver. The receiver machine replies with a TCP segment that both advertises a zero window and has the RESET flag set. This clearly indicates that the receiver is unwilling to accept any data on this incoming connection. The TCP layer on the transmitter actually tries to send a SYN packet two more times to establish a connection, but each time the receiver's response is the same. It is worth noting that the port number of the new connection is different that the previous successful connection (4958 rather than 4957).

Because the TCP layer is aware of the failure to connect, it is able to report this failure to the transmitting application. In particular, **ttcp** makes a call to open a channel and this function returns an error. This allows the transmitter to report the error to the user and avoid sending data over the network that will not be accepted on the other side.

Now, let's examine the UDP stream. It is shown in packets 15 through 35 of **udp_2transmit.cap**. As we saw in the **ttcp** output, the transmitter sends all the data oblivious that none of it reaches the other side. We see the same pattern of UDP transmissions as in the successful transmission case: one special datagram with 4 bytes, 5 datagrams each with 1000 bytes of real data, and then five more special datagrams to indicate the end of the transmission. Again note, that the port number on this set of datagrams has changed from 4961 to 4962.

We saw ICMP Destination Unreachable messages in the previous example when the UDP receiver exited after receiving a datagram indicating the end of the transmission. Similarly, in this example, we see ten ICMP Destination Unreachable messages because the receiver is not running for the duration of the transmission. Interestingly, there are eleven UDP messages sent but only ten ICMP messages. Either one UDP datagram was dropped before reaching the receiver or one ICMP message was dropped before reaching the machine on which the Ethereal capture was running. Even though this is a local network, the laptop is connected via a wireless link that is less reliable than a wired link.

QUESTIONS

Answer the following questions about the files **tcp_2transmit.cap** and **udp_2transmit.cap**.

1. Examine the UDP headers in **udp_2transmit.cap**. Does the length field include the header and the data or simply the data? Why is this sub optimal?

2. Write a display filter to isolate all of the special UDP datagrams with only 4 bytes of data.

3. We saw that ICMP messages are used to report a UDP datagram as undeliverable. Why couldn't TCP use this as indication of lost segments?

4. We computed the overhead of the successful TCP transmission to be 36 percent of 5000 bytes of real data. What was included in this overhead? What would be the overhead be if there had been no retransmission?

5. Compute the overhead of UDP in transferring the 5000 bytes of data. How did you compute your answer? What if we had sent 100 buffers of 50 bytes rather than 5 buffers of 1000 bytes?

DISCUSSION AND INVESTIGATION

1. For the purpose of testing TCP or UDP, it doesn't really matter what data is transmitted by ttcp. Use Follow TCP Stream to see what is actually sent. If you were the programmer of ttcp, what could you use this space to accomplish? For example, when **ttcp** is used to send UDP traffic (-u flag), **ttcp** could use this data area to implement certain aspects of TCP functionality in the **ttcp** application itself. Describe how **ttcp** could use this data area to allow the receiver to identify dropped or reordered packets. Could it also be used to gather information not visible in the network traces? Give some examples.

2. In this exercise, we discussed the difficulty of a UDP receiver identifying the end of a sequence of transmissions. How did **ttcp** solve this problem? What are the drawbacks of this approach? Propose another way to solve the problem.

3. Is it fair to compare TCP and UDP purely of the basis of the overhead of data transmission? Why or why not?

4. Given all the functionality provided by TCP, why do some applications use UDP?

5. Use ttcp to perform a series of tests comparing TCP to UDP. For example, send the same amount of data using 512 bytes through 8192 bytes for each TCP and UDP and plot the reported throughout numbers. Can you tell the amount of data loss for each UDP test? If you can, try repeating this same experiment for two machines on the same local network and two machines on separate networks. What conclusions can you draw from the data you have collected?

6. Investigate alternate tools for testing TCP and UDP performance such as Iperf (http://dast.nlanr.net/Projects/Iperf/).

RESOURCES

- RFC 793, Transmission Control Protocol, **ftp://ftp.rfc-editor.org/in-notes/rfc793.txt**

- RFC 768, User Datagram Protocol, **ftp://ftp.rfc-editor.org/in-notes/rfc768.txt**

- RFC 792, Internet Control Message Protocol, **ftp://ftp.rfc-editor.org/in-notes/rfc792.txt**

- NLANR/DAST's Iperf tool, **http://dast.nlanr.net/Projects/Iperf**

Transport Layer Protocols:
Exercise **3.4**

Competing TCP and
UDP Streams

INTRODUCTION

In all the exercises in the Transport Layer Section, we have been examining the details of TCP and UDP and comparing them to each other. One important aspect of this comparison that we have not yet touched upon is how they each react to contention for network resources. TCP adjusts the sending rate to avoid overwhelming both the receiver and the network. Limiting the sending rate to avoid overwhelming a receiver is called *flow control*. Limiting the sending rate to avoid overwhelming the network is called *congestion control*. UDP contains no flow control or congestion control algorithms and will send data into the network as fast as applications produces it.

TCP uses the Receiver's Advertised Window field in the TCP segment header to implement flow control. This field specifies the amount of data that the other end of the connection is willing and able to receive. It is first set during connection establishment and then it is updated with each TCP segment received. For example, if the receiver's advertised window was set to 17520, the sender should transmit no more than 17520 byes of unacknowledged data.

TCP senders maintain another limit called the *congestion window*. The congestion window typically starts at the maximum segment size (1 MSS) and then increases with each segment that is successfully acknowledged. The real limit on a TCP sender's rate is the minimum of the receiver's advertised window and the congestion window.

At first, the congestion window grows multiplicatively with each acknowledgment. This phase of multiplicative growth is called *slow start*. Multiplicative growth may not seem particularly slow, but it is slower than immediately sending the full receiver's advertised window. Even if no packet is lost, this multiplicative growth does not continue forever. Above an adaptively determined threshold, TCP switches to an additive increase in the congestion window. In this phase, called *congestion avoidance*, each successfully acknowledged segment increases the congestion window by the 1 MSS.

If at any point, a retransmission timer expires signaling the loss of a packet, then the congestion window is set back to one segment and the algorithm begins all over again. Given a long enough connection, a TCP sender will constantly increase its sending rate until it exceeds the capacity of the network and packet loss occurs. In addition to setting the congestion window back to one, TCP sets the threshold between slow-start and congestion avoidance to half of the value of the congestion window at the point the loss occurred. Thus, even though the sending rate is drastically reduced, the TCP sender will increase its sending rate to half of its previous value. During a long running connection, TCP will cycle through the slow start and congestion avoidance phases many times as it exceeds the network capacity and is forced to readjust.

Ideally, a TCP sender would use slow start and congestion avoidance to determine the maximum sending rate that does not lead to loss and then continue to transmit at exactly this rate. However, in practice, this maximum rate is not fixed. In reality, the ideal sending rate rarely stays constant. It changes as other data streams enter and leave the network. TCP adapts to these changes by varying the congestion window as well as other key parameters such as the length of time for the retransmission timer and the threshold at which it switches from slow start to congestion avoidance. These aspects of TCP allow it to balance the needs of the network as a whole while allowing each stream to achieve a fair portion of the network bandwidth.

TCP's pattern of gradual advance and aggressive retreat is an important key to the stability of Internet. Before congestion control was built into TCP, there were episodes of *congestion collapse* in the Internet. Congestion collapse occurs when senders so overwhelm the network that no data can actually reach its destination. This is much like gridlock on a city street.

UDP does nothing to limit the sending rate of applications. At first glance, it may seem advantageous to grab as much network bandwidth as possible for your application. However, this is shortsighted, as it would soon lead to congestion collapse in the Internet as a whole. Therefore, applications that use UDP to send large amounts of data are encouraged to implement congestion control algorithms themselves. Such applications are called *TCP-Friendly*. In this exercise, we will clearly demonstrate the impact that applications that are not TCP-Friendly have on other data streams.

CONFIGURATION

The traces used in this exercise were taken on a private network. A desktop PC and a laptop were connected via a hub. No traffic is exchanged with the global Internet. We will use **ttcp** to generate both TCP and UDP streams with specified properties.

Figure 3.4.1: Exercise Configuration

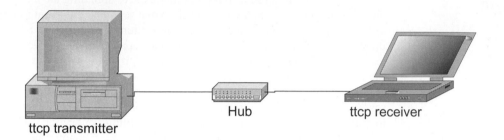

EXPERIMENT

In this experiment, we will examine concurrent data streams. In previous exercises, we have compared a TCP stream to an independent UDP stream transmitting the same data. Here, we first run two TCP streams in parallel to show how they adapt to allow each stream its fair share of the bandwidth. Then, we run a TCP stream together with a UDP stream to show how a UDP stream takes all the available bandwidth. Finally, we run two UDP streams to show how the competition between them results in data loss. We produce these streams using **ttcp**.

TWO COMPETING TCP STREAMS

With **ttcp**, we started two TCP receivers running on the laptop, each in a separate command window. We allowed one to listen on the default port, 5001 and instructed the other to listen on port 5002. We used the following command lines:

```
TCP RECEIVER 1:

      pcattcp -r -l 1000

TCP RECEIVER 2:

      pcattcp -r -l 1000 -p 5002
```

On the desktop machine, we also opened two different command windows, one for each transmitter. We typed the command lines required to run the transmitters, but did not actually execute them. We used the following command lines:

```
TCP TRANSMITTER 1:

    pcattcp -t -l 1000 192.168.0.102

TCP TRANSMITTER 2:

    pcattcp -t -l 1000 -p 5002 192.168.0.102
```

When both transmitters were ready to execute, we started an Ethereal capture. We then executed transmitter one and several seconds later executed transmitter two. The resulting trace is saved to the file **tcp_tcp.cap**. You can open this trace from the accompanying CD.

The first TCP stream begins with the SYN segment in packet 3. The endpoints of this stream are port 5001 on the laptop (192.168.0.102) and port 4421 on the desktop (192.168.0.100). This stream ends with final ACK in packet 4873.

The second TCP stream begins with the SYN segment in packet 1288. The endpoints of this stream are port 5002 on the laptop (192.168.0.102) and port 4422 on the desktop (192.168.0.100). This stream ends with final ACK in packet 6148.

The first TCP stream has exclusive access to the network for 1.7 seconds (packet 3 to packet 1287). The second stream arrives and both connections share the network for 4.9 seconds (packet 1288 to packet 4873). Finally, the second stream has exclusive access to the network for 1.8 seconds (packet 4874 through 6148).

The effect on each stream can clearly be seen using the Time-Sequence Graph tool under TCP Stream Analysis in the Analyze Menu. First examine stream one, by selecting one of the packets in the stream and then choosing the Time-Sequence Graph menu option. We are interested in the main flow of data so be careful to choose a packet sent from port 4421 to port 5001 and not a packet from port 5001 to port 4421.

Figure 3.4.2: Time-Sequence Graph for Stream One

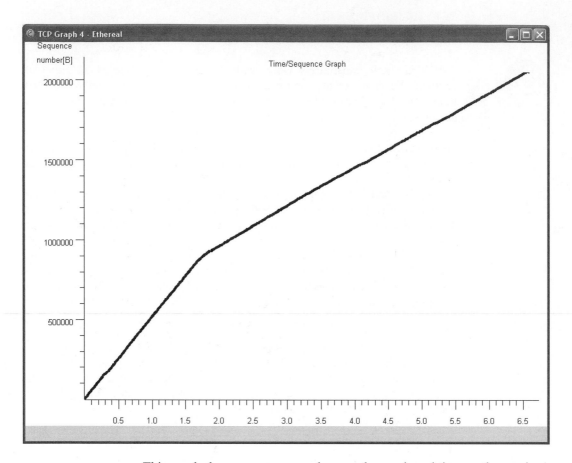

This graph shows sequence numbers on the *y*-axis and time on the *x*-axis. A steep line indicates that many bytes are being transferred per unit time, or in other words, the connection is achieving high bandwidth. A flatter line indicates that the transfer rate is slowing down. In the graph of connection one, we see that the line is steepest for the first 1.8 seconds. After this, the line becomes flatter as stream two is introduced. Although the line is flatter, stream one continues to make progress in its data transfer. We can examine a similar graph for connection two. (Warning: In order to select a packet in the second stream, you will need to reset the display filter with the Reset button at the bottom of the main Ethereal screen. Again, be careful to choose a packet from the main data flow.)

Figure 3.4.3: Time-Sequence Graph for Stream Two

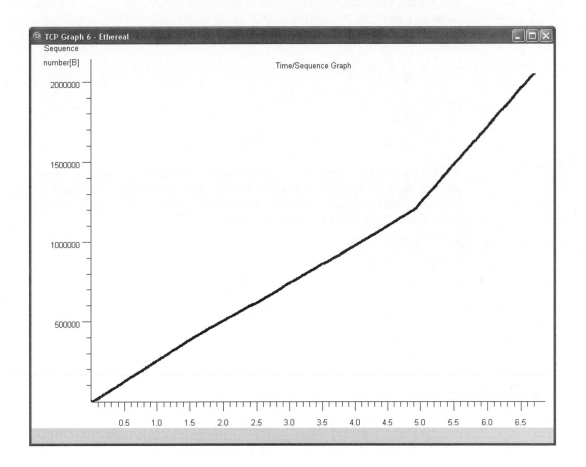

In the graph of connection two, we see that the line is steepest in the last 1.8 seconds. This corresponds to the time after stream one has completed.

These graphs show that TCP successfully adapts to share network bandwidth with other streams. In the face of competition, it decreases its sending rate. It also detects when more bandwidth becomes available and increases its sending rate appropriately.

Note that during the time when both streams are active, stream one transfers approximately 1,200,000 bytes (2,100,000 – 900,000) and stream two transfers approximately the same (1,200,000 – 0). Not only do TCP streams share available bandwidth; they share it equally.

UDP COMPETING WITH TCP

We started two **ttcp** receivers running on the laptop, each in a separate command window. We started a TCP receiver listening on the default port, 5001. We started a UDP receiver on port 5002. We used the following command lines:

```
TCP RECEIVER:

        pcattcp -r -l 1000

UDP RECEIVER:

        pcattcp -r -u -l 1000 -p 5002
```

On the desktop machine, we also opened two different command windows, one for the TCP transmitter and one for the UDP transmitter. We typed the command lines required to run the transmitters, but did not actually execute them. We used the following command lines:

```
TCP TRANSMITTER:

        pcattcp -t -l 1000 192.168.0.102

UDP TRANSMITTER:

        pcattcp -t -u -l 1000 -p 5002 192.168.0.102
```

When both transmitters were ready to execute, we started an Ethereal capture. We then executed the TCP transmitter and several seconds later executed the UDP transmitter. The resulting trace is saved to the file **tcp_udp.cap**. You can open this trace from the accompanying CD.

The TCP stream begins with the SYN segment in packet 1. The endpoints of this stream are port 5001 on the laptop (192.168.0.102) and port 4417 on the desktop (192.168.0.100). This stream ends with final ACK in packet 5132.

The first UDP datagram is packet 1822 and the last is packet 4066. The endpoints of this stream are port 5002 on the laptop (192.168.0.102) and port 4418 on the desktop (192.168.0.100).

The TCP stream has exclusive access to the network for 2.3 seconds (packet 1 to packet 1821). The UDP stream lasts for 1.2 seconds. Finally, the TCP stream again has exclusive access to the network for 1.3 seconds (packet 4419 through 5132).

As we did for the last trace, we examine the TCP connection using the Time-Sequence Graph. Notice this time, that the line is basically flat for the duration of the UDP connection. This indicates that the TCP connection made little to no progress transferring data during this time. This is a good illustration of why UDP is not "TCP-Friendly."

Figure 3.4.4: Time-Sequence Graph for TCP Stream with UDP

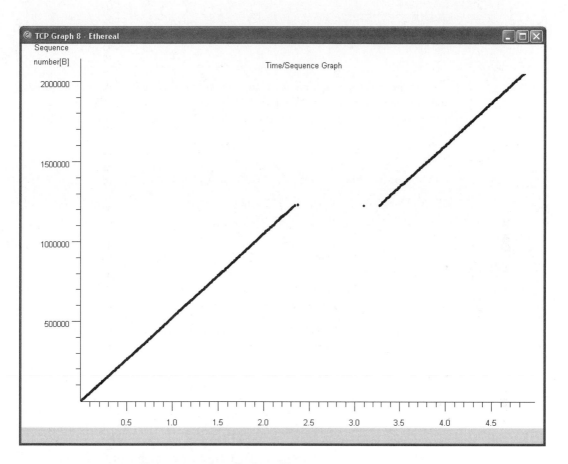

If we use the display filter `tcp.analysis.retransmission` to isolate the retransmissions, we see that they all occur between 2.33 and 3.50 seconds when the UDP stream is active.

TWO COMPETING UDP STREAMS

We started two UDP **ttcp** receivers running on the laptop, each in a separate command window. We allowed one to listen on the default port, 5001, and instructed the other to listen on port 5002. We used the following command lines:

```
UDP RECEIVER 1:

        pcattcp -r -u -l 1000

UDP RECEIVER 2:

        pcattcp -r -u -l 1000 -p 5002
```

On the desktop machine, we also opened two different command windows, one for each transmitter. We typed the command lines required to run the transmitters, but did not actually execute them. We used the following command lines:

```
UDP TRANSMITTER 1:

        pcattcp -t -u -l 1000 192.168.0.102

UDP TRANSMITTER 2:

        pcattcp -t -u -l 1000 -p 5002 192.168.0.102
```

When both transmitters were ready to execute, we started an Ethereal capture. We then executed transmitter one and several seconds later executed transmitter two. The resulting trace is saved to the file **udp_udp.cap**. You can open this trace from the accompanying CD.

The endpoints of first UDP stream are port 5001 on the laptop (192.168.0.102) and port 4445 on the desktop (192.168.0.100). This stream begins with packet 3 and ends packet 3707.

The endpoints of second UDP stream are port 5002 on the laptop (192.168.0.102) and port 4446 on the desktop (192.168.0.100). This stream begins with packet 1654 and ends packet 3711.

The first UDP stream has exclusive access to the network for 0.4 seconds (packet 3 to packet 1654). The streams share the network for the remainder of the transmission.

There can be no corresponding Time-Sequence graph tool for UDP, but we can use other metrics to analyze the impact of the competing UDP streams.

Based on the command line parameters, each transmitter should have sent 2048 datagrams with 1000 bytes each. First, we use the display filter udp.srcprt == 4445. This isolates the data packets in the first UDP stream. If we then choose the Summary option in the Analyze menu, we can see that only 1655 packets and were actually seen on the network. (Five of these 1655 are actually special 4 byte transfers used to indicate the beginning or end of the transfer.) This is a loss rate of 19 percent. Using the display filter udp.srcprt == 4446, we can isolates the second UDP stream. Interestingly, all the data from this stream appeared on the network.

The amount of data seen in the Ethereal trace paints an optimistic picture. Not all of the data seen in the trace successfully reached the receiving processes.

The receiver of the second UDP stream reports receiving only 163000 bytes, a 92 percent loss rate! The receiver of the first UDP stream does not even report statistics, presumably because all of the special end of stream packets are lost. This is likely due as much to the lack of flow control as the lack of congestion control.

QUESTIONS

Answer the following questions about the files `tcp_tcp.cap`, `tcp_udp.cap`, and `udp_udp.cap`.

1. In `tcp_udp.cap`, how many TCP packets are sent in each direction during the time that the UDP transmission is actively sending data packets? Write display filters that help you identify these packets.

2. In `tcp_udp.cap`, how many bytes of data are successfully transmitted by TCP during the time that the UDP transmission is active? How many bytes of total TCP traffic? How did you determine your answer?

3. In `tcp_tcp.cap`, examine the Time-Sequence Graph for the first TCP connection. Use the zoom feature to clearly display the point at which the slope changes (from a steeper line to a flatter line). What time does this occur? Does this correspond exactly with the beginning of the second TCP stream? Why do you think this is?

4. Do you see any retransmissions in the trace `tcp_tcp.cap`? How did you determine your answer? Why do you think this is?

5. In `udp_udp.cap`, how many UDP packets from port 4445 to 5001 occur after the second UDP transmission begins? How large is the gap between these packets and all of the other packets from 4445 to 5001? What do all of these packets have in common? Why do you think this is?

6. In `udp_udp.cap`, the second UDP transmission stream is significantly more successful in acquiring bandwidth than the first. Do you think that there is a fundamental advantage to the latecomer? Why or why not? Describe a set of experiments you could perform to test your answer.

7. Examine the traces and determine what we did when they were captured to limit the size of the traces. Estimate how large the traces would have been without this limit.

DISCUSSION AND INVESTIGATION

1. In the TCP segment header, the sequence number and acknowledgement number fields are both 32 bits and the receiver's advertised window field is 16 bits. Discuss the implication of the size of these fields.

2. A study of commercial backbone traffic in 1997 by Thompson, Miller and Wilder found that 95 percent of the bytes and 90 percent of the packets sent on the Internet were part of TCP connections. If the percentage of data sent over UDP were to rise, how would that affect the stability of the Internet?

3. "TCP-Friendly" UDP applications can implement congestion control algorithms on their own. Investigate the definition of the term "TCP-Friendly."

4. Investigate other proposed approaches to congestion control in TCP including TCP Vegas.

RESOURCES

- RFC 2581, TCP Congestion Control, **ftp://ftp.rfc-editor.org/in-notes/rfc2581.txt**

- RFC 2914, Congestion Control Principles, **ftp://ftp.rfc-editor.org/innotes/rfc2914.txt**

- The TCP-Friendly Website, **http://www.psc.edu/networking/tcp_friendly.html**

- Kevin Thompson, Gregory J. Miller, and Rick Wilder. Wide-area internet traffic patterns and characteristics. *IEEE Network Magazine*, 11(6):10-23, November/December 1997

- Web search: TCP Congestion Control

Section 4:
Network Layer Protocols

Introduction

The network layer provides end-to-end routing and delivery of messages. The Internet Protocol (IP) is *the* network layer protocol for the Internet. IP is based on the principle of packet switching. In a packet switched network, each packet is individually routed from source to destination with out regard for the path taken by other packets in the same flow. In this section, we will examine traces that illustrate how packets flow through the Internet over IP.

In Exercise 1, we discuss some of the basics of IP including the format of the IP datagram. We discuss how IP addresses are assigned to provide efficient routing and how end hosts can obtain IP addresses through DHCP. We compare the current version of IP (IP version 4) to the next generation version of IP (IP version 6). Finally, we examine how IP datagrams can be fragmented as they cross the network.

In Exercise 2, we introduce `ping` and `traceroute`, two powerful tools for exploring the Internet. We examine traces of `ping` and `traceroute` activity to understand how they rely on the Internet Control Message Protocol (ICMP), which is a companion protocol to IP. We examine a multi-hop path and illustrate how an IP datagram is changed as it traverses the path.

In Exercise 3, we discuss how Internet paths are established and maintained with dynamic routing protocols. In particular, we use Ethereal traces to examine the impact of enabling a dynamic protocol to provide end-to-end connectivity in a small local network consisting of two hosts and five intermediate routers.

In Exercise 4, we explain how the Internet is divided into administrative units called Autonomous Systems (AS) and in addition, show how dynamic routing is handled differently inside an AS than it is between them. We also introduce the Border Gateway Protocol (BGP) – the standard dynamic routing protocol for inter-AS routing.

Network Layer Protocols:
Exercise 4.1

Joining the Internet: Introduction to IP and DHCP

INTRODUCTION

The Internet Protocol (IP) is the backbone of the Internet. It defines the way in which a collection of independent networks can work together to form a global network of networks. Each host in the Internet is given an IP address. Data is sent from host to host in packets called *datagrams*. Each datagram is labeled with both source and destination IP addresses and sent out into the network. If source and destination machines are not on the same local network, then intermediate machines called *routers* receive the transmitted datagram and send it one step closer to its destination. This process is called *packet switching*.

For early Internet researchers, packet switching was an important new idea. Other global communication networks like the telephone network did not use packet switching. Instead, these networks established a fixed circuit between source and destination and sent all traffic over this connection. In packet switched networks, packets do not travel along established circuits; instead they are individually addressed and routed through the network.

The Internet Protocol allows datagrams to travel from source to destination over many different networks. Each network may have its own rules and conventions; IP allows datagrams to adapt to each network it traverses. For example, the maximum amount of data that can be sent as a unit varies from network to network. IP allows datagrams to be broken into smaller pieces (fragmented) and then reassembled at the destination.

The format of each IP datagram is shown below. The source and destination address fields in the header each contain a 32 bit IP address value. IP addresses are often written in the dotted quad format (e.g. 192.168.0.1). Each of the four numbers in this format range from 0 to 255 and each represents 8 of the 32 bits.

Figure 4.1.1: IP Datagram Header

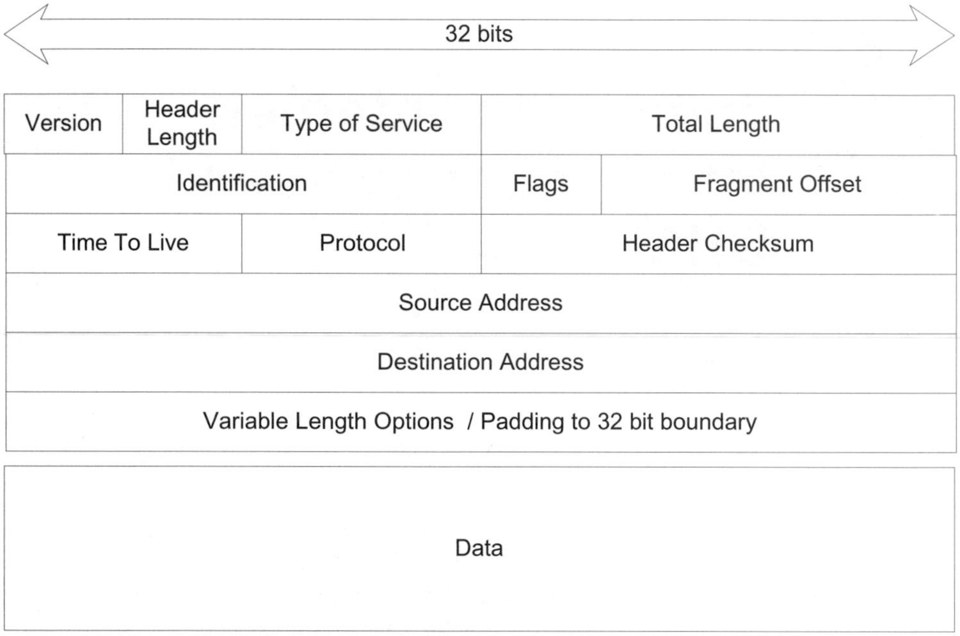

32 bits					
Version	Header Length	Type of Service	Total Length		
Identification			Flags	Fragment Offset	
Time To Live		Protocol	Header Checksum		
Source Address					
Destination Address					
Variable Length Options / Padding to 32 bit boundary					
Data					

Most IP addresses represent a single host on the Internet. To make sure that each host receives a unique IP address, the process of obtaining an IP address is carefully managed. At the highest level, an organization called the Internet Corporation for Assigned Name and Numbers (ICANN) controls the allocation of all IP addresses. ICANN delegates large portions of the IP address space to Regional Internet Registries (RIR). Each RIR allocates portions of the IP address space it manages to organizations operating within their designated geographical area. For example, the American Registry for Internet Numbers (ARIN) controls IP address allocation within the Americas. Organizations that need many IP addresses (e.g. Internet Service Providers, large corporations, universities, etc.) apply to the RIR in their area. Organizations that need a smaller number of IP addresses typically obtain them directly from their Internet Service Provider.

This system is designed to promote fair and efficient decomposition of the IP address space. IP address space is a limited and therefore valuable resource. Organizations also pay a sizable yearly fee for IP address blocks. Organizations are not allowed to tie up large unused blocks of address space simply because they have the money to do so. RIRs typically require organizations to document their need for a certain number of IP addresses before they will be granted.

It is essential for efficient routing that similar IP addresses be grouped together. When a datagram is sent into the network, routers look at its destination address and decide how to send it closer to that destination. If IP addresses were assigned randomly, then each router would need to record the location of each individual IP address. When large blocks of IP address space are handed out to regions and then to Internet Service Providers and then to organizations, it allows remote routers to maintain a single route for the entire block of addresses. Only the routers near the destination need to know its specific location. Finally, organizations allocate individual IP addresses to each machine they administer.

Often times, organizations automate the allocation of IP addresses to individual machines with a protocol called Dynamic Host Configuration Protocol or DHCP.

Not all IP addresses represent individual hosts on the Internet. For example, IP addresses in the range 224.0.0.0 to 239.255.255.255 are multicast addresses. A multicast address represents a group of multiple machines that have all subscribed to certain stream of data. There are also special broadcast addresses which are designed to reach all hosts in a specific local network or subnet. The address 255.255.255.255 is a special broadcast address that refers to anyone listening within a limited broadcast domain.

IP addresses for a single host are called unicast addresses. Unicast addresses are in the range 1.0.0.0 to 223.255.255.255. Most addresses within this range are considered globally routable, meaning that a datagram sent to these addresses anywhere in the Internet will be directed to the proper destination. However, some of these addresses have been reserved for private networks (RFC 1918). Private networks may be networks that use IP, but which do not connect to the global network. They may also be networks that sit behind firewalls or routers that translate local addresses into globally routable addresses. Many of the experiments in this book were performed in a private network using IP addresses in the range 198.168.0.0 –198.168.255.255.

The first field in the IP datagram header contains the version number. Version 4 of the Internet Protocol or IPv4 is the dominant version used in the Internet. It is described in RFC 791. A new version of IP, version 6, has also been defined. The primary motivation for the design of iPv6 was the possibility of running out of IP addresses. If demand for IP address space continues to grow at the same rate, some estimate that all available 32 bit IPv4 addresses will be consumed by 2010. In IPv6, the address size is increased from 32 bits to 128 bits. 128 bits per address provides approximately 1500 addresses per square foot of the Earth's surface! Even if every computer, PDA, car, and toaster on the planet has an IP addresses, the designers of IPv6 thought that 1500 per square foot would be sufficient. Although increasing the number of IP addresses was the primary motivation, IPv6 contains other new features such as extensible, chained headers and flow labels to support the simulation of circuits over a packet switched network.

Internet registries are already making blocks of IPv6 space available and many operating systems include an IPv6 implementation. However, the rate of adoption of IPv6 is slow at best. In part, this is because it is difficult for IPv6 and IPv4 to co-exist. IPv6 is supported on only a small percentage of hosts and routers. For these hosts and routers to communicate using IPv6, they typically must "tunnel" IPv6 over iPv4 meaning that an IPv6 datagram is placed in the data portion of an iPv4 datagram. This configuration allows IPv6 to be tested but provides few of the benefits. It is believed by some that only the actual exhaustion of IP address space will force a conversion. However, islands of IPv6 space are becoming more common in the US government and in installations with large numbers of end hosts such as cell phones.

In this exercise, we will examine several traces that explore the basics of the Internet Protocol. First, we will review a trace of a machine obtaining an IP address via DHCP. Next, we will examine IPv4 traffic that illustrates the use of several fields in the IPv4 that control fragmentation and reassembly. Finally, we will see a trace of IPv6 traffic tunneled on top of IPv4 datagrams.

CONFIGURATION

The traces used in this exercise were taken on a private network. A desktop PC and a laptop were connected via a switch that hands out IP addresses via DHCP.

Figure 4.1.2: Exercise Configuration

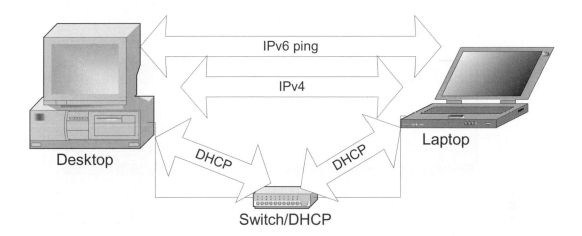

EXPERIMENT

OBTAINING AN IP ADDRESS VIA DHCP

Our first experiment in this exercise is to obtain an IP address for our desktop machine. Our desktop machine is running Windows and we opened up a command prompt. We started an Ethereal trace and then issued the following commands:

```
ipconfig /release
ipconfig /renew
ipconfig /renew
ipconfig /release
```

The command `ipconfig` is used to display information about and change the configuration of the machine's IP address.

We saved the result of these commands to the file **dhcp_isolated.cap**. You can open this file from the accompanying CD.

Packet 1 is used to release the machine's current IP address, 192.168.0.100. Notice that packet 1 lists 192.168.0.100 as the source IP address. After it is released, the machine has no valid IP address and uses the address 0.0.0.0 as the source address in packet 2.

Packet 2 is a DHCP Discovery message, and it is used by machines without an IP address to request one. It is sent to the special broadcast address, 255.255.255.255. This address will reach all connected hosts within a limited broadcast range. Logically, 255.255.255.255 means broadcast the entire Internet, but this is never literally the case because routers will not forward such a broadcast beyond the local network to avoid swamping the Internet with such requests.

Figure 4.1.3: DHCP Discover

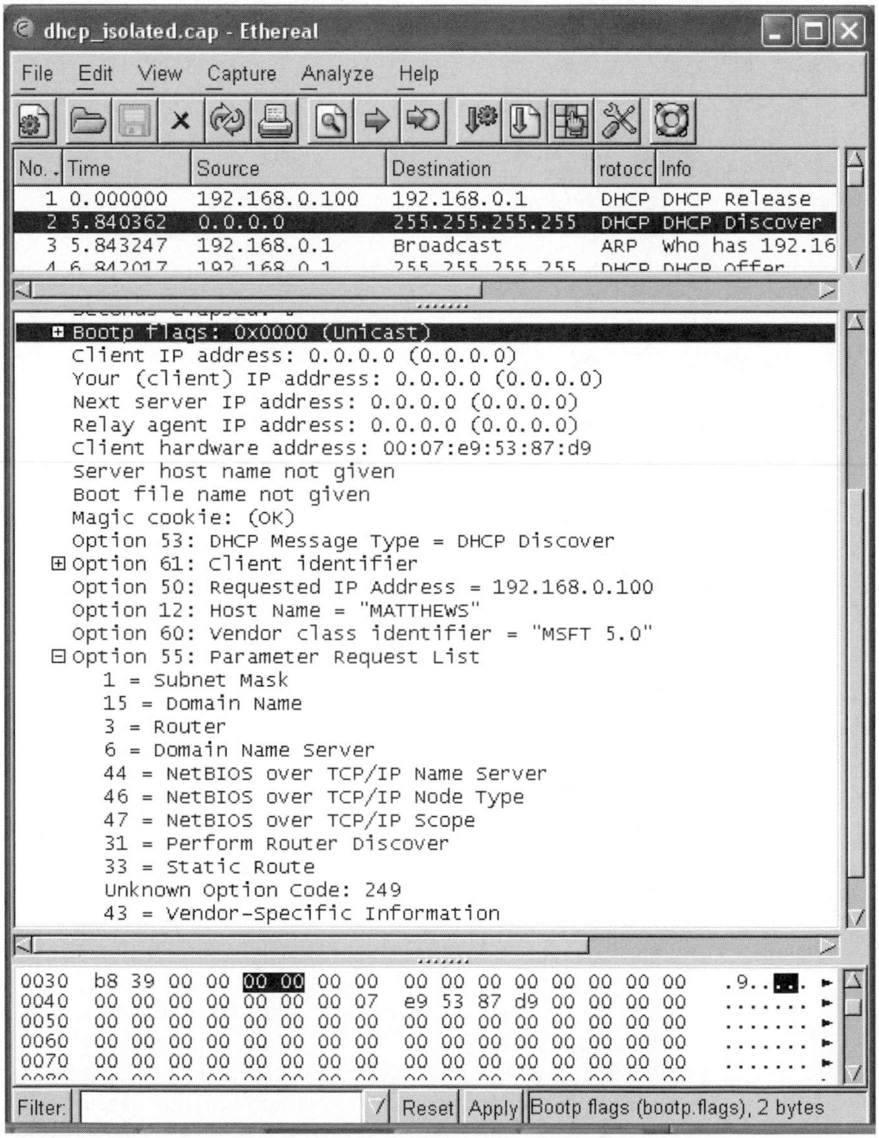

In the DHCP Discovery message, the client includes information about itself. In particular, it provides its hostname (MATTHEWS) and the physical address of its Ethernet interface (00:07:e9:53:87:d9). These values can be used by DHCP to recognize a known client. DHCP servers can use this information to implement a variety of policies such as handing out the same IP address as last time, handing out a different IP address as last time or requiring clients to register their physical layer address in order to ontain an IP address.

In the DHCP Discovery message, the client also specifies the list of information it would like to receive from the DHCP server. This "Parameter Request List" contains items in addition to an IP address that the client would like to know about the local network. Many of these values are required for a machine to fully "join" the Internet. For example, the client must know the identity of the local router. This is the machine to which it must send any datagram that is not destined for a host on the local network. In other words, this is the first intermediate machine that will direct outgoing datagrams one step closer to their final destination.

Clients must also know their subnet mask. A subnet mask is a 32 bit number which when combined with the IP address (bitwise logical AND) tells the network address. All machines that can reach each other without the assistance of an intervening router have the same network address. Thus, the subnet mask is used to determine whether a datagram should be sent to the local router or directly to a local destination.

Clients must also know their Domain Name and the identity of their local Domain Name server. A domain name is a human readable network name. For example, the machine **www.arin.net** has arin.net as its domain name. Domain Name servers translate human readable machine names such as **www.arin.net** into IP addresses.

In packet 4, the DHCP server at 192.168.0.1 responds with a DHCP OFFER message. This packet is also broadcast to 255.255.255.255 because, although the client machine does not yet know its IP address, it will receive messages sent to the broadcast address. This message contains the values requested by the client including its IP address, local router, subnet mask, domain name, and local domain name server.

In packet 5, the client indicates its acceptance of the IP address by sending a DHCP request message echoing the same information. Finally, the transaction is completed with packet 6, in which the DHCP server acknowledges the addresses requested. Notice that in packet 7, the client begins to use its new IP address as the source address.

It is interesting to note the ARP messages in packets 3 and 7 through 12. ARP stands for the Address Resolution Protocol and is used to translate IP addresses to physical layer addresses. ARP works by broadcasting a message asking for the physical layer address of the machine with a certain IP address. If that machine hears the message, they should respond with their physical layer address.

In packet 3, the DHCP server asks if anyone has the IP address 192.168.0.100. (Notice this request is sent to the broadcast address.) This allows the DHCP server to double check that no other machine has the address before it is offers the address to our desktop machine. Also after acquiring its IP address, our desktop sends three messages asking if any other machine has the same IP address.

The first four ARP requests all went unanswered. In packets 10 through 13, we see the DHCP server again ask who has the IP address 192.168.0.100. Both times the desktop machine answers that it does and supplies its Ethernet address.

IP addresses handed out through DHCP are leased for a specific period of time. To maintain their IP address, a client must renew their lease. Packets 14 and 15 illustrate the process of renewing an existing lease. They are the result of our second `ipconfig /renew` command. The DHCP Request requests the renewal of 192.168.0.1. The DHCP ACK includes the length of the lease (one day in this case.) If no DHCP request is sent before a lease expires, the DHCP server is free to reassign the IP address to another machine.

Finally, packet 16 is the result of our `ipconfig /release` command. After the DHCP server receives this message, it is no longer bound by the expiration time of the lease. It is free to reassign the IP address if desired.

FRAGMENTATION IN IPv4

In our second experiment, we examine the use of several fields in the IPv4 header. In particular, we will see how the identification field, the fragment offset field and some of the flags are used to support fragmentation and reassembly of IP datagrams.

The Internet is composed of a collection of networks with different administrative and physical different characteristics. In a packet-switched network like the Internet, the source of an datagram cannot know the characteristics of all networks over which the datagram will pass. Handling this kind of diversity is one of the big challenges in connecting heterogeneous networks together to form a single Internet.

 One example of the type of diversity encountered is that different networks set different limits on the size of datagrams transmitted over their network. IP must either require all networks to operate at the lowest bound of all possible networks or it must include a way to adapt to differences when encountered.

IP contains support for fragmentation and reassembly. Fragmentation refers to breaking a single IP datagram into multiple pieces when the original datagram is too large for the local network. Reassembly refers to putting the pieces back together properly at the destination.

To experiment with fragmentation, we used a tool called **ttcp** to send data that is too large for the local network. Specifically, we sent two messages of size 5000 bytes over a network that can support a datagram of at most 1514 bytes. Data is sent from the desktop with IP address 192.168.0.100 to the laptop with IP address 192.168.0.102.

We saved a specific portion of this trace in the file **fragment_5000_isolated.cap**. You can open this file from the attached CD and follow along.

The IP layer (the network layer) sits between the transport layer and the link layer. In this case, UDP is the transport layer protocol and Ethernet is the link layer protocol. UDP is dicussed in more detail in Section 3. Ethernet is discussed in more detail in Section 5.

Two UDP datagrams were sent, each containing 5000 bytes of data and 8 bytes of the UDP header. In **fragment_5000_isolated.cap**, packets 1 through 4 represent the first UDP datagram and packets 5 through 8 represent the second.

When the IP layer receives each 5008 byte UDP datagram, its job is to transmit it as an IP datagram over the Ethernet. However, the Ethernet permits only 1514 bytes to be transmitted at one time and 14 bytes of this are the Ethernet frame header.

IP is forced to send the datagram as multiple fragments. Each fragment must have an Ethernet frame header and an IP datagram header. Each fragment will contain a portion of the UDP payload (header and data).

IP places the first 1480 bytes of the original datagram (8 bytes of UDP header and the first 1472 bytes of data) into the first fragment. The next two fragments each contain 1480 bytes of data and the final fragment contains the remaining 568 bytes (5000 − 1472 − 1480 − 1480 = 568).

To allow the receiver to reconstruct the original datagram, IP numbers the fragments using specfic fields in the header. First the identification field is used to link all the fragments together. Packets 1 through 4 all share identification number 0xfd2b and packets 5 through 8 all share identification number 0xfd2c. The fragment offset specifies the offset into the fragment of the first byte of data in the packet. For example, packets 1 and 5 both contain fragment offset 0 because they are the first fragment.

Finally, the flags field contains a bit that indicates where additional fragments follow this one. Packets 1 through 3 and 5 through 7 all have this bit set. Packets 4 and 8 do not because they are the last fragment of their respective datagrams.

Figure 4.1.4: Fragmentation Flags

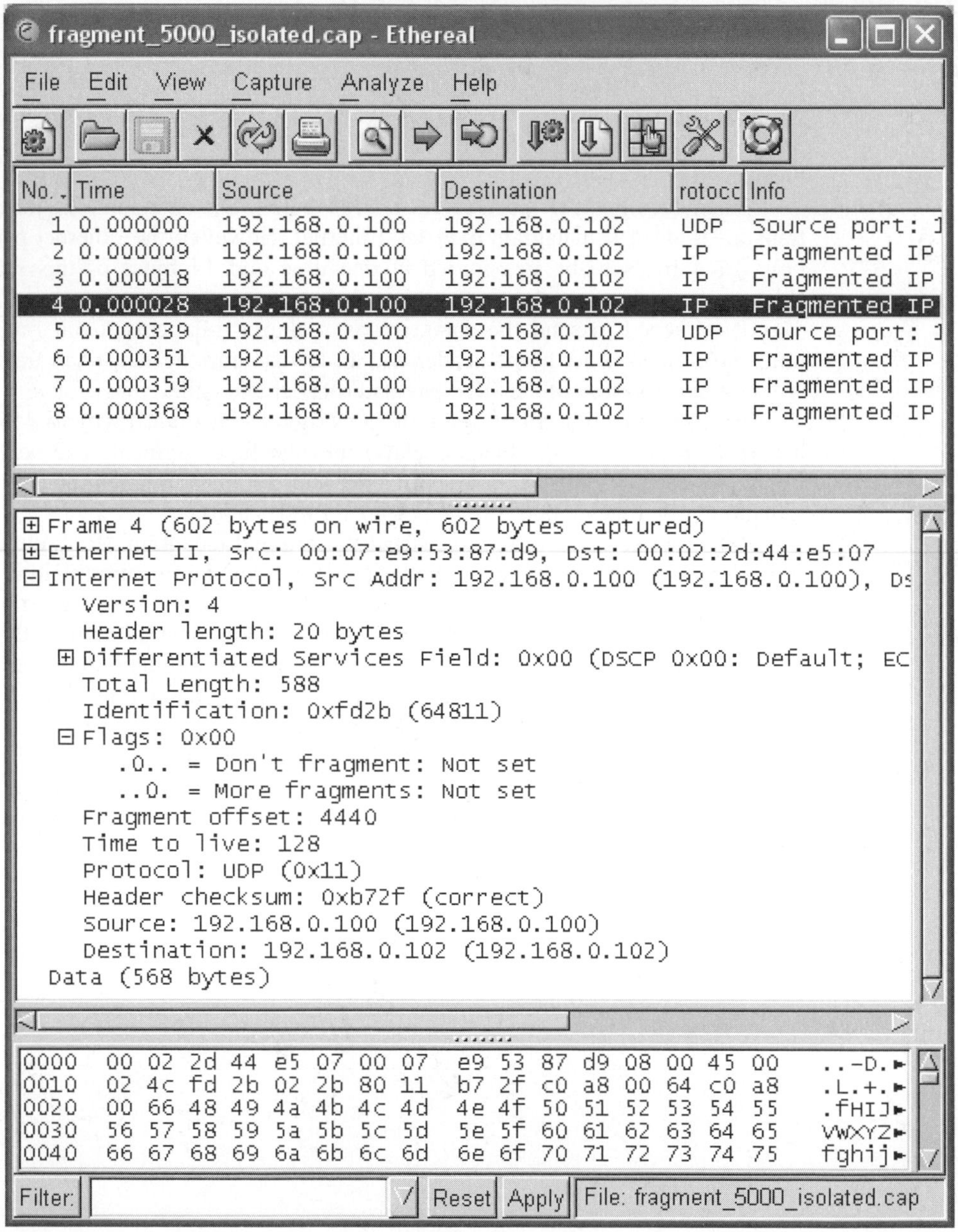

PING OVER IPv6

In our last experiment in this exercise, we use the IPv6 implementation in Windows XP to send IPv6 datagrams between the desktop and the laptop machines.

To prepare for this experiment, we issued an `ipv6 install` command at the command prompt on both the desktop and the laptop. This enabled IPv6. We then used the command `ping6` that is an IPv6 enabled version of the `ping` command which we examine in detail in the next exercise. We used this tool to send 3 datagrams from the desktop to the laptop and the laptop replied with 3 datagrams. We saved the resulting trace in the file **ping_ipv6.cap**.

This trace illustrates how IPv6 can be "tunneled" over IPv4. In particular, the IPv6 datagrams are places within the data section of an IPV4 datagram. Notice that the IPv6 source and destination addresses are much larger than the IPv4 addresses. Notice also that the IPv6 address of each machine is the same as the IPv4 address with 0xfe0800000000000000005efe in the upper 96 bits. This is because a portion of the IPv6 address space was devoted to backward compatibility with existing IPv4 addresses.

If IPv6 becomes the standard version of IP used in the Internet, the IPv6 header would immediately follow the Ethernet frame header and the IPv4 header would no longer be present.

Figure 4.1.5: IPv6 over IPv4

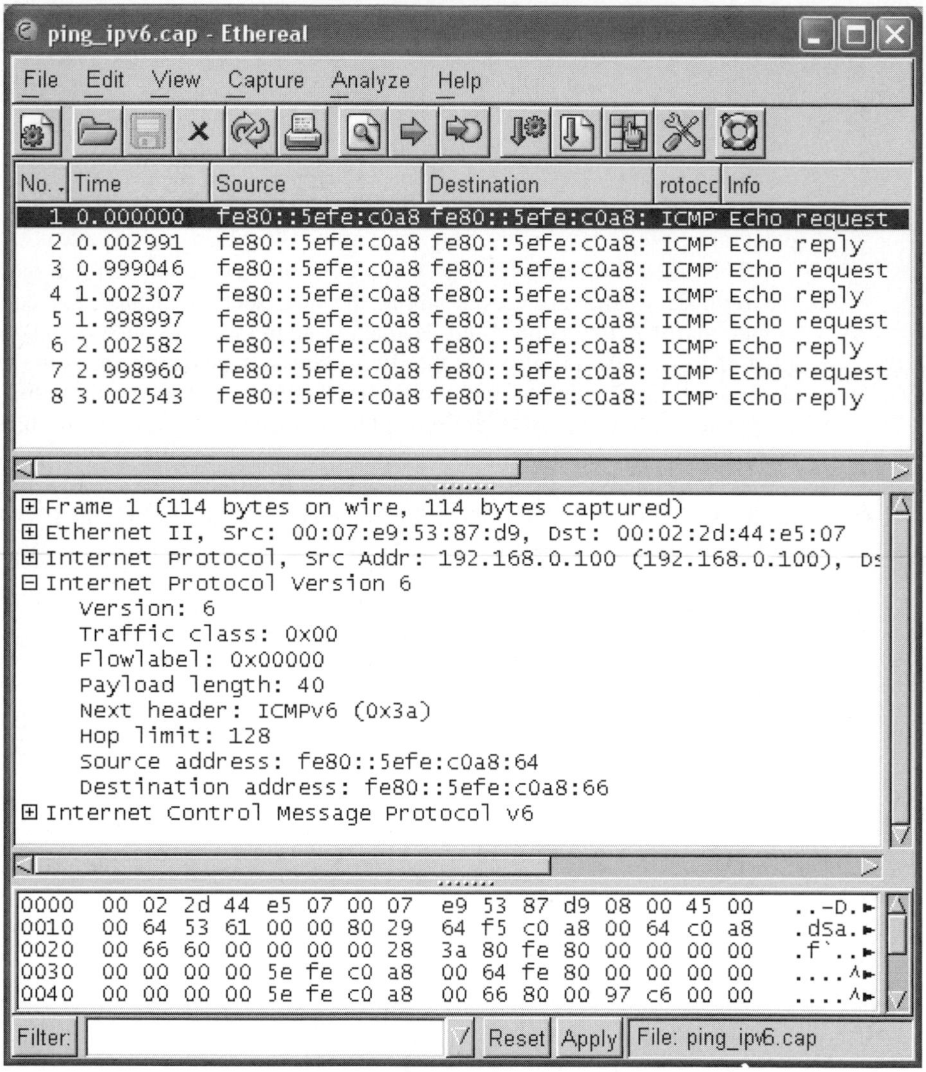

QUESTIONS

Answer the following questions about the files `dhcp_isolated.cap`, `fragment_5000_isolated.cap`, and `ping_ipv6.cap`.

1. What is the IP address of the local router or default gateway advertised by the DHCP server? How do you know? Is this the same as the DHCP server itself?

2. What is the domain name assigned by the DHCP server in `dhcp_isolated.cap`? How do you know?

3. How many domain name servers are advertised? What are their IP addresses? Are any of these machines the same as the DHCP server?

4. In `fragment_5000_isolated.cap`, we saw that 5000 bytes of data sent over UDP had to be fragmented into multiple IP datagrams. What is the largest amount of data that could be sent at once over the same network and not require fragmentation? How did you compute this?

5. How much bigger is the IPv6 header than the IPv4 header? What percentage of each header consists of source and destination addresses?

6. Consider the header overhead of IPv4 vs IPv6. How much additional overhead would there be for 1000 bytes of IP data? How much overhead would this be if IPv6 is tunneled over IPv4? What about for 100 bytes of data?

DISCUSSION AND INVESTIGATION

1. Explore the web page for the American Registry for Internet Numbers (ARIN). Summarize the process for acquiring a block of IPv4 addresses. See if you can find how much organizations must pay each year for blocks of various sizes. How do the policies for blocks on IPv6 space differ?

2. Acquire a block of IPv6 space from **www.freenet6.org**. and set up a IPv6 tunnel to your local machine. A variety of sites (e.g. http://ipv6-test.singnet.com.sg) will report whether you are connecting over IPv6.

3. Investigate the role of Classless Interdomain Routing (CIDR) and Network Address Translation (NAT) on the problem of exhaustion of IPv4 address space.

4. Search for concrete data that describes how much of IPv4 space is currently allocated.

5. When an application such as a web browser or e-mail server is called IPv6 enabled, what does that really mean? Discuss what would be involved in making an application IPv6 enabled?

6. Investigate the United States Department of Defense's decision to require a transition to IPv6. What are the likely consequences of this decision on US commercial deployment of IPv6?

RESOURCES

- Internet Corporation For Assigned Names and Numbers, **http://www.icann.org**

- American Registry for Internet Numbers, **http://www.arin.net**

- RFC 1918, Address Allocation for Private Internets, **ftp://ftp.rfc-editor.org/in-notes/rfc1918.txt**

- RFC 791, Internet Protocol, **ftp://ftp.rfc-editor.org/in-notes/rfc791.txt**

- RFC 2460, Internet Protocol, Version 6 (IPv6) Specification, **ftp://ftp.rfc-editor.org/in-notes/rfc2460.txt**

- RFC 3513, Internet Protocol Version 6 (IPv6) Addressing Architecture, **ftp://ftp.rfc-editor.org/in-notes/rfc3513.txt**

- IP OPTION NUMBERS, **http://www.iana.org/numbers.html**

- Web search: Exhaustion of IPv4 space

Network Layer Protocols:
Exercise **4.2**

Ping and Traceroute

INTRODUCTION

In this exercise, we will introduce two powerful tools for exploring the Internet—ping and traceroute. Ping sends special probe messages to a specific host in the Internet and waits for a reply indicating that the host is "alive" and functioning. The name ping was inspired by sonar equipment that uses echo-location to identify ships. Traceroute maps out all the intermediate hosts along a path to a specific Internet host.

In the following example, we used ping to probe the connection from 128.153.128.2 to www.iana.org (192.0.34.162). Notice that ping reports information about the round trip time.

```
> ping www.iana.org

PING www.iana.org: 56 data bytes
64 bytes from www.iana.org (192.0.34.162): icmp_seq=0. time=96. ms
64 bytes from www.iana.org (192.0.34.162): icmp_seq=1. time=97. ms
64 bytes from www.iana.org (192.0.34.162): icmp_seq=2. time=123. ms
64 bytes from www.iana.org (192.0.34.162): icmp_seq=3. time=97. ms
----www.iana.org PING Statistics----
4 packets transmitted, 4 packets received, 0% packet loss
round-trip (ms)  min/avg/max = 96/103/123
```

In the following example, we used traceroute to identify the intermediate nodes along the path and the round trip time to each. Traceroute is available on most platforms. The version available under Windows is called tracert instead of traceroute.

Notice that the majority of the delay occurs between hop 10 and 11. From the machine names, it seems likely that intermediate node 10 is located on the East Coast (New York City) and that intermediate node 11 is located on the West Coast (Los Angeles). This does not imply that there is a direct physical connection between these two machines. Most likely, this traffic is sent over long-haul links provided by telephone or communication companies.

```
> traceroute www.iana.org

traceroute to www.iana.org (192.0.34.162), 30 hops max, 40 byte packets

   1   128.153.4.129          (128.153.4.129)            0.669 ms
2      128.153.2.1            (128.153.2.1)              1.367 ms
   3   pts-clarkson.nysernet.net   (199.109.34.14)       1.487 ms
   4   syr-pts.nysernet.net        (199.109.34.6)        6.326 ms
   5   65.124.186.237         (65.124.186.237)           19.641 ms
   6   205.171.30.109         (205.171.30.109)           20.340 ms
   7   205.171.30.18          (205.171.30.18)            19.793 ms
   8   204.255.173.21         (204.255.173.21)           19.512 ms
   9   0.so-6-1-0.XL2.NYC8.ALTER.NET (152.63.19.50)      19.770 ms
  10   0.so-2-0-0.TL2.NYC8.ALTER.NET (152.63.0.185)      21.156 ms
  11   0.so-0-2-0.TL2.LAX9.ALTER.NET (152.63.1.97)       91.994 ms
  12   0.so-1-0-0.XL2.LAX9.ALTER.NET (152.63.115.149)    93.600 ms
  13   POS7-0.GW6.LAX9.ALTER.NET (152.63.116.101)        92.750 ms
  14   icann-gw.customer.alter.net (157.130.247.6)       95.934 ms
  15   www.iana.org                (192.0.34.162)        97.6543 ms
```

Both traceroute and ping rely on a protocol called the Internet Control Message Protocol or ICMP. ICMP is considered a companion protocol to IP. ICMP messages are sent within IP datagrams, but logically ICMP messages report on the status of network layer events.

Some ICMP messages request information. For example, in the case of ping, an ICMP echo request message is sent to the remote host. If they are alive, they are expected to return an ICMP echo reply message.

Some ICMP messages are sent in response to errors that occur at the network layer. For example, one ICMP message type specifies that a destination is unreachable. It may be unreachable for many reasons and the ICMP message attempts to identify the problem. For example, the host itself may be down or possibly its entire network is disconnected.

The host itself may be functioning, but unable to deliver the datagram. For example, one of the fields in the IP header is the Protocol field. It is this field that specifies what protocol should process the data portion of the IP datagram. Internet Assigned Numbers Authority (IANA) publishes a list of these numbers. For example, if this field contains a 6, then the data is to be interpreted as a TCP segment and the IP layer of the kernel passes the data to the TCP layer. If the field contains a 1, then the data is to be interpreted as an ICMP message and the IP layer of the kernel passes the data to the ICMP layer. If a datagram arrives with a protocol number that the operating system does not support, then it would return an ICMP message that specifies "Protocol Unreachable." The IANA also publishes a list of ICMP message types.

Traceroute is based on an ingenious use of ICMP, and another field in the IP header called the Time-To-Live field. When a datagram is sent, the Time-To-Live field is initialized to the maximum number of hops that it should take through the network. At each intermediate machine, this number is decremented. If it reaches zero, the machine holding the datagram will not forward it any further. Instead, it will send an ICMP Time-To-Live-Exceeded message back to the source IP address.

The Time-To-Live field is used to prevent datagrams from circulating forever in the Internet. Recall that the path taken by a datagram is determined as each intermediate router attempts to forward the packet one step closer to its destination. Routers determine this next step by exchanging information with other routers about good paths. The best "next step" often changes dynamically with variations in network conditions. This allows the Internet to route around severed links, but it can also result in confusion over the proper path. It is possible for datagrams to be caught in routing loops where, for example, router A thinks the datagram should go to router B and router B thinks the datagram should go back to router A!

This field is 8 bits so the maximum length of an Internet path is at most $2^8 -$ 1 or 255 hops. However, most source machines initialize this value to an even smaller number (e.g. 128 or 64). Setting the Time-To-Live field to a small number might make it impossible to reach remote destinations. Setting the Time-To-Live field to a large number means that datagrams would circulate longer in the event of an infinite loop.

Traceroute uses the Time-To-Live field to map the intermediate nodes along an Internet path. It deliberately sets the Time-To-Live field to a very low number to force intermediate nodes to send an ICMP Time-to-Live-Exceeded message, thus revealing their identity. Specifically, it begins by sending a datagram with Time-To-Live field set to 1. When it receives the ICMP Time Exceeded message, it notes the source IP address and the round trip time. It then repeats the process by sending a datagram with the Time-To-Live field set to 2 and so on until the machine sending the ICMP Time-To-Live-Exceeded message is the destination machine itself.

It is important to realize that each datagram sent by traceroute could actually take a different path through the Internet because in a packet-switched network each packet is routed individually. Each datagram samples an intermediate node along a single path and so traceroute could actually imply a connection between machines that does not exist. It is not uncommon to see variations along Internet paths. It is interesting to perform several traceroutes to the same destination on different days or at different times of day to look for such variations. Researchers have performed similar experiments using traceroute to understand variations in the end-to-end routes through the Internet.

Internet paths are determined through a complex set of dynamic routing rules and peering relationships among large Internet Service Providers. One result of this complexity is that the path from host A to host B in the Internet is often different than the path from host B to A. However, it is difficult to appreciate this aspect of Internet routing from a single vantage point. Using machines on a local network, you can only probe routes that originate from this network and most people do not have access to machines on multiple networks around the Internet.

To address the limited visibility on Internet routes, many networks maintain a traceroute server. A traceroute server will display the results of a traceroute from their local network to a specified destination. An excellent collection of pointers to traceroute servers located around the globe is available at http://www.traceroute.org.

CONFIGURATION

The traces in this exercise all use ping or traceroute to explore characteristics of the path between machines. Some traces were taken on a private home network. Others were taken on a university network.

Figure 4.2.1: Exercise Configuration

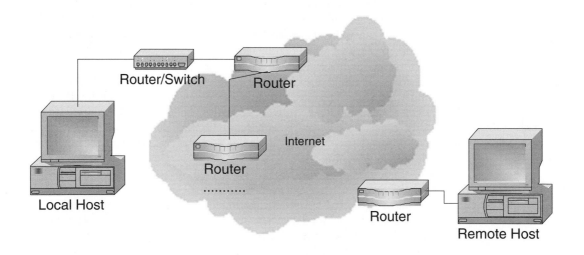

EXPERIMENT

LOCAL AND REMOTE PINGS

In the file **ping_private.cap**, we captured the network traffic that resulted from running two pings from a machine on a private network. The first ping was to the IP address 192.168.0.1, which is the address of the local router. The second ping was to the hostname www.iana.org. The output is saved to the file **ping_private_commands.txt**. You can find these files on the accompanying CD.

For each of the two destinations, four ICMP echo request packets are sent and four ICMP echo reply packets are received. Packets 3 through 10 show this exchange with 192.168.0.1, and packets 13 through 20 show the exchange with **www.iana.org**. Each request is linked with its corresponding reply by the ICMP sequence number field. The requests have ICMP type 8 and the replies ICMP type 0.

Notice how the ICMP message is contained within the data portion of the IP datagram. Notice also that the protocol field in the IP header is set to 1 indicating that the data area contains an ICMP message.

Packets 1 and 2 illustrate that in order to send the ICMP messages to 192.168.0.1 we need to know its Ethernet address (00:06:25:8d:be:1d) because it is on the local network. Packets 11 and 12 illustrate that in order to send the ICMP messages to www.iana.org, we need to know its IP address, 192.0.34.162. This IP address is not present in the local network (as determined by the source machines IP address and the local subnet mask). Therefore, the datagram will be sent first to the physical address of the local router, and it will then pass it on to the next intermediate router. That is why all of the ICMP echo request packets are sent to the same Ethernet address.

Figure 4.2.2: Ping Traffic

```
ping_private.cap - Ethereal

File  Edit  View  Capture  Analyze  Help

No. . Time      Source          Destination    Protocol  Info
   1 0.000000   192.168.0.100   Broadcast      ARP       who has 192.168.0.1?
   2 0.000930   192.168.0.1     192.168.0.100  ARP       192.168.0.1 is at 00
   3 0.000939   192.168.0.100   192.168.0.1    ICMP      Echo (ping) request
   4 0.001395   192.168.0.1     192.168.0.100  ICMP      Echo (ping) reply
   5 1.000191   192.168.0.100   192.168.0.1    ICMP      Echo (ping) request
   6 1.000575   192.168.0.1     192.168.0.100  ICMP      Echo (ping) reply
   7 2.000141   192.168.0.100   192.168.0.1    ICMP      Echo (ping) request
   8 2.000532   192.168.0.1     192.168.0.100  ICMP      Echo (ping) reply
   9 3.000101   192.168.0.100   192.168.0.1    ICMP      Echo (ping) request
  10 3.000477   192.168.0.1     192.168.0.100  ICMP      Echo (ping) reply

⊞ Frame 3 (74 bytes on wire, 74 bytes captured)
⊞ Ethernet II, Src: 00:07:e9:53:87:d9, Dst: 00:06:25:8d:be:1d
⊞ Internet Protocol, Src Addr: 192.168.0.100 (192.168.0.100), Dst Addr:
⊟ Internet Control Message Protocol
    Type: 8 (Echo (ping) request)
    Code: 0
    Checksum: 0x095c (correct)
    Identifier: 0x0200
    Sequence number: 0x4200
    Data (32 bytes)

0000  00 06 25 8d be 1d 00 07  e9 53 87 d9 08 00 45 00   ..%..... .S..
0010  00 3c e3 eb 00 00 80 01  d5 1f c0 a8 00 64 c0 a8   .<...... .....
0020  00 01 08 00 09 5c 02 00  42 00 61 62 63 64 65 66   .....\.. B.ab
0030  67 68 69 6a 6b 6c 6d 6e  6f 70 71 72 73 74 75 76   ghijklmn opqr
0040  77 61 62 63 64 65 66 67  68 69                     wabcdefg hi

Filter:                                        Reset  Apply  File: ping_private.cap
```

LOCAL TRACEROUTE

In the next experiment, we performed a traceroute between two machines that are on the same university network but separated by an intermediate router. There were a total of 2 hops along this route.

We traced this activity at both the source machine and the destination machine. These traces are saved to the files **traceroute1_src.cap** and **traceroute1_dst.cap**. The following is the output of the traceroute command run on the machine bgpdata.sclab.clarkson.edu (128.153.145.86):

```
$ ./traceroute softeng.camp.clarkson.edu
 traceroute to softeng.camp.clarkson.edu (128.153.11.150), 30 hops max,
38 byte packets
  1  gw (128.153.144.1)  0.629 ms  0.657 ms  0.590 ms
  2  128.153.11.150 (128.153.11.150)  0.522 ms  0.525 ms  0.520 ms
```

First, let's examine the traffic from the perspective of the source machine in the file **traceroute1_src.cap**. Packets 1 and 2 contain DNS packets that translate softeng.camp.clarkson.edu into its IP address 128.153.11.150.

Traceroute sends its first probe packet in packet 3. It is a UDP packet and the Time-To-Live field in the IP header is set to one. The intermediate router, 128.153.144.1, responds with an ICMP Time-To-Live-Exceeded message. Traceroute then issues a DNS PTR query to translate this IP address into the human readable hostname, gw.sclab.clarkson.edu. In packets 7 and 9, traceroute repeats the probe with the Time-To-Live field set to one. Each time the same machine replies with the ICMP Time-To-Live-Exceeded message. These additional probes allow traceroute to warn about variations encountered in the path and also to report an average round trip time measurement.

Figure 4.2.3: Traceroute Traffic

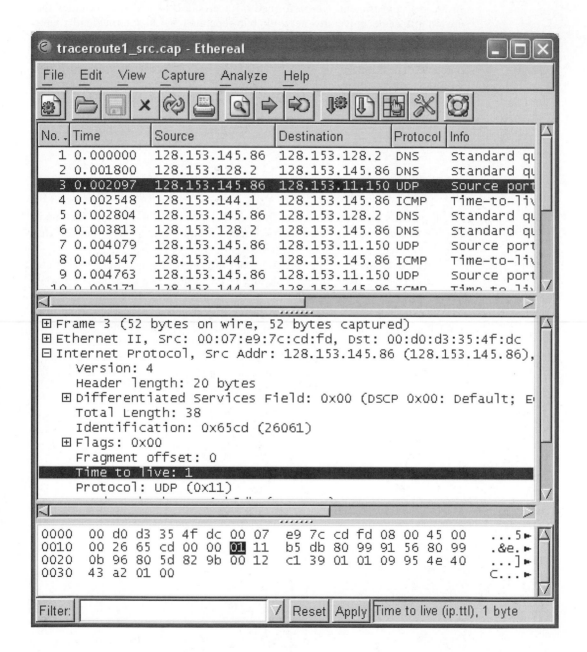

Packet 11 contains the first probe with time-to-live set to 2. The machine 128.153.11.150 replies. This is the destination machine. Traceroute sends another two probes with time to live 2.

Now let's examine this same network activity from the perspective of the destination machine. This is found in the file **traceroute1_dst.cap**. Most of the traffic does not reach the actual destination, including the probes with Time-to-Live 1 and the DNS requests.

The traffic that does reach the destination can be directly correlated with packets in the previous trace. For example, packet 1 is equivalent to packet 11 in **traceroute1_src.cap**. Comparing this packet carefully in each trace illustrates a great deal about the multi-hop nature of IP traffic. Notice for instance that the Time-To-Live field is 1 by the time it reaches the destination machine. This is because the count was decremented as the packet passed through gw.sclab.clarkson.edu. Notice also that although the source and destination IP addresses are the same, the source and destination Ethernet addresses are different. On the first local network, the packet is sent from the Ethernet interface on bgpdata.sclab.clarkson.edu to the Ethernet interface of gw.sclab.clarkson.edu. This machine actually has multiple Ethernet interfaces – one on the same network as bgpdata.sclab and the other on the same network as softeng.camp. Each of these interfaces has their own Ethernet address, their own IP address and even their own hostname.

We also performed a traceroute in the opposite direction, from softeng to bgpdata. Again we traced the traffic at both ends. These traces are saved to the files **traceroute2_src.cap** and **traceroute2_dst.cap**. The output of the traceroute was as follows:

```
$ traceroute bgpdata.sclab.clarkson.edu
 traceroute to bgpdata.sclab.clarkson.edu (128.153.145.86), 30 hops max,
38 byte packets
  1  gw (128.153.8.1)  0.429 ms  0.413 ms  0.394 ms
  2  bgpdata.sclab.clarkson.edu (128.153.145.86)  0.337 ms  0.347 ms
0.339 ms
```

These traces are similar to the first set, but they also add a few important pieces of information. For example, the traceroute from softeng probes the other interface of the gateway and determines its IP address, 128.153.8.1. Each interface on a router has its own IP address. Interestingly, the Ethernet address for each of these interfaces is the same. This is rarely the case as Ethernet addresses are typically assigned to the interface card itself by the manufacturer. It is often possible to reset these Ethernet addresses, and this must be the case here.

From this information, we could draw a fairly detailed network diagram of the connection between the two machines. This illustrates the power of tools like ping and traceroute in mapping out the connections between hosts on the Internet.

Figure 4.2.4: Network Diagram

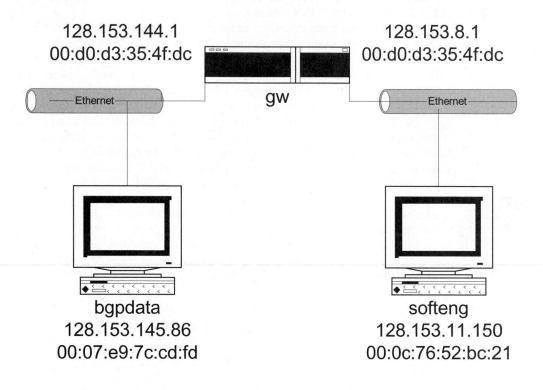

128.153.144.1
00:d0:d3:35:4f:dc

128.153.8.1
00:d0:d3:35:4f:dc

gw

Ethernet

Ethernet

bgpdata
128.153.145.86
00:07:e9:7c:cd:fd

softeng
128.153.11.150
00:0c:76:52:bc:21

REMOTE TRACEROUTE

In our final experiment, we used a traceroute server at UC Berkeley to perform a traceroute to softeng.camp.clarkson.edu. Then we performed a traceroute back to the traceroute server. We captured a trace on softeng and saved it to the file **tracerouteBerkeley.cap**. We also saved the output of both traceroutes to the file **tracerouteBerkeleyOutput.txt**. Both files are available on the accompanying CD.

It is interesting to examine the differences in the incoming and outgoing paths. Although they are similar, not a single intermediate IP address is repeated. In some cases, it is likely different interfaces on the same machine. In other cases, it is likely a different path through a large transit network. There is even one more hop on the path from softeng to Berkeley than on the reverse path.

QUESTIONS

Answer the following questions. Refer to the files used in this exercise as necessary.

1. Compare times reported by ping in **ping_private_commands.txt** to the difference in packet timestamps as reported by Ethereal in **ping_private.cap**. Consider the first ICMP echo request and reply pair for each destination.

2. Examine the ICMP echo requests and replies in **ping_private.cap**. What links the request with the corresponding reply? Examine the UDP packets sent by traceroute and the corresponding ICMP Time-To-Live-Exceeded messages. What links the UDP packet with its corresponding ICMP reply? (Hint: Examine the ICMP details in the protocol pane.)

3. Could traceroute send ICMP echo request packets (like ping does) instead of UDP packets? Why or why not?

4. In the file **tracerouteBerkeley.cap**, identify the packets that are the result of the traceroute from **http://www.net.berkeley.edu** to softeng.camp.clarkson.edu? How do you know?

5. In the file **tracerouteBerkeley.cap**, the majority of the traffic is the result of the traceroute from softeng.camp.clarkson.edu to **www.net.berkeley.edu**. Identify the first ICMP Time-To-Live-Exceeded packets from each of the hops along that path. For each of these packets, what is the value of the Time-To-Live field? How did these machines initialize the Time-To-Live field when they sent the ICMP replies? Is there any variation?

6. Examine the traceroute output in the file **tracerouteBerkeley Output.txt**. Consider the traceroute from www.net.berkeley.edu to softeng.camp.clarkson.edu. The three numbers at the end of each line represent the three measured round trip times. Were most of these times consistent? Which hop appears to have the most consistent measurements? Which hop appears to have the most variation? (Optional: Try importing the traceroute data into a spreadsheet and computing the average and standard deviation of the measurements for each hop.)

7. Examine the traceroute output in the file **tracerouteBerkeley Output.txt.** Consider the traceroute from

softeng.camp.clarkson.edu to www.net.berkeley.edu. Line 10 begins with a star and only contains 2 measurements. This indicates that no reply was received on one of the probes. Write a filter to isolate the ICMP Time-To-Live-Exceeded replies from this machine. What filter did you use and which packets were shown? Which probe packet went unanswered? How do you know?

DISCUSSION AND INVESTIGATION

1. Choose a traceroute server from **www.traceroute.org**. Do a traceroute to your local machine and then do a reverse traceroute to that machine. Record the traceroute output from both operations. Comment on the similarity of the two paths. (Reminder: Try `tracert` at a Window's command prompt.)

2. Read Vern Paxon's 1997 paper on "End-to-end routing behavior in the Internet." If you were going to repeat his results today, how would you go about choosing servers to contact? How would you expect the results to change?

3. Investigate CAIDA's skitter project (**http://www.caida.org/tools/measurement/skitter/index.xml**) and its approach to visualizing Internet connectivity. Summarize their goals, their methods for collecting data, and some of their results.

4. Some sites have chosen not to return ICMP requests in response to worms or viruses that exploit them. Investigate the role of ICMP in documented attacks. What would be the consequences to disabling ICMP completely?

5. An alternate approach to traceroute, the Record Route IP option, uses the option field in the IP header. In this approach, each node that handles an IP datagram places its address in the option field. What is an advantage of the Record Route approach? What is a drawback of this approach?

RESOURCES

- The Story of the PING program, Mike Muuss, **http://ftp.arl.mil/~mike/ping.html**

- Traceroute.org, **http://www.traceroute.org**

- RFC 792, Internet Control Message Protocol, **ftp://ftp.rfc-editor.org/in-notes/rfc792.txt**

- IANA's Protocol Numbers,
  http://www.iana.org/assignments/protocol-numbers

- IANA's ICMP Type Numbers,
  http://www.iana.org/assignments/icmp-parameters

- V. Paxson, End-to-end routing behavior in the Internet, IEEE/ACM Transactions on Networking, Volume 5, Issue 5, pages 601-615, October 1997

- CAIDA skitter project,
  http://www.caida.org/tools/measurement/skitter/index.xml

Network Layer Protocols:
Exercise **4.3**

Dynamic Routing with RIP

INTRODUCTION

In Exercise 4.2, we examined several end-to-end paths through the Internet using traceroute. In this exercise, we will examine how these paths are established and maintained.

On a path from source to destination, datagrams often pass through many intermediate router machines. Each router is responsible for directing datagrams one step closer to their final destination. Routers can be compared to a police officer directing traffic at an intersection. Cars enter the intersection from one direction and the police officer directs them to leave the intersection in the direction that takes them closer to their destination. Routers have multiple network interfaces that act like the street leaving an intersection. Datagrams arrive on one of the router's network interfaces and are retransmitted from another network interface, ideally the one closest to its destination.

You may wonder how a router knows which way a datagram should go. In some cases, a human operator manually configures the router with a set of static rules. For example, the router shown in Figure 4.3.1 would need only two simple rules. If a datagram is destined for an IP address in the 145.45.32.0/24 network, then it should be sent out the interface labeled B; otherwise it should be sent out the interface labeled A. (Note: 145.45.32.0/24 means that the last 8 bits are free to be allocated to hosts within the network and that the remaining 24 bits indicate the network ID. The 8 free bits allow for 256 IP addresses in the range 145.45.32.0 to 145.45.32.255. This is the same as specifying the subnet mask 255.255.255.0.)

Figure 4.3.1: Router for a Stub Network

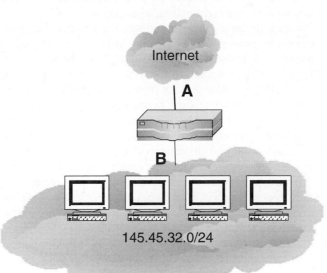

However, in many cases, static rules are insufficient. For example, links can fail and with static routing there is no way to choose an alternate path even if one exists. In general, any changes in the network topology require a manual change to the static configuration. Finally, some network topologies are so complicated that entering the rules manually would be difficult even without considering changes.

As an alternative to static routing, routers can also communicate with each other to learn about good routes to other networks. As conditions in the network change, news of changing routes will spread from router to router. This is called dynamic routing and the types of messages sent from router to router are determined by the specific dynamic routing protocol chosen

There are two primary types of dynamic routing algorithms—link state and distance vector.

In a link state algorithm, each router sends messages to all other routers notifying them of the state of their local links. Once a router has received messages from all other routers, it knows about every connection in the network. In other words, it has complete knowledge of the entire network, and it uses this information to identify the best route from itself to every possible destination. In some sense, this is more information than is needed. A router does not absolutely need to know the complete path that a datagram will take towards its final destination. It simply needs to know which direction to send the packet.

Returning to our earlier example, a police officer does not need to know every turn you will need to take on your way home. They simply need to know that you want to turn right in their intersection.

In a distance vector algorithm, each router does not attempt to assemble a complete picture of the network. In fact, in a distance vector algorithm, each router only knows about the rest of the network through "gossip" it receives from its immediate neighbors. Routers begin by gossiping with their neighbors about all their other directly connected neighbors, but after one "gossip" session they will learn about their neighbor's neighbors and in two sessions they will learn about their neighbor's neighbor's neighbor and so on. In this way, news of good routes through the network spread from router to router.

Link state and distance vector protocols both allow a group of routers to dynamically determine the best routes through a network. However, they require different types of communication. In link state, each router sends small messages containing information about their own links to everyone (many small messages). In distance vector, neighboring routers exchange information about the best route they have heard of to each destination (fewer large messages).

In both cases, it might seem as if this communication phase would be relatively short. In link state, once each router had heard from all other routers, there would be nothing more to say and in distance vector, once the "gossip" had spread to all routers then there would be nothing new to say. However, the larger the network, the more likely that something is changing somewhere and this change must be propagated to the rest of the routers. For example, if a link is disconnected and then later reconnected, this will cause a ripple of dynamic routing protocol activity to flow through the network. This effect is even more pronounced if the routing protocol considers current traffic volume when determining the best route. For example, if the most direct route is heavily congested, it may be preferable to take a different path. The amount of traffic on each link is always changing and would result in constant updates to the dynamic routing protocol information. In addition, dynamic routing protocols typically require routers to send periodic updates to one another even if nothing has changed.

In this exercise, we will experiment with a simple distance vector protocol called the Routing Information Protocol or RIP. We will also see a small example of a link-state protocol called Open Shortest Path First or OSPF.

CONFIGURATION

In this exercise, we used a network consisting of 5 routers communicating routes to one another via a dynamic routing protocol. One of the links is labeled with a question mark in the network diagram. Notice that without this link, routers 1 through 5 are arranged in a straight line.

We number the routers from left to right as Router1 though Router5. Notice that each router has multiple network interfaces. This is essential for routers or they would be unable to direct traffic one step closer to their destination. For each router, we refer to the leftmost interface as interface A and the rightmost interfaces as interface B.

Several laptops are also placed in the network as monitors so that we can trace the traffic. The laptops are given the letters A through D from left to right. In this configuration, Laptop A would be monitoring on the 201.100.1.0/24 network to the far right, and Laptop D would be monitoring on the 201.100.6.0/24 network to the far left. (Note: There are actually two laptops monitoring on the 201.100.6.0 network and if you look carefully you will see evidence of this in the traces.)

Four of the networks are Ethernet networks (201.100.1.0/24, 201.100.2.0/24, 201.100.5.0/24, and 201.100.6.0/24). There is a laptop monitor in each of these networks. The last two networks (201.100.3.0/24 and 201.100.4.0/24) are actually direct connections between Routers 2 and 3 and Routers 3 and 4. There are no laptops monitoring these networks.

The link labeled with a question mark creates a cycle or a loop in the network graph. Without this link, there is only one possible route from any source to any destination. Including this link introduces alternate routes and the routers will use the dynamic routing protocols to reach agreement on the best alternatives in each case.

Figure 4.3.2: Exercise Configuration

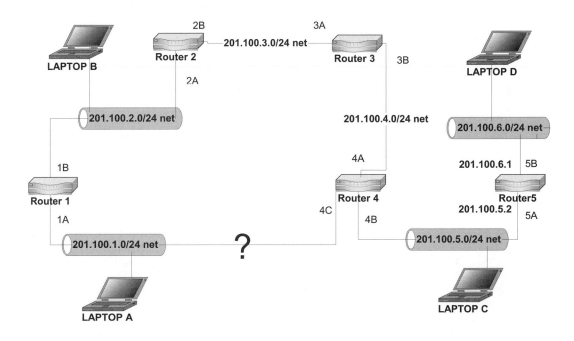

EXPERIMENT

In this experiment, we begin with a network in which there is no connectivity between machines. We then systematically enable dynamic routing on each of the routers and watch the increase in connectivity. Eventually, routes will be established between all machines.

NO RIP ENABLED

Initially, all of the router interfaces were disabled and the laptops had no IP addresses. We began by assigning each network interface an IP address and a subnet mask. Interfaces that share a network segment were configured with corresponding IP addresses. For example, LaptopA and Router1's A interface were both configured with addresses on the 201.100.1.0/24 network. We also set Router1 to be the LaptopA's default gateway. This means that Laptop1 will send any datagram destined for an IP address outside the 201.100.1.0/24 network to Router1. Similarly, we assigned a default gateway for the other three laptops.

We did not enable the connection from Router4 to the 201.100.1.0/24 network. This is the connection labeled with a question mark in Figure 4.3.2.

When this step was complete, each machine could communicate with its directly connected neighbors. However, communication between network segments was impossible. For example, LaptopA could communicate with Router1's A interface, but not with Routers 2-5 or the other laptop.

At this point, we started Ethereal on all the laptops and captured traces of some successful pings between directly connected neighbors. We saved the trace from LaptopA to a file **1_LAPA_NoRIP.cap**. Similarly, we save the traces from each of the other laptops. In addition to the ping activity, this illustrates some routine activity from the routers. For example, the routers routinely send "loopback" frames on their own interfaces. They also periodically send Cisco Discovery Protocol (CDP) messages that allow neighboring routers to discover one another. No RIP packets are present in these traces because RIP is not yet enabled.

In **1_LAPA_NoRIP.cap**, there are five sets of ping request and reply messages from LaptopA to Router1. In this first stage, LaptopA is only able to ping Router1. It cannot reach Routers 2-5 or any of the other laptops.

RIP ENABLED ON THE ENDPOINTS

In the second stage, we enable RIP on Routers 1 and 5. We trace the resulting network activity on all laptops. We save LaptopA's trace in **2_LAPA_RIP_R1_R5.cap**. Similarly, we save the traces from each of the other laptops.

With RIP enabled on Router 1 and 5, we begin to see RIP messages in **2_LAPA_RIP_R1_R5.cap** and **2_LAPD_RIP_R1_R5.cap**. If we examine one of the RIP announcements in **2_LAPA_RIP_R1_R5.cap** (e.g. packet 2), we see that it advertises a route to the 201.100.2.0 network with metric 1. The 201.100.2.0 network is the network connecting Router1 to Router2. Metric 1 means that it can reach this network in 1 hop.

LaptopB can also see RIP announcements from Router1 on the 201.100.2.0 network. For example, packet 3 in **2_LAPB_RIP_R1_R5.cap** shows Router1 announcing a route to the 201.100.1.0 network. Thus, on each network, Router1 announces a route to the other network. In other words, Router1 talks to each of its neighbors about the other neighbor.

Notice that RIP messages are sent approximately every 30 seconds. Even if there are no changes, neighbors update one another every 30 seconds. If there are changes, however, they will send updates earlier.

In the second stage, we see no increase in connectivity. LaptopA is still only able to ping Router1. Even though RIP is enabled on two routers, their messages do not reach each other and so they are unable to learn of new routes. They are "gossiping" to their neighbors, but the neighbors aren't actually listening or speaking back to them.

RIP ENABLED ON ALL MACHINES BUT ONE

In the third stage, we enable RIP on Routers 2 and 4. We save LaptopA's trace in **3_LAPA_RIP_R1_R2_R4_R5.cap**. Similarly, we save the traces from each of the other laptops.

In **3_LAPA_RIP_R1_R2_R4_R5.cap**, we see that Router 1 is now advertising its directly connected network (201.100.2.0) but also a network it learned about from Router 2 (201.100.3.0). Notice it advertises a metric of 2 for this new network. Router2 advertised it with a metric of 1 and when Router1 repeats this route it adds the additional hop that is required when passing through Router1 itself.

In this third stage, we do see an increase in connectivity. However, the network is still divided into two pieces. Machines to the right of Router3 can communicate with each other and machines to left of Router3 can communicate with each other, but no traffic crosses Router3.

Figure 4.3.3: RIP Traffic

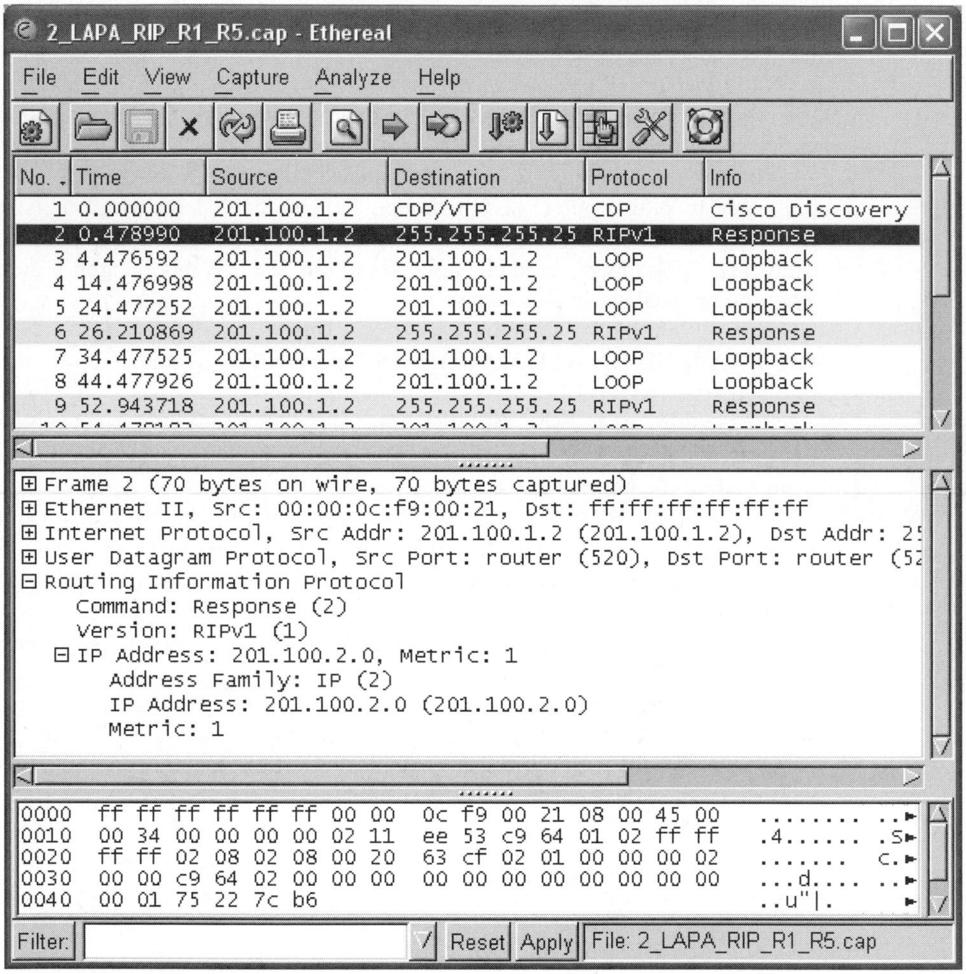

```
┌─────────────────────────────────────────────────────────────────────────┐
│ @ 2_LAPA_RIP_R1_R5.cap - Ethereal                          [_][□][X]      │
├─────────────────────────────────────────────────────────────────────────┤
│  File   Edit   View   Capture   Analyze   Help                            │
├─────────────────────────────────────────────────────────────────────────┤
│  No. ▪│ Time       │ Source      │ Destination    │ Protocol │ Info        │
│      1 0.000000     201.100.1.2    CDP/VTP          CDP        Cisco Discovery│
│      2 0.478990     201.100.1.2    255.255.255.25   RIPv1      Response      │
│      3 4.476592     201.100.1.2    201.100.1.2      LOOP       Loopback      │
│      4 14.476998    201.100.1.2    201.100.1.2      LOOP       Loopback      │
│      5 24.477252    201.100.1.2    201.100.1.2      LOOP       Loopback      │
│      6 26.210869    201.100.1.2    255.255.255.25   RIPv1      Response      │
│      7 34.477525    201.100.1.2    201.100.1.2      LOOP       Loopback      │
│      8 44.477926    201.100.1.2    201.100.1.2      LOOP       Loopback      │
│      9 52.943718    201.100.1.2    255.255.255.25   RIPv1      Response      │
├─────────────────────────────────────────────────────────────────────────┤
│ ⊞ Frame 2 (70 bytes on wire, 70 bytes captured)                           │
│ ⊞ Ethernet II, Src: 00:00:0c:f9:00:21, Dst: ff:ff:ff:ff:ff:ff             │
│ ⊞ Internet Protocol, Src Addr: 201.100.1.2 (201.100.1.2), Dst Addr: 25    │
│ ⊞ User Datagram Protocol, Src Port: router (520), Dst Port: router (52     │
│ ⊟ Routing Information Protocol                                             │
│     Command: Response (2)                                                  │
│     Version: RIPv1 (1)                                                     │
│   ⊟ IP Address: 201.100.2.0, Metric: 1                                     │
│       Address Family: IP (2)                                              │
│       IP Address: 201.100.2.0 (201.100.2.0)                               │
│       Metric: 1                                                            │
├─────────────────────────────────────────────────────────────────────────┤
│ 0000  ff ff ff ff ff ff 00 00  0c f9 00 21 08 00 45 00   ........  ..►     │
│ 0010  00 34 00 00 00 00 02 11  ee 53 c9 64 01 02 ff ff   .4......  .S►     │
│ 0020  ff ff 02 08 02 08 00 20  63 cf 02 01 00 00 00 02   ........  c.►     │
│ 0030  00 00 c9 64 02 00 00 00  00 00 00 00 00 00 00 00   ...d....  ..►     │
│ 0040  00 01 75 22 7c b6                                  ..u"|.     ►      │
├─────────────────────────────────────────────────────────────────────────┤
│ Filter:│                          │√│ Reset │ Apply │ File: 2_LAPA_RIP_R1_R5.cap│
└─────────────────────────────────────────────────────────────────────────┘
```

Figure 4.3.4: Metric of Two

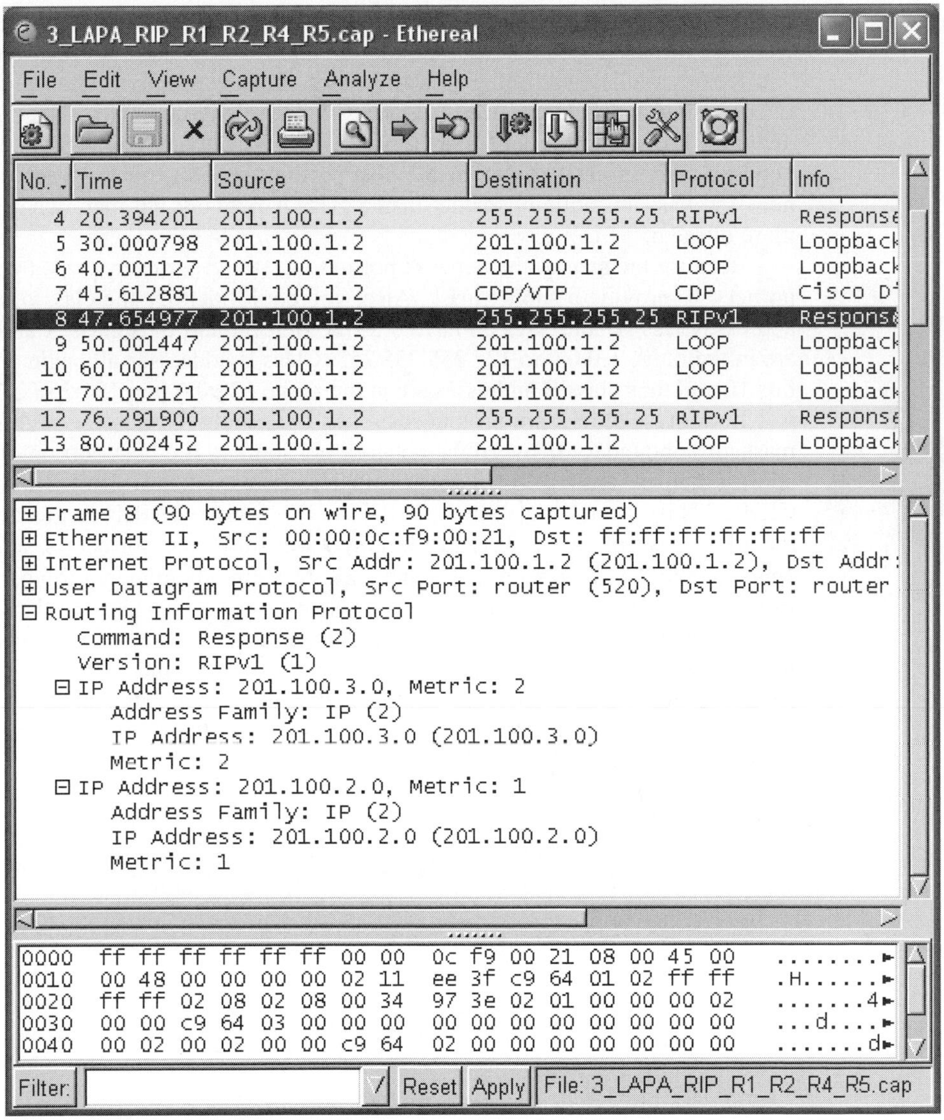

```
© 3_LAPA_RIP_R1_R2_R4_R5.cap - Ethereal                        _ □ X

File   Edit   View   Capture   Analyze   Help

No. .  Time        Source          Destination      Protocol   Info
    4  20.394201   201.100.1.2     255.255.255.25   RIPv1      Response
    5  30.000798   201.100.1.2     201.100.1.2      LOOP       Loopback
    6  40.001127   201.100.1.2     201.100.1.2      LOOP       Loopback
    7  45.612881   201.100.1.2     CDP/VTP          CDP        Cisco D
    8  47.654977   201.100.1.2     255.255.255.25   RIPv1      Response
    9  50.001447   201.100.1.2     201.100.1.2      LOOP       Loopback
   10  60.001771   201.100.1.2     201.100.1.2      LOOP       Loopback
   11  70.002121   201.100.1.2     201.100.1.2      LOOP       Loopback
   12  76.291900   201.100.1.2     255.255.255.25   RIPv1      Response
   13  80.002452   201.100.1.2     201.100.1.2      LOOP       Loopback

⊞ Frame 8 (90 bytes on wire, 90 bytes captured)
⊞ Ethernet II, Src: 00:00:0c:f9:00:21, Dst: ff:ff:ff:ff:ff:ff
⊞ Internet Protocol, Src Addr: 201.100.1.2 (201.100.1.2), Dst Addr:
⊞ User Datagram Protocol, Src Port: router (520), Dst Port: router
⊟ Routing Information Protocol
     Command: Response (2)
     Version: RIPv1 (1)
   ⊟ IP Address: 201.100.3.0, Metric: 2
       Address Family: IP (2)
       IP Address: 201.100.3.0 (201.100.3.0)
       Metric: 2
   ⊟ IP Address: 201.100.2.0, Metric: 1
       Address Family: IP (2)
       IP Address: 201.100.2.0 (201.100.2.0)
       Metric: 1

0000  ff ff ff ff ff ff 00 00   0c f9 00 21 08 00 45 00   .........►
0010  00 48 00 00 00 00 02 11   ee 3f c9 64 01 02 ff ff   .H......►
0020  ff ff 02 08 02 08 00 34   97 3e 02 01 00 00 00 02   .......4►
0030  00 00 c9 64 03 00 00 00   00 00 00 00 00 00 00 00   ...d....►
0040  00 02 00 02 00 00 c9 64   02 00 00 00 00 00 00 00   .......d►

Filter:                          / Reset Apply  File: 3_LAPA_RIP_R1_R2_R4_R5.cap
```

It may surprise you that each network in a RIP announcement is denoted simply with a single IP address (i.e. simply 201.100.1.0 rather than with a network address and subnet mask). When RIP was developed, each IP address belonged to one of 5 classes, A through E. Within each class, the sizes of the network and host portions were fixed. For example, in class A addresses, 8 bits were used to designate the network address and the remaining 24 bits were free to allocate to hosts within the network. Since there were only 8 bits of network ID, the number of distinct class A networks is relatively small. Each class A network, however, can contain 2^{24} hosts. Class B networks had 16 bits for the network address and 16 bits for the host portion. This meant that each class B network was substantially smaller than a class A network but there where many more of them.

Because the size of the network portion was fixed for each class, there was no need to provide a subnet mask. Also, you could identify the class of any IP address. Class A addresses all have 0 as the first bit and thus class A addresses are in the range 1.0.0.0 to 127.255.255.255. Class B addresses all begin with the bits 10 and thus class B addresses are in the range 128.0.0.0 to 191.255.255.255.

IP address blocks are no longer broken up strictly by classes. With subnet masks, the boundary between the network portion and the host portion of an IP address can be anywhere. This is called Classless Inter-Domain Routing or CIDR. This is one limitation of RIP. In RIP version 2, RIP announcements include a subnet mask. In **RIPv2.cap**, we show the format of a RIPv2 announcement taken on a different network. It is not advertising a route, but the format of RIPv2 announcement can be clearly seen. This packet also shows what happens when a RIP enabled router has no network reachability information to report. The packet contains only an announcement of "Address Not Specified" with metric 16. In RIP, a metric of 16 means that a destination is unreachable. Thus, 15 hops is the longest path a RIP network can advertise. This is another limitation of RIP.

Figure 4.3.5: RIPv2

```
@ 1 0.000000 210.93.105.1 224.0.0.9 RIPv2 Re...   [_][□][X]

⊞ Frame 1 (66 bytes on wire, 66 bytes captured)
⊞ Ethernet II, Src: 00:60:70:35:ad:29, Dst: 01:
⊞ Internet Protocol, Src Addr: 210.93.105.1 (21
⊞ User Datagram Protocol, Src Port: router (52C
⊟ Routing Information Protocol
    Command: Request (1)
    Version: RIPv2 (2)
    Routing Domain: 0
  ⊟ Address not specified, Metric: 16
      Address Family: Unspecified (0)
      Route Tag: 0
      Netmask: 0.0.0.0 (0.0.0.0)
      Next Hop: 0.0.0.0 (0.0.0.0)
      Metric: 16

0000  01 00 5e 00 00 09 00 60  70 35 ad 29 08►
0010  00 34 00 00 00 00 02 11  9d 51 d2 5d 69►
0020  00 09 02 08 02 08 00 20  00 00 01 02 00►
0030  00 00 00 00 00 00 00 00  00 00 00 00 00►
0040  00 10                                  ►
```

RIP ENABLED END-TO-END

In the fourth stage, we enable RIP on Routers 3. We save LaptopA's trace in **4_LAPA_RIP_ALL_LINE.cap**. Similarly, we save the traces from each of the other laptops.

In **4_LAPA_RIP_ALL_LINE.cap**, we can clearly see the increase in reachability information as routers share information once RIP is enabled on Router3. The first RIP announcements in packet 3 contains only the announcements for the 201.100.2.0 and 201.100.3.0 network as in the last stage. Packet 8 adds the 201.100.4.0 network. Packet 13 adds the 201.100.5.0 network and the 201.100.6.0 network.

Notice the appropriate hop metrics for each network. Similarly, in **4_LAPA_RIP_ALL_LINE.cap**, RIP announcements shows all the other networks. However, the hop metrics are different from those in **4_LAPA_RIP_ALL_LINE.cap**. This is because the networks closest to Laptop A are the farthest from Laptop D and vice versa.

With routing fully configured, we issued a set of pings and traceroutes between LaptopA and LaptopD to illustrate the full connectivity of the network. Traceroute output from LaptopA is shown below. Notice that each router sends a response using an IP address ending in a 2. This is because they reply using the IP address of the interface that is closest to the destination.

```
% traceroute 210.100.6.98

Tracing route to 210.100.6.98
over a maximum of 30 hops:

    1     2 ms     1 ms     3 ms   201.100.1.2
    2     4 ms     3 ms     2 ms   201.100.2.2
    3    23 ms    20 ms    35 ms   201.100.3.2
    4    40 ms    37 ms    37 ms   201.100.4.2
    5    41 ms    37 ms    36 ms   201.100.5.2
    6    45 ms    40 ms    41 ms   201.100.6.98


Trace complete.
```

If instead we do the traceroute from Laptop D to A, the same routers are involved but this time they respond from the IP address of the interface closest to D.

```
% traceroute 210.100.1.99

Tracing route to 210.100.6.98
over a maximum of 30 hops:

    1     1 ms     1 ms     1 ms   201.100.6.1
    2     3 ms     3 ms     3 ms   201.100.5.1
    3    29 ms    19 ms    19 ms   201.100.4.1
    4    38 ms    35 ms    35 ms   201.100.3.1
    5    36 ms    35 ms    34 ms   201.100.2.1
    6    34 ms    36 ms    35 ms   201.100.1.99


Trace complete.
```

ADDING A LOOP IN THE NETWORK GRAPH

In the fifth stage, we enabled the connection between Router4 and the 201.100.1.0 network. This creates an alternate path in the network. We save LaptopA's trace in **5_LAPA_RIP_ALL_CIRCLE.cap**. Similarly, we save the traces from each of the other laptops.

In **5_LAPA_RIP_ALL_CIRCLE.cap**, we can see the impact of this new path on the routing messages exchanged. Packet 32 is the first RIPmessage sent by Router4 on its newly connected network. It is a Request rather than a response. Router4 begins not by announcing routes but by requesting routes routes from other routers. In packet 33, Router1 replies by sending all of the network reachability information it has.

Packet 34 is quite interesting. Router4 reports that it can reach the 201.100.4.0 and 201.100.5.0 networks in one hop and the 201.100.3.0 and 201.100.6.0 networks in two hops. It does not report anything about the 201.100.2.0 network. This is because Router1 had already reported a better path to that network. In RIP, the routers don't gossip about bad news as much as they brag about good news.

Routers report the best-cost path they have heard of, unless that best cost path came from the same neighbor they are talking to. Router4 will send traffic destined for the 201.100.2.0 to Router1 and as a result it does not repeat this best cost path information back to Router1. This is important to avoiding routing loops in which two routers keep sending a packet back and forth between them; each thinking that the other one is one step closer. Similarly, when Router1 speaks again in packet 39, it only reports routes to 201.100.2.0 network and the 201.100.3.0 network. It has decided to use the cheaper routes advertised by Router1 to the other networks and therefore it does not readvertise these routes back to Router4.

We repeat the traceroute from LaptopA to Laptop D. The output is shown below. This traceroute takes the new shorter path. Interestingly, the first hop is still to 201.100.1.2, which is Router1. This is because Router1 is the default gateway for LaptopA. All traffic not destined for the local network is sent to Router1 first. Router1 then sends it across the local network to Router4 for final delivery.

```
% traceroute 210.100.6.98

Tracing route to 210.100.6.98
over a maximum of 30 hops:

    1      2 ms      1 ms      1 ms    201.100.1.2
    2      *         3 ms      4 ms    201.100.1.1
    3      5 ms      3 ms      2 ms    201.100.5.2
    4      2 ms      3 ms      2 ms    210.100.6.98


Trace complete.
```

ADJUSTING TO A FAILED LINK

Finally, we disconnect Router5 from the network. We save LaptopA's trace in **6_LAPA_RIP_FAILEDLINK.cap**. Similarly, we save the traces from each of the other laptops. Notice that in packet 100, router 4 is still advertising that the 201.100.6.0 network is reachable in 2 hops even though we are receiving no response to the traceroute probes sent starting with packet 51. Finally, the RIP announcement in packet 114 changes the metric to 16 for the 201.100.6.0 network meaning that the network is unreachable. Router1 responds immediately in packet 115 indicating that it does not have a route to that network either.

OPEN SHORTEST PATH FIRST

We performed a similar experiment with a link-state routing protocol called Open Shortest Path First or OSPF. To illustrate how link state protocols differ from distance vector protocols, we include a sample link state advertisement in the trace in **OSPF.cap**. This traces was taken in the same topology with Laptop A. This link-state advertisement originated with Router1 and has been relayed onto the 201.100.1.0 network. Notice that Router5 (201.100.6.1) is the advertising router and that it reports on its two attached links. It correctly identifies the 201.100.6.0/24 network as a stub network and the 201.100.5.0/24 network as a transit network.

Figure 4.3.6: OSPF

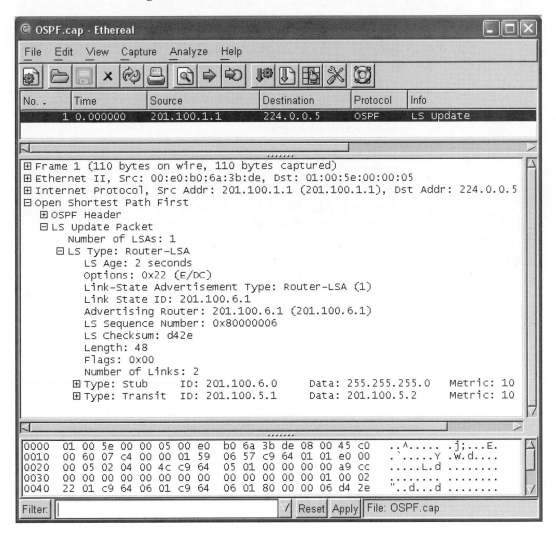

QUESTIONS

Answer the following questions. Refer to the files used in this exercise as necessary. There are a total of 24 trace files: 6 traces for each of the 4 laptop monitors. There is a subdirectory for each laptop containing all the traces taken for that laptop.

1. Before RIP was enabled on any router, we could ping Router1's A interface from Laptop1. Why is that? We could not however ping Router1's B interface. What does that say about how routers view their multiple network interfaces?

2. Using **2_LAPD_RIP_R1_R5.cap**, determine when RIP was enabled on Router5. How do you know? Can you tell when RIP was enabled from 2_LAPA_RIP_R1_R5.cap? Why or why not?

3. After we enabled RIP on Routers 1 and 5, we saw no increase in connectivity even though RIP packets were being sent. Why is that?

4. After we enabled RIP on Routers 1 and 5, we saw no increase in connectivity. Think carefully about why a ping from Laptop1 to Router2 would be unsuccessful. Consider that Router1 advertised a route to the 201.100.2.0/24 network. What would happen to the ping request? What would happen to the ping reply?

5. Modify the network diagram shown in Figure 4.3.2 by labeling each laptop and router interface with the proper IP address. Can you determine them all? (Note: There are actually two laptops monitoring on the 201.100.6.0 network. Look for evidence of the IP addresses assigned to each one.)

6. Since we have laptops monitoring at several locations in the network, we can follow a single IP packet as it travels along the path. Consider packet 144 in **4_LAPA_RIP_ALL_LINE.cap**. It is one of the last probes in a traceroute from Laptop A to D. When sent from LaptopA, its time to live is set high enough that it can travel all the way to LaptopD. The same IP packet can be found in **4_LAPB_RIP_ALL_LINE.cap**, **4_LAPC_RIP_ALL_LINE.cap** and **4_LAPD_RIP_ALL_LINE.cap** as well. Can you write a filter that will help find it in each of these traces? Hint: Consider the IP Identification field. Note the packet number, transmission time, Time-To-Live field, source, and destination IP addresses for this packet on each hop. What other packets are identified by your filter? Why?

DISCUSSION AND INVESTIGATION

1. How often are RIP announcements sent out if there are no changes? Can you find a value specified in the RFCs that describe RIP? Provide a reference including RFC number and page number.

2. In RIP, neighboring routers "gossip" with one another about the best distance they know of to all locations in the network. In this way, knowledge of available routes spreads through the entire network. RIP was designed to be used between routers on a local network. What would happen if all the routers in the Internet "gossiped" in this way? Consider what would happen each time a link somewhere in the Internet failed or was recovered. How much traffic would be required for each change?

3. RIP was one of the earliest routing protocols developed, and it has a number of well-documented limitations including slow convergence in the face of changing routes, the possibility of routing loops where datagrams circle endlessly because routers do not agree on the best routes, and the "count-to-infinity" problem. Investigate these and other limitations of RIP.

RESOURCES

- RFC 1058, Routing Information Protocol, **ftp://ftp.rfc-editor.org/in-notes/rfc1058.txt**

- RFC 1923, RIPv1 Applicability Statement for Historic Status, **ftp://ftp.rfc-editor.org/in-notes/rfc1923.txt**

- RFC 2543, RIP Version 2, **ftp://ftp.rfc-editor.org/in-notes/rfc2543.txt**

- RFC 1519, Classless Inter-Domain Routing (CIDR): an Address Assignment and Aggregation Strategy, **ftp://ftp.rfc-editor.org/in-notes/rfc1519.txt**

- RFC 1817, CIDR and Classful Routing, **ftp://ftp.rfc-editor.org/in-notes/rfc1817.txt**

- RFC 2328, OSPF Version 2.0**, ftp://ftp.rfc-editor.org/in-notes/rfc2328.txt**

- Web search: RIP routing problems

Network Layer Protocols:
Exercise **4.4**

Border Gateway Protocol

INTRODUCTION

In Exercise 4.3, we explored dynamic routing protocols. We saw that in distance vector routing protocols, news of available paths spreads through the network as neighboring routers exchange information about the best paths to each destination in the network. We also discussed that in link-state routing protocols, each router sends information about the state of their local links to every other router allowing each router to build a full picture of the entire network.

Now consider what would happen if we used either a distance vector or link-state protocol to exchange information on every route in the Internet. In the case of link-state, an announcement would be sent to every router each time a link changed state anywhere in the Internet! In the case of distance vector, neighboring routers would be periodically exchanging their best-known path to every destination! In either case, the dynamic routing protocol messages would gobble up much of the available bandwidth.

The primary strategy for avoiding these problems is "divide and conquer." The Internet as a whole is first divided up into smaller networks called Autonomous Systems (AS). Routing within each AS is hidden from the rest of the Internet and then routing is done between ASes. For example, a university AS may have many routers and many sub networks. Within the university, these routers will communicate with each other to determine the best path to each sub network. However, when communicating with routers from another AS, the routers will simply report the set of network prefixes (e.g. the 1.0.0.0/8 network) that are available within the university. IP datagrams from the rest of the Internet will be directed toward the university based on the set of reported network prefixes. Then once a datagram arrives at the university, the local routers will determine the best path to follow within the university to their final destination.

This is similar to the way in which road maps are published. You may get a roadmap of an entire country that shows how to get from one city to another, but then you need another roadmap with more details to know how to reach a particular street within a city.

Each AS is assigned a unique Autonomous System Number. This is handled by the regional registries like ARIN or RIPE. Organizations apply to a regional registry for an autonomous system number much like they apply for blocks of unique IP address space.

The routing protocols we examined in Exercise 4.3, such as RIP and OSPF, are all designed to support dynamic routing within an AS. They are called Interior Gateway Protocols or IGPs. The network administrator of an AS determines which Interior Gateway Protocol to use. However, between ASes, an Exterior Gateway Protocol or EGP is used. To allow communication, all ASes must agree on a standard dynamic routing protocol. This standard protocol is the Border Gateway Protocol or BGP.

BGP is considered a path-vector protocol. Path-vector protocols are similar to distance-vector protocols in that nearest neighbors tell each other about the best paths they know to all destinations. However, in a path-vector protocol, neighbors do not simply report that they know a path of cost X to a destination as we saw with RIP. Instead, they report the entire path to each destination. In the case of BGP, this path would take the form of a list of AS numbers indicating which ASes are encountered along the path.

Information about full paths is advantageous for several reasons. First, it can help avoid routing loops in which routers keep passing a packet back and forth because each thinks the other is closer to the destination. In the case of BGP, such a routing loop would be obvious if an autonomous system appeared multiple times in a path. Second, having a list of the AS numbers, allows organizations to make policy decisions such as "I don't want my data to traverse my competitor's network."

IGPs such as RIP or OSPF are primarily concerned about finding the fastest path from a source to a destination while BGP allows for configuration based on more intricate policy decisions. For example, BGP neighbors do not automatically share all the routes they know. Instead, administrators only advertise routes that they want other ASes to use. Some networks, called stub networks, only advertise routes to their own network because they do not want traffic destined for other networks to use their resources. Other networks called transit networks are in the business of providing Internet connectivity. These networks advertise routes from many stub networks to each other. Transit networks must be multi-homed meaning that they have connections to more than one other autonomous system. Stub networks can also be multi-homed (e.g. multiple connections in case one fails), but they can refuse to allow transit traffic between these connections by not advertising routes to these connections.

Another interesting distinction between IGPs and BGP is that IGPs identify neighboring routers by direct connections while in BGP, administrators manually determine the list of BGP peers for each router. These peers need not be directly connected. A router within an AS that is advertising routes via BGP is called a BGP speaker. To exchange route information with another AS, their BGP speakers establish a TCP connection over which they exchange routing information. These BGP peering sessions are established manually by the network administrators in each AS.

Some routers in the Internet specifically establish peering sessions with many other ASes to collect information about the overall routes available within the Internet. These routers are called route servers. They typically do not route packets or share the routes they have learned among their BGP peers. They are simply used as a window into the inter-AS routing within the Internet.

It is interesting to see the number of distinct network prefixes that are reported. More distinct network prefixes or independent Internet destinations means that it is harder for routers within the core of the Internet to do their job. For example, if the entire 1.0.0.0/8 network was available within the same Autonomous system, then the path to 2^{24} hosts can be summarized with a single path. However, if the 1.0.0.0/8 network is divided into the 1.0.0.0/16 network through the 1.255.0.0/16 network and each is located in a different AS, then 256 paths must be maintained. If it was divided into /24 networks, then 38400 paths must be maintained. For each distinct path, a core Internet router must store the path and it must then search through the list of possible paths for each IP datagram that must be routed!

Similarly, it is interesting to know the average size of the network prefixes that are announced, the average number of ASes in a path, the percentage of IPv4 address space being announced, and how often routes change and other such statistics. These and other statistics can be computed by looking at the data reported by route servers. Researchers study data like this to determine the health and stability of routes in the Internet and to assemble high level maps of Internet connectivity.

I used a bgp.potaroo.net to examine the BGP statistics reported by a route server at the University of Oregon's Route Views Project (AS 6447). It reported close to 170,000 active BGP entries. Data from AS 1221 (Telstra) indicated that the most common network prefix is a /24 (45% of all the prefixes) with the next most common being a /32 (7%).

In this exercise, we are going to examine traces of a simple network of BGP peers. Questions at the end of the chapter will encourage you to explore some of the publicly available data on inter-AS routing in the Internet as a whole.

CONFIGURATION

In this exercise, we used a network consisting of three routers – each acts as the border router for an Autonomous System. Each AS was assigned an AS number

(100,200 and 300) and allocated a /8 network (1.0.0.0/8, 2.0.0.0/8 and 3.0.0.0/8). We simulated the Autonomous System itself with a loopback interface on the router. The loopback interface was given an IP address in the /8 network (1.0.0.1, 2.0.0.1 and 3.0.0.1). We connected the three routers in a circle with Ethernet hubs and attached laptops to each hub to monitor the resulting traffic. The hubs were each assigned a /24 network (201.100.1.0/24, 201.100.2.0/24 and 201.100.3.0/24). We established BGP peeing sessions between each pair of routers.

Figure 4.4.1: Exercise Configuration

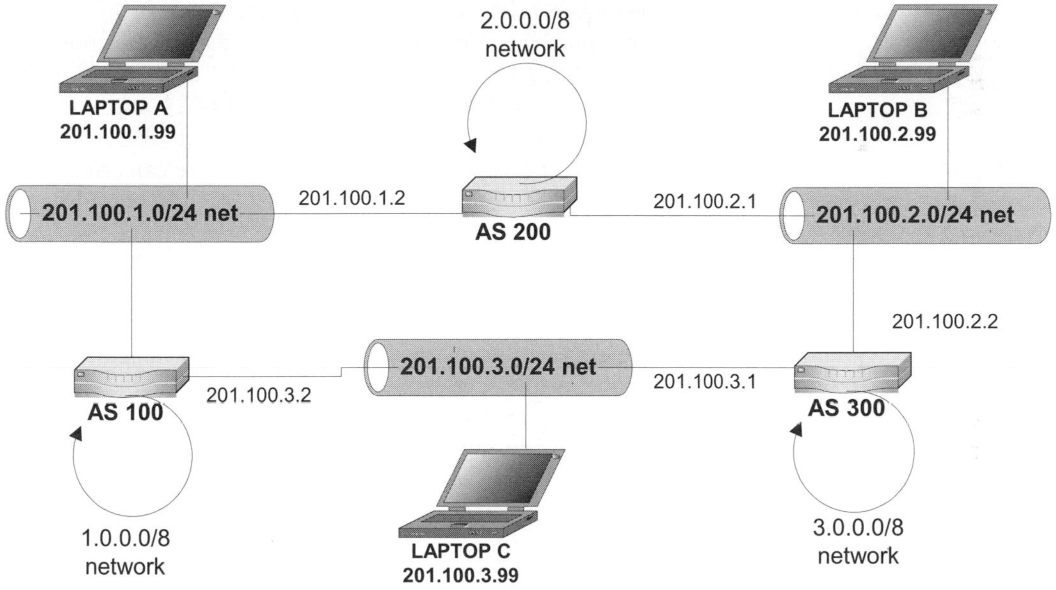

EXPERIMENT

ESTABLISHING BGP PEERING SESSIONS

When we began this experiment, the network was fully assembled as illustrated in Figure 4.4.1, but BGP was not enabled on any of the routers. We began tracing on each of the three laptops and then enabled BGP on the three routers. We saved LaptopA's trace in `1_LAPA_BGP_INITIALCIRCLE.cap`. Similarly, we save the traces from the other 2 laptops in `1_LAPB_BGP_INITIALCIRCLE.cap` and `1_LAPC_BGP_INITIAL CIRCLE.cap`.

In the trace captured by LaptopA, we can see the BGP peering session between the BGP speaker for AS 100 and the BGP speaker for AS 200. The TCP session for this peering session begins with packet 15. If you use "Follow TCP Stream" under the Analyze menu, you will see that BGP is not a text based as many other protocols are. However, Ethereal provides excellent support for decoding the BGP messages that are sent over the connection.

Notice the port numbers for each end of the connection in `1_LAPA_BGP_INITIALCIRCLE` are 11004 on 201.100.1.1 and the traditional BGP port 179 on 201.100.1.2. In `1_LAPB_BGP_INITIALCIRCLE`, we can see a BGP peering session established between 201.100.2.2 port 16839 and port 179 on 201.100.2.1. In `1_LAPC_BGP_INITIALCIRCLE`, we can see a BGP peering session established between 201.100.3.2 port 11003 and port 179 on 201.100.3.1.

The first messages sent over a BGP peering session are OPEN messages. These are sent by each side and are required to establish the session. Packet 18 shows some details of the OPEN message sent by the BGP speaker for AS 100. It contains an announcement of its AS number and of its BGP identifier. The BGP identifier is a unique number that will identify this router. In this case, the router sends the lowest IP address on any of its interfaces, 1.0.0.1. Similarly, packet 19 contains the OPEN message from the BGP speaker for AS 200. The OPEN does not advertise reachable networks. It simply introduces the BGP peers to one another and establishes the session.

Figure 4.4.2: BGP OPEN Messages

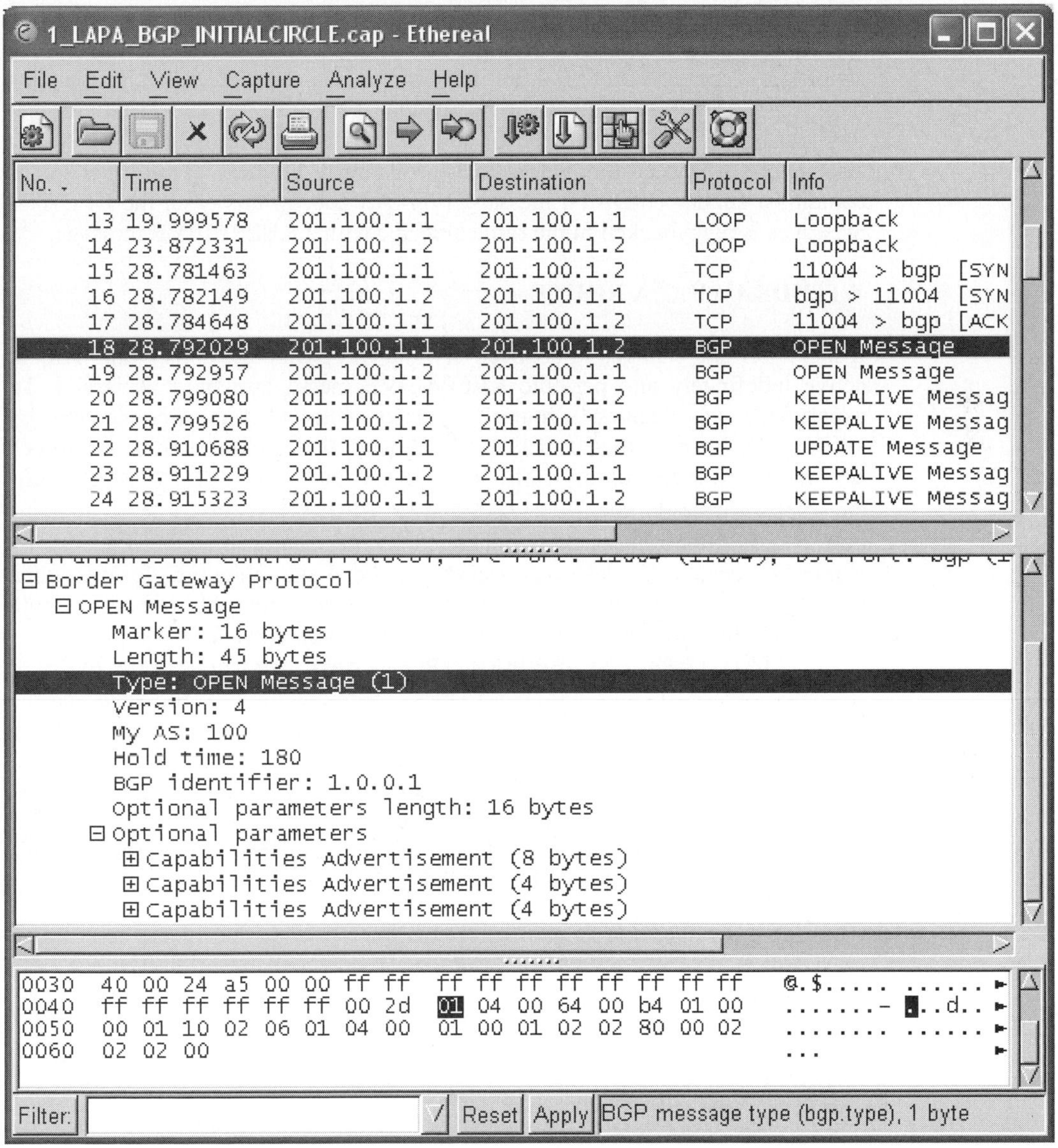

The successful OPEN messages transition the BGP peering session into an established state. In this state, peers will notify one another of changes in paths via UPDATE messages and will periodically exchange KEEPALIVE messages even if there are no changes to report. Packets 20 and 21 show the initial KEEPALIVE messages sent in each direction.

Packet 22 contains the first UPDATE message from AS 100 to AS 200. It advertises a route to the 1.0.0.0/8 network. In this case, the AS path contains only AS 100 because this is the network that is local to AS 100. It reports that the next hop is 201.100.1.1, the IP address of the router closest to AS 200. It also reports it learned this via an Interior Gateway Protocol or IGP. Packet 23 contains a similar UPDATE message from AS 200. In this case, the UPDATE messages is piggybacked in the same message with a KEEPALIVE message.

WITHDRAWING A ROUTE

If there were no changes in connectivity, our three BGP sessions would remain active indefinitely and periodic KEEPALIVE messages would be issued. To experiment with changes in routes, we disconnected the cables connecting AS 100 and AS 300 over the 201.100.3.0/24 network that is monitored by Laptop C.

We saved the resulting traffic in **2_LAPA_BGP_BROKEN CIRCLE.cap** etc. Not surprisingly, the file **2_LAPC_BGP_BROKEN CIRCLE.cap** contains only a few Loopback packets generated by the routers just before the disconnection occurs. The last such packet is packet 4 and in the time for this frame (frame.time) is 13:26. After this packet, we see no other activity because both routers are disconnected from the hub and only laptop C remains connected.

In **2_LAPA_BGP_BROKENCIRCLE.cap**, we can see how the BGP speakers for AS 100 and 200 react to these changes. First, we observe that the BGP session is undisturbed. It continues on the same ports as before. Second, we can see UPDATEs sent over this connection in reaction to the change in connectivity. Specifically, packet 7 contains an UPDATE message from AS 100 that withdraws a route to the 3.0.0.0/8 network. This packet also has time 13:26. (Be aware that the clocks on the laptop are not synchronized precisely.) This update message is generated when the link fails.

Figure 4.4.3: BGP UPDATE Messages

```
1_LAPA_BGP_INITIALCIRCLE.cap - Ethereal                         _ □ X
File  Edit  View  Capture  Analyze  Help

No. .  Time        Source         Destination     Protocol  Info
                   201.100.1.2    201.100.1.1     BGP       OPEN Message
  20 28.799080     201.100.1.1    201.100.1.2     BGP       KEEPALIVE Message
  21 28.799526     201.100.1.2    201.100.1.1     BGP       KEEPALIVE Message
  22 28.910688     201.100.1.1    201.100.1.2     BGP       UPDATE Message
  23 28.911229     201.100.1.2    201.100.1.1     BGP       KEEPALIVE Message, UPDATE Message
  24 28.915323     201.100.1.1    201.100.1.2     BGP       KEEPALIVE Message
  25 29.212275     201.100.1.2    201.100.1.1     TCP       bgp > 11004 [ACK] Seq=118 Ack=134
  26 29.999290     201.100.1.1    201.100.1.1     LOOP      Loopback
  27 33.872193     201.100.1.2    201.100.1.2     LOOP      Loopback
  28 39.008217     201.100.1.1    CDP/VTP         CDP       Cisco Discovery Protocol
  29 39.009859     201.100.1.1    CDP/VTP         CDP       Cisco Discovery Protocol
  30 39.623877     201.100.1.1    201.100.1.2     BGP       KEEPALIVE Message
  31 39.624306     201.100.1.2    201.100.1.1     TCP       11011 > bgp [RST] Seq=0 Ack=23020!

 Transmission Control Protocol, Src Port: 11004 (11004), Dst Port: bgp (179), Seq: 85, Ack
□ Border Gateway Protocol
  □ UPDATE Message
      Marker: 16 bytes
      Length: 50 bytes
      Type: UPDATE Message (2)
      Unfeasible routes length: 0 bytes
      Total path attribute length: 25 bytes
    □ Path attributes
      ⊞ ORIGIN: IGP (4 bytes)
      ⊞ AS_PATH: 100 (7 bytes)
      ⊞ NEXT_HOP: 201.100.1.1 (7 bytes)
      ⊞ MULTI_EXIT_DISC: 0 (7 bytes)
    □ Network layer reachability information: 2 bytes
      ⊞ 1.0.0.0/8

0000  00 e0 1e bb f5 70 00 e0  b0 6a 3b de 08 00 45 c0   .....p.. .j;...E.
0010  00 5a 00 04 00 00 01 06  24 0f c9 64 01 01 c9 64   .Z...... $..d...d
0020  01 02 2a fc 00 b3 87 c2  eb 01 44 64 af f3 50 18   ..*..... ..Dd..P.
0030  3f d0 70 c4 00 00 ff ff  ff ff ff ff ff ff ff ff   ?.p..... ........
0040  ff ff ff ff ff ff 00 32  02 00 00 00 19 40 01 01   .......2 .....@..

Filter:                                  / Reset Apply File: 1_LAPA_BGP_INITIALCIRCLE.cap
```

Figure 4.4.4: BGP Withdrawal Messages

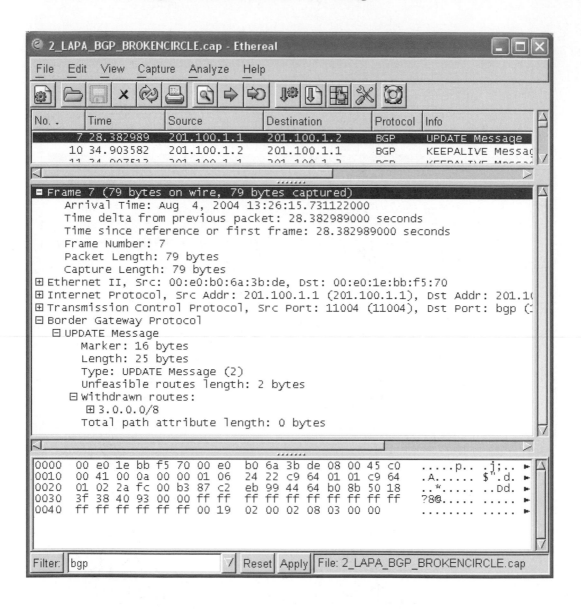

REPAIRING A CONNECTION

We reconnected the cables connecting AS 100 and AS 300 over the 201.100.3.0/24 network monitored by Laptop C. We saved the corresponding traces in **`3_LAPA_BGP_REPAIR.cap`**, **`3_LAPB_BGP_REPAIR.cap`** and **`3_LAPC_BGP_REPAIR.cap`**.

In **`3_LAPC_BGP_REPAIR.cap`**, we see that the old BGP peering session is officially closed with a NOTIFCATION message in packet 10 and is then reset with packet 11. In packet 23, a new BGP peering session is established between port 16840 on 201.100.3.1 and port 17 on 201.100.3.2. OPEN messages are sent by each side to complete the connection.

Over this new connection, we see several UPDATE messages. Let's focus on the routes advertised by AS 300. First, packet 32 contains the announcement of a route to 2.0.0.8/8 network. This path is a multi-hop path consisting of two autonomous systems AS 300 and AS 200. Notice that each AS is listed explicitly in the path. Similarly, packet 34 advertises two paths – one of length 1 to the 3.0.0.0/8 network and one of length 3 to the 1.0.0.0/8 network. Again notice that all ASes in the path are listed.

We can also see new routes advertised as a result of the repaired connection in the traces from Laptop A and B. For example, packet 53 in **`3_LAPA_BGP_REPAIR.cap`** shows a path containing AS 100 and 300 to the 3.0.0.0/8 network.

Figure 4.4.5: Multi-hop Path Announcement

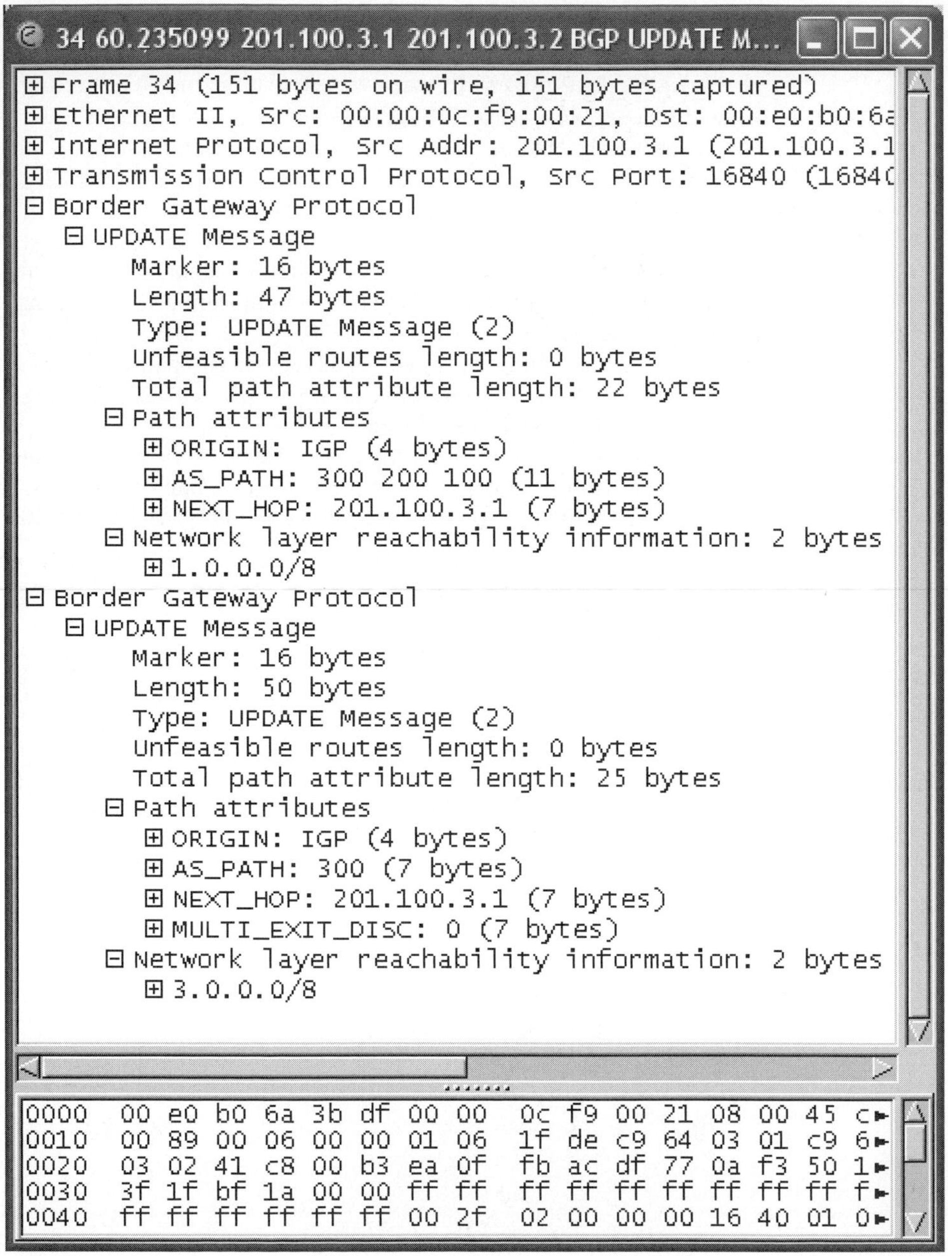

```
@ 34 60.235099 201.100.3.1 201.100.3.2 BGP UPDATE M...   _ □ X
⊞ Frame 34 (151 bytes on wire, 151 bytes captured)
⊞ Ethernet II, Src: 00:00:0c:f9:00:21, Dst: 00:e0:b0:6a
⊞ Internet Protocol, Src Addr: 201.100.3.1 (201.100.3.1
⊞ Transmission Control Protocol, Src Port: 16840 (16840
⊟ Border Gateway Protocol
   ⊟ UPDATE Message
       Marker: 16 bytes
       Length: 47 bytes
       Type: UPDATE Message (2)
       Unfeasible routes length: 0 bytes
       Total path attribute length: 22 bytes
     ⊟ Path attributes
       ⊞ ORIGIN: IGP (4 bytes)
       ⊞ AS_PATH: 300 200 100 (11 bytes)
       ⊞ NEXT_HOP: 201.100.3.1 (7 bytes)
     ⊟ Network layer reachability information: 2 bytes
       ⊞ 1.0.0.0/8
⊟ Border Gateway Protocol
   ⊟ UPDATE Message
       Marker: 16 bytes
       Length: 50 bytes
       Type: UPDATE Message (2)
       Unfeasible routes length: 0 bytes
       Total path attribute length: 25 bytes
     ⊟ Path attributes
       ⊞ ORIGIN: IGP (4 bytes)
       ⊞ AS_PATH: 300 (7 bytes)
       ⊞ NEXT_HOP: 201.100.3.1 (7 bytes)
       ⊞ MULTI_EXIT_DISC: 0 (7 bytes)
     ⊟ Network layer reachability information: 2 bytes
       ⊞ 3.0.0.0/8

0000  00 e0 b0 6a 3b df 00 00   0c f9 00 21 08 00 45 c►
0010  00 89 00 06 00 00 01 06   1f de c9 64 03 01 c9 6►
0020  03 02 41 c8 00 b3 ea 0f   fb ac df 77 0a f3 50 1►
0030  3f 1f bf 1a 00 00 ff ff   ff ff ff ff ff ff ff f►
0040  ff ff ff ff ff ff 00 2f   02 00 00 00 16 40 01 0►
```

QUESTIONS

Answer the following questions. Refer to the files used in this exercise as necessary. There are a total of 9 trace files- 3 traces for each of the 3 laptop monitors. There is a subdirectory for each laptop containing all the traces taken for that laptop.

1. Which packet in **2_LAPB_BGP_BROKENCIRCLE.cap** withdraws a route in response to the broken connection between AS 100 and AS 300? What route is withdrawn and what time was the UPDATE sent? Does this time correspond to the time at which the connection was actually broken?

2. In **3_LAPB_BGP_REPAIR.cap**, which packet shows the advertisement of a new route as a result of the repaired connection between AS 100 and 300? What network is advertised and what is the AS path for this route?

3. What do packets 10 and 11 in **3_LAPC_BGP_REPAIR.cap** suggest about the routers view of their BGP peering session while the connection was broken?

DISCUSSION AND INVESTIGATION

1. Notice that the OPEN messages specify a hold down timer value of 18- and that the NOTIFICATION message in trace **3_LAPC_BGP_REPAIR.cap** specifies that the Hold-down timer expired. Investigate the role of hold-down timers in BGP. Search for the term "Hold Timer" in RFC 1771 and summarize its purpose.

2. Telnet to an available route server (e.g. route-views.oregon-ix.net.) This gives a direct look at the IP routing tables of the route server's automous system. Some good commands to type once you gain access are "show ip bgp summary" which shows a summary of the routing information (how many networks are reachable etc.) and a list of all active BGP peers. You can get a sense of the instability of routes with "show ip bgp dampening dampened-paths" or "show ip bgp dampening flap-statistics." You can request information on the route to a specific network prefix with "show ip bgp <prefix> <netmask>" or "show ip route <prefix> <netmask>." In general, the command "show ip bgp ?" will give you information on the BGP information you can request.

3. Read about the Oregon Route View Project. What type of data is made available? Summarize several research projects that have used this data.

4. Read the paper by Rexford et. al on the stability of BGP routing in the Internet. Summarize its conclusions.

RESOURCES

- RFC 1771, A Border Gateway Protocol 4 (BGP-4), **ftp://ftp.rfc-editor.org/in-notes/rfc1771.txt**

- RFC 1772, Application of the Border Gateway Protocol In the Internet, **ftp://ftp.rfc-editor.org/in-notes/rfc1772.txt**

- Merit Network's Router Asset Database, **http://www.radb.net**

- University of Oregon Route Views Project, **http://routeviews.org**

- Jennifer Rexford, Jia Wang, Zhen Xiao, and Yin Zhang. BGP Routing Stability of Popular Destinations. *Proceedings of ACM SIGCOMM Internet Measurement Workshop, November, 2002*

- Web search: BGP Route Instability

Section 5:
Link Layer
Protocols

Introduction

The link layer deals with networks of machines that are directly connected by a shared physical medium. This physical medium may be copper wire, fiber optic cables or wireless frequencies, but a shared medium is fundamental to any communication. One device "speaks" into the medium and another device or devices "hear." As with any shared resource, there must be rules that govern access. It is the link layer specifications that answer questions such as "Can more than one device speak at once?," "How can data be directed to one of many listening devices?," etc.

In Exercise 1, we begin by discussing how unique addresses are assigned for link layer protocols. We discuss the role of the IEEE in administering the space of 48 bit MAC addresses. We explain how ARP is used to translate from the IP addresses found on the local network to their corresponding MAC addresses. We examine traces of ARP and of MAC address spoofing.

In Exercise 2, we cover the dominant link layer technology, Ethernet. We discuss its evolution from an experimental network at Xerox PARC to a global standard. We also describe the many physical layer implementations of Ethernet from 10BaseT to Gigabit Ethernet. Finally, we explain the difference between shared and switched Ethernet and examine Ethereal traces that highlight the differences between a hub-based Ethernet network and a switch-based network.

In Exercise 3, we cover wireless networks. We describe the differences between the various IEEE 802.11 standards for wireless. We also discuss the role of Wired Equivalent Privacy (WEP) in making wireless networks more secure.

Link Layer Protocols:
Exercise **5.1**

MAC Addresses and the Address Resolution Protocol (ARP)

INTRODUCTION

At every layer of the network protocol stack, unique numbers are assigned to differentiate entities. IP addresses are used to identify hosts on the Internet and port numbers are used to distinguish network applications executing on a host. At the link layer, there are Media Access Control or MAC addresses.

Within a local area network, each network device must have a unique MAC address. Devices listen to the shared communication medium for packets with a destination MAC address that matches their own. If two devices had the same MAC address, they would both attempt to act upon and reply to the same messages.

MAC addresses are typically hardcoded into the network interface card itself. For example, if you install an Ethernet card or a wireless card into your computer, the card itself contains its unique MAC address.

MAC addresses are 48 bits or 6 bytes in length. They are typically written in a colon-separated hexadecimal format such as 00:06:5b:e3:4d:1a. In this format, each colon-separated number represents a byte of the address.

To ensure the uniqueness of MAC addresses, the IEEE (Institute of Electrical and Electronics) Registration Authority administers these addresses. Companies that manufacture network interface cards apply to the IEEE for a 24 bit OUI or Organizationally Unique Identifier. Typically, this involves an application fee and a yearly renewal fee. This company ID can then be used as the first 24 bits of the MAC address of any network interface card they produce.

Once a company has obtained a 24 bit OUI, they can assign the remaining 24 bits to 2^{24} or 16777216 individual network interface cards. The company is responsible for tracking their use of each one of these addresses to ensure that unique addresses are hardcoded into each device produced. If a company needs more unique MAC addresses, it can apply to the IEEE for another OUI but it must prove that 95 percent of the previously allocated address space has been used. This prevents companies from buying up address space to prevent competition.

Organizations that need fewer than 4097 unique MAC addresses can request an Individual Address Block or IAB. Each IAB is actually a subset of a special OUI belonging to the IEEE Registration Authority itself. Each IAB has 36 bit specified by the IEEE leaving 12 bits free to allocate to individual devices. IABs cost significantly less than a full OUI. A list of allocated OUIs and IABs is available on-line from the IEEE. However, companies can ask to be excluded from this list for an additional fee.

Ethereal can translate the OUI portion of a MAC address into a string representing the manufacturer. For example, 00:06:5b:e3:4d:1a can also be displayed as Dell:e3:4d:1a because the OUI 00:06:5b belongs to Dell. Not surprisingly, there are other OUIs allocated to Dell as well. You can see all of these by searching for "Dell Computer" in http://standards.ieee.org/regauth/oui/oui.txt.

The address ff:ff:ff:ff:ff:ff is a special MAC address meaning that the data should be broadcast to all devices on the local network. Also, if the first bit of any address is set to one, then it is a multicast address.

Despite the fact that unique MAC addresses are hardcoded into the interface hardware by the manufacturer, the MAC address of most network interfaces can be reset in software. This does not change the value in the hardware itself, but it configures the card to use a different MAC address. This is called MAC Address Spoofing.

MAC Address spoofing relies upon the fact that it isn't really necessary for a MAC address to be unique among all devices in the world. It is simply necessary that all devices on the same local network have different MAC addresses. With 48 bit addresses, even if MAC addresses were assigned randomly, the chance of conflicting with another address would be very small.

MAC address spoofing can be used for legitimate purposes such as providing a unique MAC address for virtual guest operating systems with products such as VMWare. It can also be used for testing networks. However, MAC address spoofing can also be used to attack networks or to gain illegitimate access to network resources. For example, some network administrators require that every machine in the network register its MAC address and then they use the list of registered addresses to grant access to network resources. By spoofing a registered MAC address, any machine could use the network without registration. For this reason, access control or authentication mechanisms based on MAC address may deter attacks, but in general, are not reliable.

In the Internet, IP addresses are used for communication between hosts whether or not they belong to the same local network. Before data is transmitted between machines on the same local network, the sender must first translate the destination IP addresses into a corresponding MAC address. This is done by way of the Address Resolution Protocol (ARP). RFC 826 defines ARP for Ethernet networks, but ARP has been applied to other local area network technologies as well.

Each machine maintains a list of known IP address to MAC address translations known as the ARP cache. Before sending an IP datagram to a specific destination address, the ARP cache is consulted. If a corresponding MAC address is found, the IP datagram is placed in the data section of a link layer frame and destination address of the frame is set to the MAC address found in the ARP cache. If no translation for an IP address is found, then the machine will broadcast a message asking the machine with that IP address to respond with its MAC address. The machine with that IP address responds directly to the requester and a new entry is added to the ARP cache.

Sending a datagram to a machine that is not on the local network involves traversing a set of individual local networks connected by intermediate machines called gateways or routers. Gateways have multiple network interface cards and use them to connect to multiple local networks at the same time. The original sender or source machine sends the datagram directly to the local gateway across the local network and that gateway sends the datagram to another gateway and so forth until finally reaching a gateway that is on the same local network as the destination machine.

Link layer and physical layer networking technologies are often standardized by the Institute of Electrical and Electronics (IEEE). IEEE 802 is a family of standards that describe various local area network technologies. They are open or nonproprietary standards, meaning that anyone can produce devices that will interoperate as long as they adhere to the standard. For example, IEEE 802.3 defines networks like Ethernet that are based on the CSMA/CD Access Methods. IEEE 802.5 defines networks like FDDI that are based on the Token Ring Access Method. IEE 802.11defines wireless network technologies. Each of these networks use the 48 bit MAC addresses described earlier.

Thus, data flows through the Internet by traversing a set of local networks. This is the origin of the term "Internet" meaning a network of networks. Each local network uses a different link layer technology such as Ethernet, wireless, token ring, satellite. On a single path through the Internet, a datagram could be transmitted over a wireless network to an Ethernet network to FDDI network to another Ethernet network.

In this exercise, we will examine traces of ARP activity as well as an example of MAC spoofing.

CONFIGURATION

In this exercise, we connected two machines to an Ethernet hub. Machine A will maintain the same Ethernet MAC address and IP address for the duration of the experiment. Machine B however will be assigned a variety of MAC addresses.

A cable modem router was also connected to the network and configured to act as a DHCP server in the network. A DHCP server hands out IP addresses to machines in the network based on their MAC address. Each time Machine B's MAC address is changed, the DHCP server thinks it is a new machine and assigns it a new IP address. DHCP is discussed in more detail in Exercise 4.1.

Figure 5.1.1: Exercise Configuration

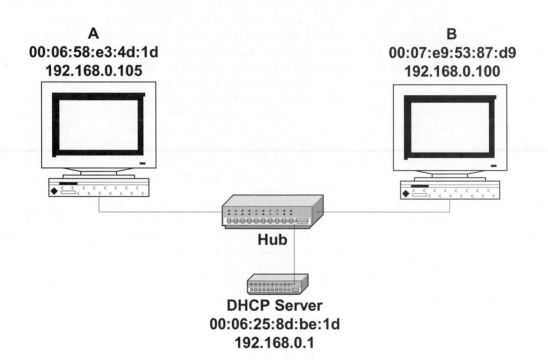

EXPERIMENT

ADDRESS RESOLUTION PROTOCOL

The first experiment performed in this configuration illustrates how the Address Resolution Protocol (ARP) is used to determine the MAC address corresponding to an IP address on the local network. During the experiment, we captured an Ethereal trace on Machine A and saved the trace in the file. You can open the file **arp.cap** from the attached CD and follow along as we discuss the contents.

On most platforms a tool called `arp` can be used to view and manipulate the contents of the local ARP cache. On machine A, we executed the command `arp -a` to display the contents of its ARP cache. There are translations for both the DHCP server and machine B.

```
>arp -a

Interface: 192.168.0.105 --- 0x10004
  Internet Address        Physical Address        Type
  192.168.0.1             00-06-25-8d-be-1d       dynamic
  192.168.0.100           00-07-e9-53-87-d9       dynamic
```

After checking the ARP cache, we executed the command `ping -n 192.168.0.100`. The result of this command is for machine A to send one small request message to machine B and for B to reply. Packets 1 and 2 in **arp.cap** are the result of this ping. Notice the source and destination address for both packet 1 and 2. Packet 1 is sent from 00:06:5b:e3:4d:1d to 00:07:e9:53:87:d9. Packet 2 is sent in the opposite direction.

Figure 5.1.2: Ping Before and After Flushing the ARP Cache

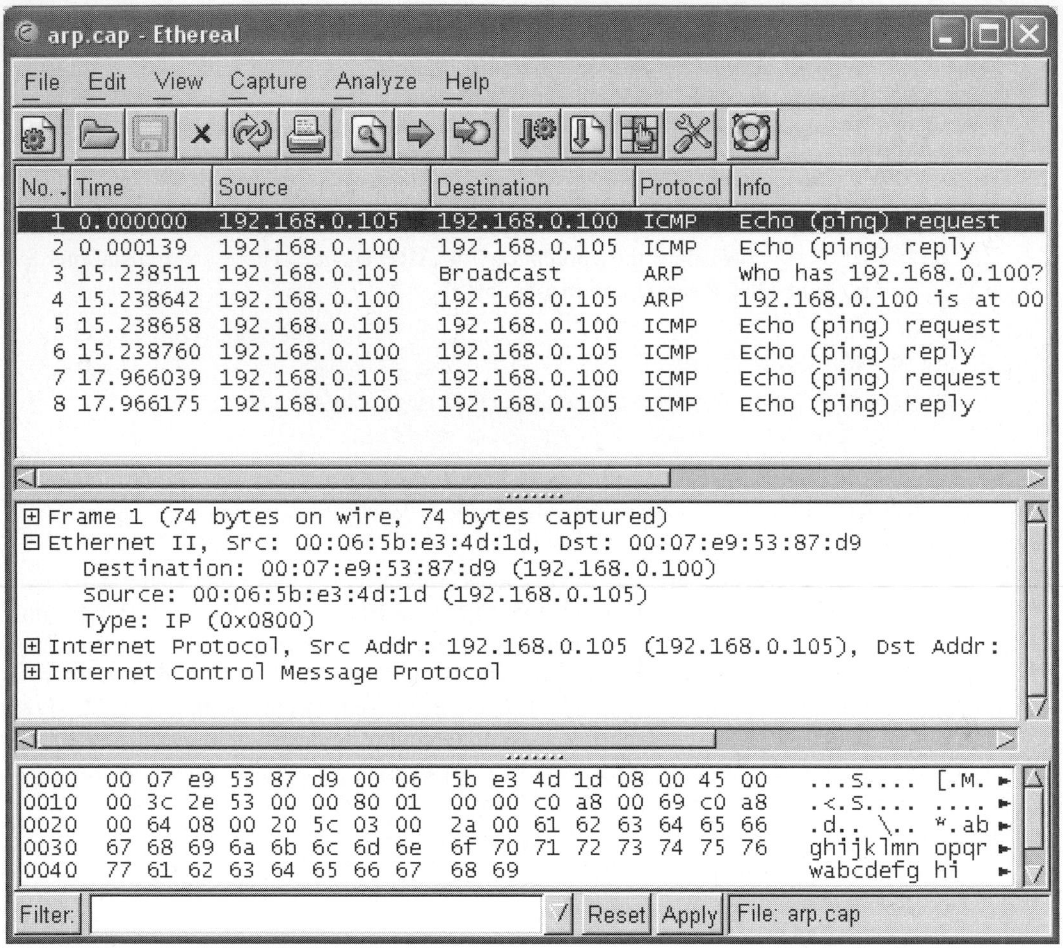

```
arp.cap - Ethereal                                          [_][□][X]

File   Edit   View   Capture   Analyze   Help

[toolbar icons]

No. . Time       Source            Destination       Protocol  Info
    1 0.000000   192.168.0.105     192.168.0.100     ICMP      Echo (ping) request
    2 0.000139   192.168.0.100     192.168.0.105     ICMP      Echo (ping) reply
    3 15.238511  192.168.0.105     Broadcast         ARP       who has 192.168.0.100?
    4 15.238642  192.168.0.100     192.168.0.105     ARP       192.168.0.100 is at 00
    5 15.238658  192.168.0.105     192.168.0.100     ICMP      Echo (ping) request
    6 15.238760  192.168.0.100     192.168.0.105     ICMP      Echo (ping) reply
    7 17.966039  192.168.0.105     192.168.0.100     ICMP      Echo (ping) request
    8 17.966175  192.168.0.100     192.168.0.105     ICMP      Echo (ping) reply

⊞ Frame 1 (74 bytes on wire, 74 bytes captured)
⊟ Ethernet II, Src: 00:06:5b:e3:4d:1d, Dst: 00:07:e9:53:87:d9
     Destination: 00:07:e9:53:87:d9 (192.168.0.100)
     Source: 00:06:5b:e3:4d:1d (192.168.0.105)
     Type: IP (0x0800)
⊞ Internet Protocol, Src Addr: 192.168.0.105 (192.168.0.105), Dst Addr:
⊞ Internet Control Message Protocol

0000  00 07 e9 53 87 d9 00 06   5b e3 4d 1d 08 00 45 00   ...S.... [.M...
0010  00 3c 2e 53 00 00 80 01   00 00 c0 a8 00 69 c0 a8   .<.S.... ....
0020  00 64 08 00 20 5c 03 00   2a 00 61 62 63 64 65 66   .d.. \.. *.ab
0030  67 68 69 6a 6b 6c 6d 6e   6f 70 71 72 73 74 75 76   ghijklmn opqr
0040  77 61 62 63 64 65 66 67   68 69                     wabcdefg hi

Filter:                                   / Reset Apply  File: arp.cap
```

After this first ping, we deliberately delete the ARP cache entry for 192.168.0.100.

```
>arp -d 192.168.0.100
>arp -s
Interface: 192.168.0.105 --- 0x10004
  Internet Address        Physical Address        Type
  192.168.0.1             00-06-25-8d-be-1d        dynamic
```

We then executed a second ping -n 192.168.0.100. With the ARP cache entry deleted, Machine A was forced to issue the ARP request show in packet 3. The ARP request is sent to the broadcast address ff:ff:ff:ff:ff:ff. Machine B hears this broadcast request and replies in packet 4. This replenishes the ARP cache and allows Machine A to send the ping request in packet 5.

Finally, we issued a third `ping -n 192.168.0.100`. The resulting packets are shown in packets 7 and 8. No ARP exchange is required before packet 7 because the ARP cache once again contains an entry for 192.168.0.100.

MAC ADDRESS SPOOFING

Our next experiment began in the same configuration as the previous experiment. On Machine B, we used the command `ipconfig /release` to release IP address 192.168.0.100. We then renewed it with the command `ipconfig /renew`. We traced this activity on Machine A and saved it to the file **dhcpRealMAC.cap**. This file is available on the attached CD.

Notice that packet 2 is sent from Ethernet address 00:07:e9:53:87:d9. The first three bytes 00:07:e9 are an OUI registered to Intel. The IP address of this packet is listed as 0.0.0.0 because we have released the previous address. Notice also that the hostname is listed as "MATTHEWS."

Figure 5.1.3: DHCP Discovery

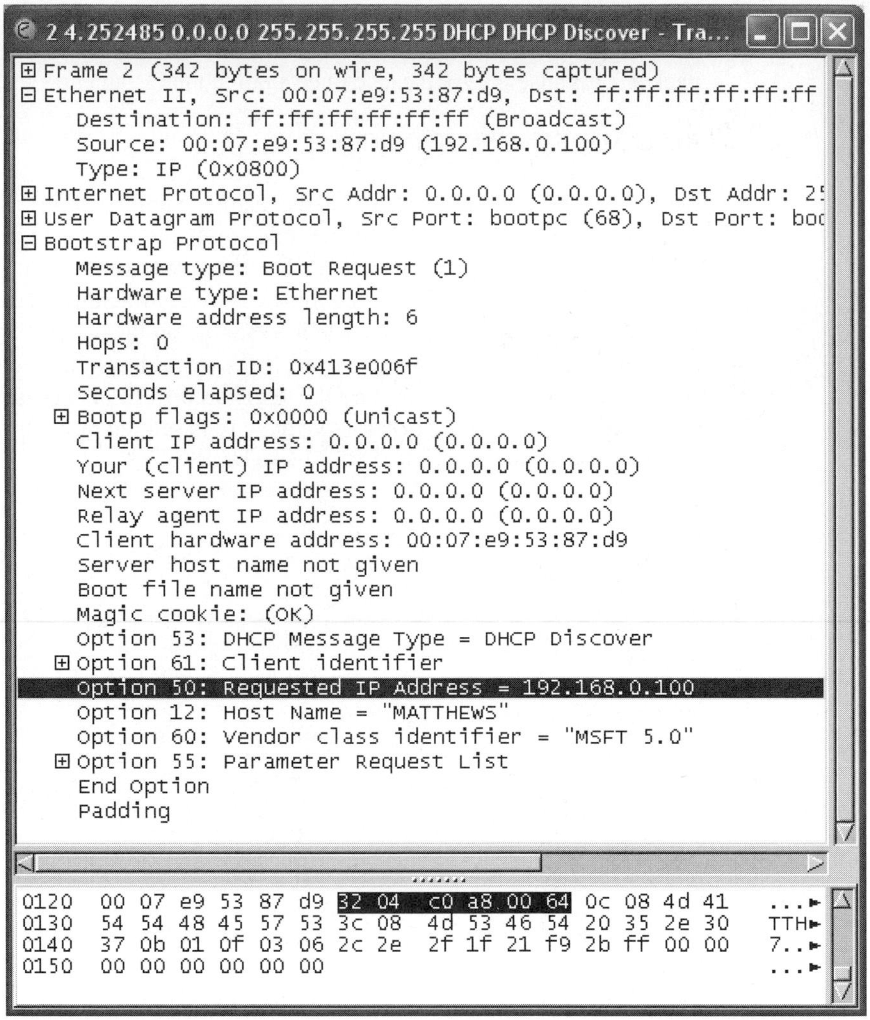

```
┌──────────────────────────────────────────────────────────────────┐
│ ⊚ 2 4.252485 0.0.0.0 255.255.255.255 DHCP DHCP Discover - Tra...  [_][□][X] │
├──────────────────────────────────────────────────────────────────┤
│ ⊞ Frame 2 (342 bytes on wire, 342 bytes captured)                  △│
│ ⊟ Ethernet II, Src: 00:07:e9:53:87:d9, Dst: ff:ff:ff:ff:ff:ff      │
│     Destination: ff:ff:ff:ff:ff:ff (Broadcast)                     │
│     Source: 00:07:e9:53:87:d9 (192.168.0.100)                      │
│     Type: IP (0x0800)                                              │
│ ⊞ Internet Protocol, Src Addr: 0.0.0.0 (0.0.0.0), Dst Addr: 2!    │
│ ⊞ User Datagram Protocol, Src Port: bootpc (68), Dst Port: boo    │
│ ⊟ Bootstrap Protocol                                              │
│     Message type: Boot Request (1)                                 │
│     Hardware type: Ethernet                                        │
│     Hardware address length: 6                                     │
│     Hops: 0                                                        │
│     Transaction ID: 0x413e006f                                     │
│     Seconds elapsed: 0                                             │
│   ⊞ Bootp flags: 0x0000 (Unicast)                                 │
│     Client IP address: 0.0.0.0 (0.0.0.0)                          │
│     Your (client) IP address: 0.0.0.0 (0.0.0.0)                   │
│     Next server IP address: 0.0.0.0 (0.0.0.0)                     │
│     Relay agent IP address: 0.0.0.0 (0.0.0.0)                     │
│     Client hardware address: 00:07:e9:53:87:d9                    │
│     Server host name not given                                    │
│     Boot file name not given                                      │
│     Magic cookie: (OK)                                            │
│     Option 53: DHCP Message Type = DHCP Discover                 │
│   ⊞ Option 61: Client identifier                                  │
│     ▓Option 50: Requested IP Address = 192.168.0.100▓            │
│     Option 12: Host Name = "MATTHEWS"                             │
│     Option 60: Vendor class identifier = "MSFT 5.0"              │
│   ⊞ Option 55: Parameter Request List                            │
│     End Option                                                    │
│     Padding                                                       │
│                                                                  ▽│
├──────────────────────────────────────────────────────────────────┤
│ ◁                          ········                          ▷   │
├──────────────────────────────────────────────────────────────────┤
│ 0120  00 07 e9 53 87 d9 32 04  c0 a8 00 64 0c 08 4d 41   ...►    △│
│ 0130  54 54 48 45 57 53 3c 08  4d 53 46 54 20 35 2e 30   TTH►    │
│ 0140  37 0b 01 0f 03 06 2c 2e  2f 1f 21 f9 2b ff 00 00   7..►    │
│ 0150  00 00 00 00 00 00                                  ...►    ▽│
└──────────────────────────────────────────────────────────────────┘
```

We reset the MAC address of this computer to 00:10:7b:59:18:64. The first three bytes of this address, 00:10:79, are an OUI registered to Cisco, not a MAC address you would expect to find on a network interface card for a PC. The MAC address change takes place on reboot so we proceeded to reboot Machine B.

While Machine B was booting, we captured an Ethereal trace of the resulting network traffic and isolated the DHCP packets. We saved the resulting

trace to the file **dhcpRebootNewMAC.cap**. This file is available on the attached CD.

In packet 1, Machine B sends a DHCP request message attempting to renew the same IP address it had before. Notice that this packet is sent from 00:10:7b:59:18:64.. It requests the IP address 192.168.0.100 and contains the hostname MATTHEWS as before.

Figure 5.1.4: DHCP Request

```
1 0.000000 0.0.0.0 255.255.255.255 DHCP DHCP Request  - T...

⊞ Frame 1 (348 bytes on wire, 348 bytes captured)
⊟ Ethernet II, Src: 00:10:7b:59:18:64, Dst: ff:ff:ff:ff:ff:f
      Destination: ff:ff:ff:ff:ff:ff (Broadcast)
      Source: 00:10:7b:59:18:64 (Cisco_59:18:64)
      Type: IP (0x0800)
⊞ Internet Protocol, Src Addr: 0.0.0.0 (0.0.0.0), Dst Addr:
⊞ User Datagram Protocol, Src Port: bootpc (68), Dst Port: k
⊟ Bootstrap Protocol
      Message type: Boot Request (1)
      Hardware type: Ethernet
      Hardware address length: 6
      Hops: 0
      Transaction ID: 0xce685329
      Seconds elapsed: 0
   ⊞ Bootp flags: 0x0000 (Unicast)
      Client IP address: 0.0.0.0 (0.0.0.0)
      Your (client) IP address: 0.0.0.0 (0.0.0.0)
      Next server IP address: 0.0.0.0 (0.0.0.0)
      Relay agent IP address: 0.0.0.0 (0.0.0.0)
      Client hardware address: 00:10:7b:59:18:64
      Server host name not given
      Boot file name not given
      Magic cookie: (OK)
      Option 53: DHCP Message Type = DHCP Request
   ⊞ Option 61: Client identifier
      Option 50: Requested IP Address = 192.168.0.100
      Option 12: Host Name = "MATTHEWS"
      Option 81: Client Fully Qualified Domain Name (12 bytes
      Option 60: Vendor class identifier = "MSFT 5.0"
   ⊞ Option 55: Parameter Request List
      End Option

0120  00 10 7b 59 18 64 32 04  c0 a8 00 64 0c 08 4d 41   .►
0130  54 54 48 45 57 53 51 0c  00 00 00 4d 41 54 54 48   T►
0140  45 57 53 2e 3c 08 4d 53  46 54 20 35 2e 30 37 0b   E►
0150  01 0f 03 06 2c 2e 2f 1f  21 f9 2b ff               .►
```

The DHCP server responds with a negative acknowledgement or NACK message to informing Machine B that the IP address 192.168.0.100 is already taken. From the DHCP's perspective, this message is not coming from the same machine B to which it granted the IP address 192.168.0.100. In packet 4, it instead offers Machine B a new IP address, 192.168.0.106.

We then reset the MAC address one more time to the same MAC address as Machine A (00:06:5b:e3:4d:1d). When we rebooted with this new MAC address, the DHCP server gave out the IP address 192.168.0.107. (It did not give it the address 192.168.0.105 because Machine A was on the network and responded to that IP address.)

We captured a trace of Machine B pinging Machine B in the file **duplicateMACs.cap**. Notice that each of these packets has different IP addresses, but the same MAC address. This is just one example of the kind of confusion that can result if multiple machines on the same network have the same MAC address.

Figure 5.1.5: Duplication MAC Addresses on a LAN

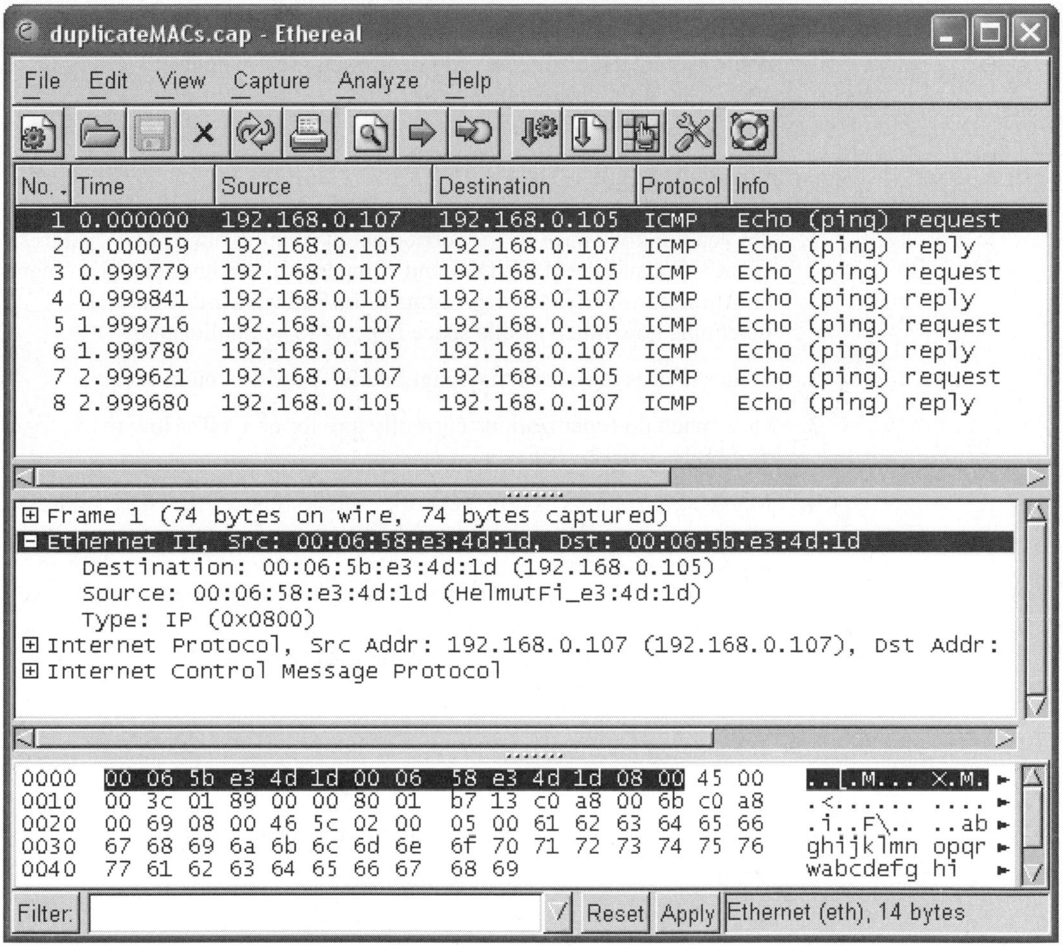

```
duplicateMACs.cap - Ethereal                                    _ □ ✕

File  Edit  View  Capture  Analyze  Help

No. .  Time        Source            Destination       Protocol  Info
    1  0.000000    192.168.0.107     192.168.0.105     ICMP      Echo (ping) request
    2  0.000059    192.168.0.105     192.168.0.107     ICMP      Echo (ping) reply
    3  0.999779    192.168.0.107     192.168.0.105     ICMP      Echo (ping) request
    4  0.999841    192.168.0.105     192.168.0.107     ICMP      Echo (ping) reply
    5  1.999716    192.168.0.107     192.168.0.105     ICMP      Echo (ping) request
    6  1.999780    192.168.0.105     192.168.0.107     ICMP      Echo (ping) reply
    7  2.999621    192.168.0.107     192.168.0.105     ICMP      Echo (ping) request
    8  2.999680    192.168.0.105     192.168.0.107     ICMP      Echo (ping) reply

⊞ Frame 1 (74 bytes on wire, 74 bytes captured)
⊟ Ethernet II, Src: 00:06:58:e3:4d:1d, Dst: 00:06:5b:e3:4d:1d
    Destination: 00:06:5b:e3:4d:1d (192.168.0.105)
    Source: 00:06:58:e3:4d:1d (HelmutFi_e3:4d:1d)
    Type: IP (0x0800)
⊞ Internet Protocol, Src Addr: 192.168.0.107 (192.168.0.107), Dst Addr:
⊞ Internet Control Message Protocol

0000  00 06 5b e3 4d 1d 00 06  58 e3 4d 1d 08 00 45 00   ..[.M... X.M...
0010  00 3c 01 89 00 00 80 01  b7 13 c0 a8 00 6b c0 a8   .<....... ....
0020  00 69 08 00 46 5c 02 00  05 00 61 62 63 64 65 66   .i..F\.. ..ab
0030  67 68 69 6a 6b 6c 6d 6e  6f 70 71 72 73 74 75 76   ghijklmn opqr
0040  77 61 62 63 64 65 66 67  68 69                     wabcdefg hi

Filter:                                    √  Reset  Apply  Ethernet (eth), 14 bytes
```

QUESTIONS

Answer the following questions. Refer to the files used in this exercise as necessary.

1. In our first experiment, if we were timing how long it took for the ping command to return successfully, we would find that the second ping took longer due to the ARP request. How much time is added by the ARP request and reply? How do you know?

2. How much larger are Ethernet addresses than IP addresses? How many unique MAC addresses can be represented? How many unique IP addresses can be represented?

3. When we assigned a duplicate MAC address to Machine B, describe one way the DHCP server could determine not to allocate 192.168.0.105 to Machine B?

DISCUSSION AND INVESTIGATION

1. Do you think we need to be worried about running out of MAC address space? Consult the IEEE OUI and company_id Assignments document at **http://standards.ieee.org/regauth/oui/index.shtml**. Can you determine how much of this space appears to be unallocated?

2. Which OUI is used for IAB assignments? How do you know?

3. How much do organizations currently pay for an OUI? How much for an IAB?

4. Many organizations ask the network users to register the MAC address of their machine. Does this seem like an effective strategy for preventing unauthorized use of network resources? If an intruder has physical access to the network, how could they determine a valid MAC address? Would there be any problem using someone else's MAC address? What does this say about the importance of physical security to protecting a network from attack?

RESOURCES

- IEEE Registration Authority, **http://standards.ieee.org/regauth**

- IEEE OUI and Company_id Assignments, **http://standards.ieee.org/regauth/oui/index.shtml**

- MAC address Organization Unique Identifier (OUI) listing, **http://standards.ieee.org/regauth/oui/oui.txt**

- IANA, **http://www.iana.org/assignments/ethernet-numbers**

- MAC Changer, **http://www.alobbs.com/macchanger**

- RFC 826, An Ethernet Address Resolution Protocol, **ftp://ftp.rfc-editor.org/in-notes/rfc826.txt**

- GetIEEE802™, **http://standards.ieee.org/getieee802**

Link Layer Protocols:
Exercise **5.2**

Ethernet

INTRODUCTION

The majority of desktop computers sold today come equipped with Ethernet interfaces. Ethernet is actually a family of local area network technologies. Variants of Ethernet vary widely in the format of the link layer frame headers, the type of cabling used and the speed of transmission.

The first Ethernet was developed in 1972 by Robert Metcalf at Xerox PARC to connect Alto computers to each other and other local resources like printers. In the original Ethernet, all connected devices tapped into a single shared network segment called the "Ether." When any device transmitted data, all the other devices would receive the transmission. Typically, a device simply ignores the data sent if the transmission was not intended for them (i.e. the destination address does not match their own). However, when put into promiscuous mode, devices will report all traffic seen if it was sent to another destination. This is the origin of the "capture packets in promiscuous mode" option in the Ethereal Capture dialog.

Only one device could transmit at a time because simultaneous transmissions would corrupt each other. The Ethernet specification included rules to govern how to avoid these conflicting transmissions. These rules are often referred to as CSMA/CD, which stands for Carrier Sense Multiple Access/ Collision Detection. This means that before a device can transmit data it must sense or listen to the channel to make sure that no other device is currently transmitting. If so, it must wait until the other device completes.

Multiple devices may listen to the channel at the same time, find it free and begin transmitting. In this case, a collision will result and the data transmitted by each station will be garbled. Devices detect such a collision by listening to the signal on the Ether at the same time they are transmitting. If the signal they hear is different than the one they are sending, then they know that a collision has occurred. To make sure that all other devices know that a collision has occurred, any device that detects a collision sends a special jamming signal. This jamming signal is heard by all devices and lets them know not to accept the corrupted transmission.

To make sure that each transmission is heard clearly by all devices and that collisions can always be detected, the Ethernet specification includes restrictions on the physical length of cabling as well as the minimum size of an Ethernet frame. The restrictions on cable length vary with the type of physical cable used and are related to the signal strength in the cable medium. A minimum transmission size is required to ensure that devices can detect any collision with its own transmission before it stops transmitting. When sending a small amount of data, padding is required to bring the frame above the minimum size.

Ethernet has evolved significantly from the original version developed by Xerox PARC. The first commercial version was called Ethernet I and defined and promoted by a consortium of companies including Xerox. An enhanced version of this standard, Ethernet II, was published in 1985.

The Institute of Electrical and Electronics (IEEE) often standardizes link layer and physical layer networking technologies. In the case of Ethernet, IEEE used the Ethernet II specification as the basis for their 802.3 standard. There are some differences in the frame format as shown below. They begin the same, with a 7 byte Preamble, a 1 byte Start Frame Delimiter and two 6 bytes addresses (destination followed by source). However, where Ethernet II has a 2 byte Type field, IEEE 802.3 has a Frame Length field followed by three additional 1 byte fields.

Figure 5.2.1: Ethernet Frame Formats

Ethernet II Frame Format

Preamble	S F D	Destination Address	Source Address	Type	Data 46-1500 bytes	FCS

IEEE 802.3 Frame Format

Preamble	S F D	Destination Address	Source Address	Len	D S A P	S S A P	C n t r l	Data 46-1500 bytes	FCS

Despite these differences, Ethernet II and IEEE 802.3 are interoperable with each other because the 2 bytes that are used for Type in the Ethernet II case and

Frame Length in the IEEE 802.3 case can be used to distinguish the two standards. All types in Ethernet II are greater than the maximum frame size of 1500. Therefore, if the 2 bytes are greater than 1500 (0x05DC in hex) then the frame is an Ethernet II frame and otherwise it is an IEEE 802.3 frame.

In addition to variation in the frame format, Ethernet networks also vary in their physical layer characteristics such as the type of cabling used and the speed at which they operate. Some common physical Ethernet types are 10BASE-T, 100BASE-T, and Gigabit Ethernet. 10BASE-T sends data at 10 Mbps (megabits per second) over twisted-pair copper wire. 100BASE-T and Gigabit Ethernet both run over either twisted-pair copper wires or fiber at 100 Mbps and 1000 Mbps respectively. There are also many other less common types such as early 10Base5 that ran over thick coaxial cable and 10Base2 that ran over thin coaxial cable.

In early versions of Ethernet that were run over coaxial cable, it was typical for multiple devices to literally tap into the same physical cable. This is called a straight bus topology. Today, it is more common for multiple computers to be linked in a star topology. In this topology, each computer has its own cable linking it to a shared networking device, often a hub or a switch.

Figure 5.2.2: Bus vs. Star Topology

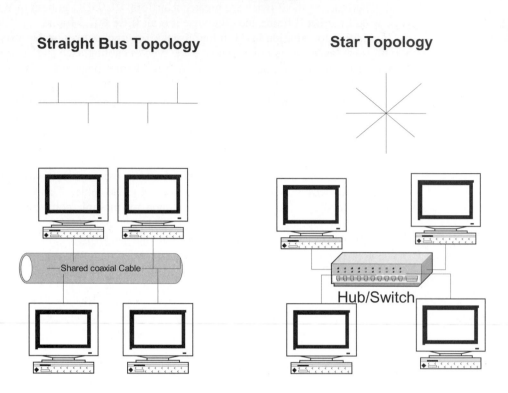

Hubs and switches both connect multiple devices with Ethernet interfaces. However, they differ substantially in how they achieve this. A hub-based network behaves much like the shared bus network. Data sent by any device connected to the hub is seen by all the devices connected to the hub. Hubs are sometimes called concentrators because they concentrate the behavior of a long cable into a single device. Switches learn which machines are located on each switch port by recording the source address of data coming in that port. Once a switch has learned that the machine with address A is located on port P, then any transmission sent to address A will only be forward on port P.

Switches provide several advantages. The first is that unlike hubs they can support simultaneous transmissions. Only transmissions that use the same ports can collide with one another. This leads to fewer collisions and a more effective use of network resources. The second advantage is privacy. Using a tool like Ethereal on a shared network segment, one can capture traffic to and from other machines in the same network segment. As many of the exercises in this book demonstrate, data transmitted over the network can contain private or sensitive data such as e-mails, web browsing patterns, and even passwords. On a switched network, even when capturing in promiscuous mode, one typically sees only data sent to and from the local machine. (Of course, if multiple people were remotely logged into the same computer, this would not eliminate problem.)

Switches are sometimes called learning bridges. They automatically learn which machines are located off each switch port. This information does not have to be configured into the machine. At initialization, a switch does not know which machines are connected to it. Over time as data is transmitted by connected machines, the switch will record the source of each frame that arrives on a port. Later, if data is transmitted to that address, it will be sent out the same port. If data is transmitted to an address that the switch has never seen as a source address, then it will send the frame out all of the switch ports in an attempt to find the machine.

Switches are considered Layer 2 devices because they process the Layer 2 or link layer frame information (i.e. learning based on source and destination addresses). Some switches offer additional capabilities such as full-duplex transmission (i.e. the ability for two communicating machines to use a set of switch ports to simultaneously send and receiver).

Hubs are considered Layer1 devices because they operate at physical layer. Hubs repeat data seen on one port to all other ports. Sometimes they perform other physical layer functions such as regenerating, amplifying or retiming a signal.

A common topology involves a switch with a hub connected to each of the switch ports and then computers connected to the hub. In this configuration, all machines on the same hub would see each other's transmissions and only one transmission could take place at a time. However, transmissions could take place on multiple hubs simultaneously. From the perspective of the switch, it would appear as if multiple computers were connected to each of its ports.

In this exercise, we will examine a set of network traces that highlight the differences between Ethernet hubs and switches.

CONFIGURATION

To prepare for this exercise, we first connected three machines with a switch to form an isolated test network. A cable modem router was also connected to the network and configured to act as a DHCP server.

After traces of experimental activity were taken in the first configuration, the switch was replaced with a hub. The experimental activity was repeated in the new configuration.

The network diagram below gives the Ethernet address of each machine along with the IP address assigned by the DHCP server.

Figure 5.2.3: Exercise Configuration

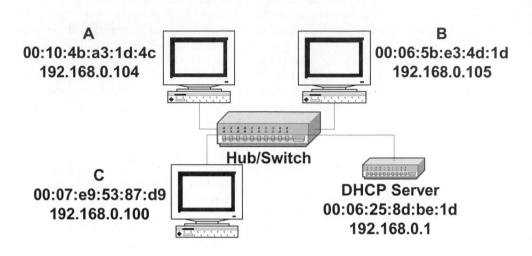

A
00:10:4b:a3:1d:4c
192.168.0.104

B
00:06:5b:e3:4d:1d
192.168.0.105

Hub/Switch

C
00:07:e9:53:87:d9
192.168.0.100

DHCP Server
00:06:25:8d:be:1d
192.168.0.1

EXPERIMENT

ETHERNET SWITCH

In our first experiment, three machines (A, B and C) were connected to a switch. We started an Ethereal capture on both B and C. On A, we issued the command `ping 192.168.0.105`. The result of this command is for machine A to send small request messages to machine B and for B to reply.

Next, we issued the command `192.168.0.255`. The result of this command is for machine A to broadcast small messages to all machines on the local network.

We saved the traces captured on B and C to the files **ping_switch_B.cap** and **ping_switch_C.cap** respectively. You can open these files from the attached CD and follow along as we discuss them.

First, we will examine the trace in **ping_switch_B.cap**. This trace contains 1 ARP request and reply and 2 sets of ping request/replies separated by a set of SSDP packets.

The ARP request in packet 1 comes from machine A. Before it can send ping packets to 192.168.0.105, it must know its corresponding Ethernet address. This request is broadcast to all machines on the local network. The destination address ff:ff:ff:ff:ff:ff indicates that the packet should be sent to all machines. Machine B hears the broadcasted ARP request and sends a response directly to machine A in packet 2. This reply is not broadcast.

Figure 5.2.4: Ethernet Broadcast

```
 ping_switch_B.cap - Ethereal                                    _ □ X

File   Edit   View   Capture   Analyze   Help

 [toolbar icons]

No. . Time       Source            Destination       Protocol  Info
   1 0.000000    192.168.0.104     Broadcast         ARP       who has 192.168.0.105?
   2 0.000041    192.168.0.105     192.168.0.104     ARP       192.168.0.105 is at 00:
   3 0.000381    192.168.0.104     192.168.0.105     ICMP      Echo (ping) request
   4 0.000416    192.168.0.105     192.168.0.104     ICMP      Echo (ping) reply
   5 1.003543    192.168.0.104     192.168.0.105     ICMP      Echo (ping) request
   6 1.003601    192.168.0.105     192.168.0.104     ICMP      Echo (ping) reply
   7 2.003557    192.168.0.104     192.168.0.104     ICMP      Echo (ping) request
   8 2.003615    192.168.0.105     192.168.0.104     ICMP      Echo (ping) reply
   9 3.003569    192.168.0.104     192.168.0.105     ICMP      Echo (ping) request
  10 3.003626    192.168.0.105     192.168.0.104     ICMP      Echo (ping) reply

⊞ Frame 1 (60 bytes on wire, 60 bytes captured)
⊟ Ethernet II, Src: 00:10:4b:a3:1d:4c, Dst: ff:ff:ff:ff:ff:ff
     Destination: ff:ff:ff:ff:ff:ff (Broadcast)
     Source: 00:10:4b:a3:1d:4c (192.168.0.104)
     Type: ARP (0x0806)
     Trailer: 00000000000000000000000000000000...
⊟ Address Resolution Protocol (request)
     Hardware type: Ethernet (0x0001)
     Protocol type: IP (0x0800)
     Hardware size: 6
     Protocol size: 4
     Opcode: request (0x0001)
     Sender MAC address: 00:10:4b:a3:1d:4c (192.168.0.104)
     Sender IP address: 192.168.0.104 (192.168.0.104)
     Target MAC address: 00:00:00:00:00:00 (00:00:00_00:00:00)
     Target IP address: 192.168.0.105 (192.168.0.105)

0000  ff ff ff ff ff ff 00 10  4b a3 1d 4c 08 06 00 01    ........ K..L...►
0010  08 00 06 04 00 01 00 10  4b a3 1d 4c c0 a8 00 68    ........ K..L...►
0020  00 00 00 00 00 00 c0 a8  00 69 00 00 00 00 00 00    ........ .i.....►
0030  00 00 00 00 00 00 00 00  00 00 00 00                ........ ....   ►

Filter:                                    √ Reset Apply File: ping_switch_B.cap
```

Notice that packet 1 is an Ethernet II frame. It has a 2 byte type field that contains 0x0806 or 2054 decimal. This is greater than 1500 and thus is not confused with an IEEE 802.3 frame.

Packets 3 through 16 are the ping requests from machine A and the ping replies from machine B. Packet 3 is sent directly from machine A (00:10:4b:a3:1d:4c) to machine B (00:06:5b:e3:4d:1d). Similarly, packet 4 is sent directly from machine B to machine A.

Packets 27 through 35 are the ping request from machine A to the broadcast address 192.168.0.255. At the Ethernet layer, this is translated into a ping reply sent to ff:ff:ff:ff:ff:ff. Although machine B hears the ping requests, it is configured not to respond to ping requests sent to a broadcast address.

The SSDP packets are sent from the cable modem router which has Ethernet address 00:06:25:8d:be:1d. It uses these packets to announce that it is an available Internet Gateway device. A similar set of SSDP packets is discussed in Exercise 1.1. These packets act like broadcast packets but they are sent to a special Ethernet address 01:00:5e:7f:ff:fa.

This same traffic is shown from the perspective of machine C in **ping_switch_C.cap**. Machine C sees only the traffic sent to the broadcast address. Specifically, it sees the ARP request in packet 1, but not the ARP reply. It sees the set of SSDP packets and the ping requests sent to the broadcast address, but neither the ping requests sent directly to B nor B's replies. Machine C does not see the packets sent directly to other Ethernet addresses because the switch has learned that those machines are not located on the same switch port as C.

We saw that machine C could not see the ping traffic between A and B. Similarly, if A and B were exchanging e-mail or hosting an instant messenger conversation, C would not see the data. For machines on a hub, however, it is a different matter.

We replaced the switch with a hub and started new Ethereal captures on machines B and C. We repeated the exact same experiment. On machine A, we issue `ping 192.168.0.105` followed by `ping 192.168.0.255`.

ETHERNET HUB

We saved the traces captured on B and C to the files **ping_hub_B.cap** and **ping_hub_C.cap** respectively. As with the last set of traces, you can open these files from the attached CD and follow along as we discuss them.

The trace as seen by B is basically the same as it was on the switch. B sees both sets of ping requests and replies. Interestingly, packet 12 contains an ARP reply from the DHCP server to machine A that B would not have seen on the switch. Also, B can see some replies the second ping request to 192.168.0.255. Unlike machines B and C, the DHCP server is configured to respond to pings of a broadcast address. Neither machines B nor C could see these responses on the switch.

On the hub, the trace as seen by C contains the exact same traffic as seen by B. In fact, **ping_hub_B.cap** and **ping_hub_C.cap** contain the exact same number and set of packets. This is not surprising as the hub places all machines on a shared network segment.

Under Statistics in the Analyze menu, choose Ethernet from the Conversation List menu. It will generate a list of all Ethernet conversations. There are 4 entries in the list for **ping_hub_C.cap** and only 2 entries in the list for **ping_switch_C.cap**. The list for **ping_hub_C.cap** is shown below.

Figure 5.2.5: Ethernet Conversation List on a Hub

EP1 Address	EP2 Address	Frames *	Bytes	-> Frames	-> Bytes	<- Frames	<- Bytes
00:06:25:8d:be:1d	01:00:5e:7f:ff:fa	40	13344	40	13344	0	0
00:06:5b:e3:4d:1d	00:10:4b:a3:1d:4c	17	1628	9	844	8	784
00:06:25:8d:be:1d	00:10:4b:a3:1d:4c	8	708	7	648	1	60
00:10:4b:a3:1d:4c	ff:ff:ff:ff:ff:ff	7	648	7	648	0	0

Ethernet Conversations: ping_hub_C.cap — Ethernet Conversations

Together, these traces illustrate the fundamental difference between Ethernet hubs and switches. Hubs allow all machines on the network to see the exact same set of traffic. Each machine can hear all other transmissions. Normally, a machine will discard data not addressed to it, but when put in promiscuous mode it will see all traffic sent by any machine. Switches are able to direct traffic to the single switch port containing the specified destination. Broadcast traffic is still sent to all switch ports, but the majority of conversations will not be visible at all nodes.

It is important to realize that the privacy offered by switches is not absolute. Switches typically have a fixed size table in which they record the mapping between Ethernet addresses and switch ports. One attack on switched networks is to overflow this table by generating a large number of packets from random forged Ethernet addresses. These forged addresses can dislodge the real machines from the switch's table and then when data is transmitted to a real address, the switch will be forced to broadcast the data on all of its ports. One defense against this attack is locking some static values in the switches tables. However, this requires a manual update each time a machine joins the network or moves to a new port. Another defense is to watch for this type of attack and either alert a human administrator or close the port from which the attack is originating.

QUESTIONS

Answer the following questions. Refer to the files used in this exercise as necessary.

1. Which machine is the source of all pings in this experiment? Is tracing done on this machine?

2. Are there any differences between `ping_hub_B.cap` and `ping_hub_C.cap`? Why or why not?

3. In `ping_hub_B.cap`, there are two sets of ping requests and replies—one is a ping of single IP address and the other is a ping of the broadcast address. Identify the last packet of the first set and the first packet of the second set. How did you know?

4. Only one machine answers the ping of the broadcast address. Which machine is that? Why is this contrary to the intention of a broadcast ping?

5. Consider the ARP requests and replies in `ping_hub_B.cap` and `ping_hub_C.cap`. How many ARP requests are shown in each trace and how many ARP replies? Give the packet numbers. Are the ARP requests broadcast or sent directly to a single machine? Are the ARP replies broadcast or sent directly to a single machine?

6. We see a number of SSDP packets in `ping_hub_B.cap` and `ping_hub_C.cap`. Are these broadcast or sent directly to a single machine? Would you expect them to be visible to all machines on a switch?

7. Which types of traffic seen in `ping_hub_B.cap` and `ping_hub_C.cap` are broadcast and which types are unicast (or sent directly to a single machine)? Consider SSDP, ARP requests, ARP replies, ping requests, ping replies. On a hub, broadcast and unicast traffic is treated identically. How does a switch handle unicast traffic versus broadcast traffic? To illustrate the differences between hubs and switches, should we focus on the unicast traffic or the broadcast traffic and why?

8. How many conversations are shown in the Ethernet conversation list for `ping_switch_B.cap`? How does this compare to the number of conversations seen by C for the same experiment? Explain the differences.

9. What types of transmissions does machine B see when on a hub that it does not see on the switch? Look in `ping_hub_B.cap` for traffic that B would not be able to see if it were on a switch and then look for that traffic in `ping_switch_B.cap`. Identify the packet numbers in `ping_hub_B.cap` and explain why that traffic does not appear in `ping_switch_B.cap`.

10. What types of transmissions does machine C see when on a hub that it does not see on the switch? Look in `ping_hub_C.cap` for traffic that B would not be able to see if it were on a switch and then look for that traffic in `ping_switch_C.cap`. Identify the packet numbers in `ping_hub_C.cap` and explain why that traffic does not appear in `ping_switch_C.cap`.

11. Suppose that machines A and B were connected to a hub and then the hub was connected to a switch with machine C. Would machine B see the same traffic that it saw when all machines were connected to the hub? Why or why not? Would machine C see the same traffic that it saw when all machines were connected to the hub? Why or why not?

12. On the attached CD, there is a trace file, **frameFormat.cap**, which contains one Ethernet II and one IEEE 802.3 frame. Which field allows Ethereal to interpret the frames correctly? What is the value of this field for each of the packets in this trace?

DISCUSSION AND INVESTIGATION

1. Many versions of ping do not allow a user to specify a broadcast address and many machines (like B and C in these traces) are configured not to respond to pings on the broadcast address. Why might some machines be configured not to respond to pings on a broadcast addresses? Can you think of a legitimate use of a broadcast ping? Can you think of a malicious use of a broadcast ping?

2. We described an attack in which a switch is overwhelmed with more unique Ethernet addresses than it has room to record. Try to write an Ethereal rule that would highlight such an attack. Would you need a more powerful language than Ethereal's capture or display languages? Describe how you would detect such an attack with a more powerful rule language.

RESOURCES

- Charles Spurgeon's Ethernet (IEEE 802.3) Web Site, **http://www.ethermanage.com/ethernet/ethernet.html**

- GetIEEE802™, IEEE 802.3 CSMA/CD Access Method, **http://standards.ieee.org/getieee802/802.3.html**

- Data Communications Cabling FAQ, **http://www.faqs.org/faqs/LANs/cabling-faq**

Link Layer Protocols:

Exercise **5.3**

Wireless LANs

INTRODUCTION

Today, it seems that wireless LANs are available everywhere—in homes, hotels, airports, coffee shops and office buildings. The IEEE 802.11 standards define the technology underlying this increasingly ubiquitous convenience.

In an 802.11 wireless LAN, client nodes associate with a wireless Access Point (AP) to form a Basic Service Set or BSS. A wireless AP is the center of a local area network segment that is shared by many clients. Access points can then connected to the rest of the Internet, often through wired connections to a switch or router.

In many ways, wireless access points are similar to the Ethernet hubs we discussed in Exercise 5.2. However, in an Ethernet network, the hub itself *creates* the shared medium and in the wireless case, the shared medium, a range of frequencies, is already present. As a result, the IEEE 802.11 standards also allow for a BSS in which no access point is present. These BSS are called Independent Basic Service Sets or ad-hoc networks. These ad-hoc networks provide connectivity between a set of local machine but do not provide a link to the rest of the Internet.

Figure 5.3.1 Basic Service Sets

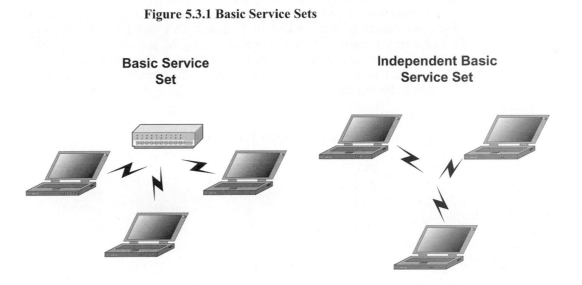

In some environments, a client has multiple access points available in range. When a client wants to associate to an access point, it will hop through all available channels looking for "beacons" sent out by the wireless access points. Even if a client detects beacons from more than one access point, it will choose one and associate. Clients can also actively send probes requesting that any available access point in range respond.

The beacons contain information about the access point, including its Service Set Identifier or SSID. An SSID is human-readable network name assigned by the network administrator. If you have a laptop with a wireless interface card, you may have been presented with a list of SSIDs and asked to choose which network you want your machine to join.

Another factor in choosing an access point is signal strength. Not surprisingly, the strength of the signal diminishes the farther away the client is from the access point. How far the signal can travel depends on number of factors including the types of obstacles (walls, furniture, etc.) and the frequency range being used. In general, as a client moves away from the access point they will experience a gradual decrease in signal strength and thus achievable bandwidth. It is not sufficient simply to be able to receive beacon frames; the signal strength must be sufficient to support the data rates required by the client.

Access points can operate on a variety of channels. When the coverage area of two access points overlaps substantially, they are typically configured to operate on different channels to avoid interfering with one another. If a large number of clients in the same area must be supported together (e.g. a densely packed office or auditorium), then multiple access points can also deployed over the same coverage area but each using a different channel.

A collection of BSSs with a common administrator can be combined to form an Extended Service Set or ESS. Within an ESS, mobile clients can move between access points without losing connectivity. All the machines in an ESS share a common connection to the rest of the Internet. This allows traffic to be easily routed to a mobile client from remote machines regardless of their location within the ESS.

Figure 5.3.2: Extended Service Set

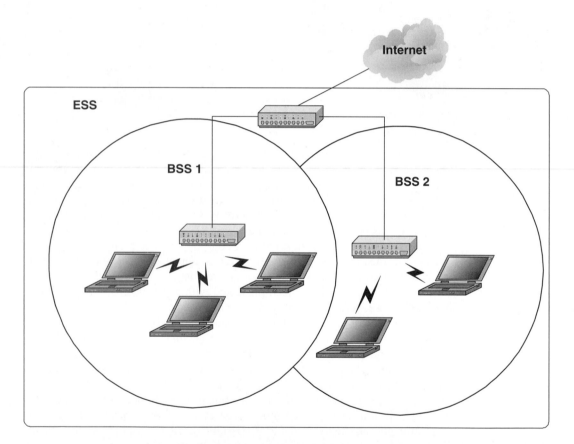

The 802.11 standard is actually divided into several specifications, 802.11a, 802.11b, and 802.11g, each of which specify a frequency range and maximum data rate for transmission. 802.11b or Wi-Fi is currently the most commonly deployed version. It operates in the 2.4 GHz spectrum with a bandwidth of 11

Mbps. 802.11g operated in the same frequency range, and it is interoperable with 802.11g but supports data rates up to 54Mbps. 802.11a is not interoperable with either b or g. It operates in the 5 GHz frequency range with a maximum data rate of 54 Mbps. 802.11b/g products also have better range than 802.11a products.

The main advantage to 802.11a is that it has approximately 12 nonoverlapping channels available. 802.11b and have only 3 nonoverlapping channels. In an environment with many clients located, 802.11a can support 12 access points in the same area each on a separate channel and thus can provide higher aggregate bandwidth, without the problem of signals overlapping and canceling each other out.

Other IEEE 802.11 standards are being developed to address other issues in wireless LAN technologies. 802.11e specifies quality of service, 802.11h specifies spectrum and power control management, and 802.11i specifies enhanced security.

Like Ethernet, wireless hosts listen before transmitting so that they do not interrupt other clients. This is called Carrier Sense Multiple Access or CSMA. This does not prevent collisions from occurring because two hosts wishing to transmit may listen and find the channel free at the same time. In Exercise 5.2, we saw that Ethernet does collision detection (CSMA/CD) to avoid this problem. Ethernet hosts listens to the signal as they transmit to verify that it is not corrupted by a collision. This is significantly more difficult for wireless hosts for several reasons. First, wireless interfaces typically cannot transmit and listen at the same time. Second, wireless networks must deal with something called the "Hidden Terminal Problem." This problem occurs when two machines, A and B, both sense the network to be idle because they are out of range of each other. However, another machine, C, between A and B is in range of both and their transmissions collide at C. For these reasons, wireless networks are based on collision avoidance (CSMA/CA) rather than collision detection.

IEEE 802.11 uses a collision avoidance scheme together with positive acknowledgments. The channel can be reserved by sending a short "Request To Send" or RTS frame. If the RTS frame arrives correctly at the intended recipient (i.e. no collisions), then they respond with a "Clear To Send" or CTS frame. These two transmissions avoid the Hidden Terminal Problem by ensuring that all machines in range of both the sender and the receiver are contacted. Together, these two transmissions reserve or allocate the network for some period of time. Note that the RTS/CTS exchange is typically used only for transmissions longer than a certain threshold.

Positive acknowledgments can also be used to verify that no collisions have occurred. In this case, the sender computes a mathematical summary of the entire frame called the cyclic redundancy code (CRC) or checksum. This CRC is sent along with the data. The receiver computes the same function over the data once it arrives and compares it to the transmitted CRC. If they are not the same, the receiver knows that some corruption has occurred in transit. If they are the same, it sends a positive acknowledgement frame to the sender letting them know that the data arrived without problem. If the sender does not receive such an acknowledgment, they can retransmit the data.

IEEE 802.11 defines a wireless frame format. Figure 5.3.3 shows the Frame Format with expanded details for the MAC Data section and then again for the Frame Control section. The Frame Control section contains type and subtype fields that indicate the purpose of the frame.

There are 3 main types of 802.11 frames, Management (type 00), Control (type 01), and Data (type 10). Type 11 is reserved for future use. There are also subtypes within each of these main types. Management frames relate to association and authentication and include beacons and association requests. Control frames deal with access to the media and include RTS, CTS, and acknowledgement frames. Data frames always carry data but different subtypes can also indicate some control and coordination functions.

A frame may contain up to four addresses. In general, address one is the destination address and address two is the source address. The exact meaning of each address is determined by the settings of the "To DS" and "From DS" bits in the Frame Control Field of the MAC Data. When the "To DS" bit is set, then the frame is addressed to the AP and the AP is supposed to forward it to the final destination. If the "To DS" bit is set, then address one is the address of the access point and not the final destination. The address of the final destination would be stored in either address three or four. Similarly, if the "From DS" bit is set, then address two is the address of the access point and not the actual sender. The address of the actual sender would be stored in address three or four. Address three and four are both used only when the "To DS" and "From DS" bits are both set.

Figure 5.3.3: IEEE 802.11 Frame Format

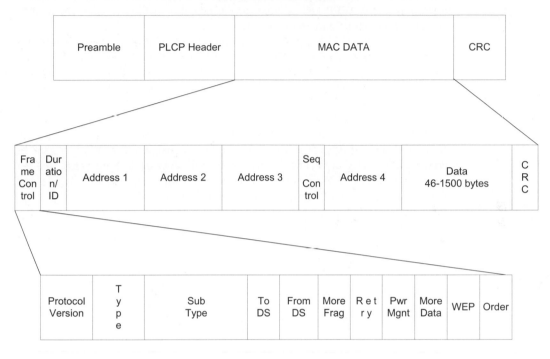

IEEE 802.11 Frame Format

Security is an important concern for wireless networks because an attacker does not need to gain physical access to join a wireless network. A building may be secured but if the range of the wireless network extends outside then the network is vulnerable to intrusion.

One aspect of the 802.11 specification is Wired Equivalent Privacy or WEP. WEP uses encryption to prevent intruders from joining a network and from eavesdropping on conversations within the network. As is suggested by the name, the goal of WEP was to provide privacy equivalent to that on a wired network. When WEP is enabled, any client wishing to join the network must prove that they know a shared secret key. Specifically, when a client wishes to join the network, the access point will send them a random number which they must encrypt using the shared key and return. This proves that they know the key without transmitting the key over the network. Exercise 6.1 contains more information about encryption.

It is important to realize that WEP is not an iron-clad protection system. Programs such as AirSnort have been developed that by collecting a large amount of encrypted traffic it is possible to determine the secret WEP key. Even with this flaw, however, WEP does introduce a significant barrier to intruders especially if the WEP key is changed periodically making it more difficult to capture enough traffic to break the key.

In June 2004, IEEE approved a long-awaited 802.11i specification for enhanced wireless security. However, Wi-Fi Protected Accesses or WPA, an enhanced security system developed by an industry consortium based on early drafts of the 802.11i specification, has been available since 2002. Both 802.11i and WPA use stronger key management schemes that changes keys automatically based on a shares master key.

Still any security mechanism is useless if not enabled. Surveys consistently find that the majority of wireless networks are using out-of-the-box default configurations. This typically means that they do not enable even WEP, that the access points allow any machine in range to join the network via DHCP, and that the access points themselves have the default IP address and password. As this exercise will illustrate, if you have a wireless network at home or at work, it is well worth your time to enable WEP and change the default settings.

CONFIGURATION

In this exercise, we used a cable modem router with a 4-port switch and an 802.11b access point. To this we attached one laptop via a wired connection and two via a wireless 802.11 interface. All three laptops were running Linux.

We ran an FTP server on the wired machine (A) and connected using one of the wireless machines (B). On the second, wireless machine (C) we ran the tracing software. Dedicating a machine specifically to tracing is important because wireless interface cards unlike wired interfaces cannot efficiently transmit and listen at the same time.

It is important to note that putting the wireless network interface into promiscuous mode and capturing with Ethereal was not sufficient. For this experiment, we needed it to be in monitor mode to see the 802.11 frames. To do this, we used an open source application called kismet. However, the traces taken with kismet can still be viewed in Ethereal.

Machine C represents a roaming wireless machine that is not officially part of the network containing A and B. It does not have an IP address and when a WEP key is in place for the network, C does not know it. C can be considered an intruder and potential attacker.

Figure 5.3.4: Exercise Configuration

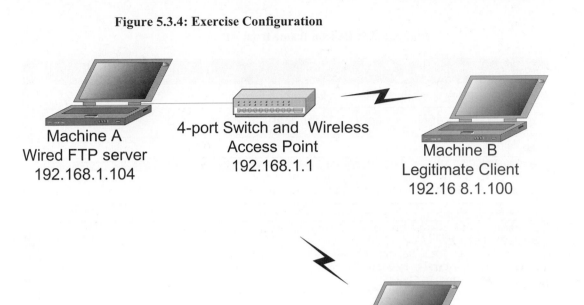

Machine A
Wired FTP server
192.168.1.104

4-port Switch and Wireless
Access Point
192.168.1.1

Machine B
Legitimate Client
192.16 8.1.100

Machine C
Wireless Laptop Running Tracer

EXPERIMENT

In this experiment, we explore aspects of IEE 802.11 traffic in general and we illustrate the difference between a network without WEP enabled and with WEP enabled.

In our first configuration, WEP is not enabled. On an "intruder" machine, we traced an FTP session between a wired FTP server and the legitimate wireless client. We saved the traces captured in the file **nowep.cap**.

BEACON FRAMES

First, let's look at the beacon frame in packet 1. Its Frame Control section contains type 0 for Management frame and subtype 8 indicating it is a beacon. It is sent from MAC address 00:0c:41:f3:f1:c9 which is the address of the wireless access point, and it is broadcast to ff:ff:ff:ff:ff:ff. Notice that the WEP flag is disabled.

Figure 5.3.5: Beacon frame from AP

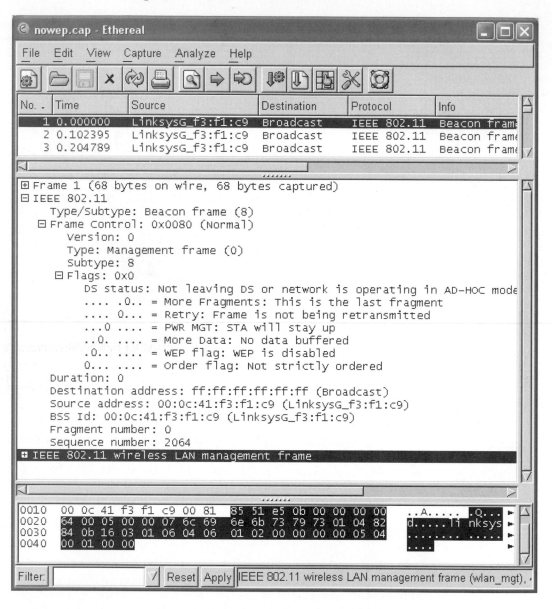

If you open the "IEEE 802.11 Wireless LAN management frame" section, you can find a wealth of information about this access point including the beacon interval, the channel on which the AP is operating, and the SSID of this network.

In this case, the beacon interval is 0.102400 seconds. This is why the majority of packets in the trace are beacons. To filter out the beacons, you can use the following filter: !((wlan.fc.type == 0) &&(wlan.fc.type_subtype == 8)). The remaining packets are either data frames or Probe Request/Response frames.

WEP DISABLED

Without WEP enabled, plain text data streams are clearly visible. To see this, we want to examine some of the FTP connections. FTP is discussed in more detail in Exercise 2.3. For the purpose of this exercise, we do not care to examine the details on the FTP streams. However, to show that the streams are in plain text, we choose packet 422, one of the data frames carrying FTP traffic and then choose Follow TCP Stream under the Analyze menu. This extracts the contents of the FTP session for each packet. In this case, the stream contains the username and password exchange with the FTP server. This was easily captured in plain text by an eavesdropping intruder! Notice that in packet 422, the FTP section of the packet actually contains the password itself in plain text.

Figure 5.3.6: Plain Text Exchange without WEP

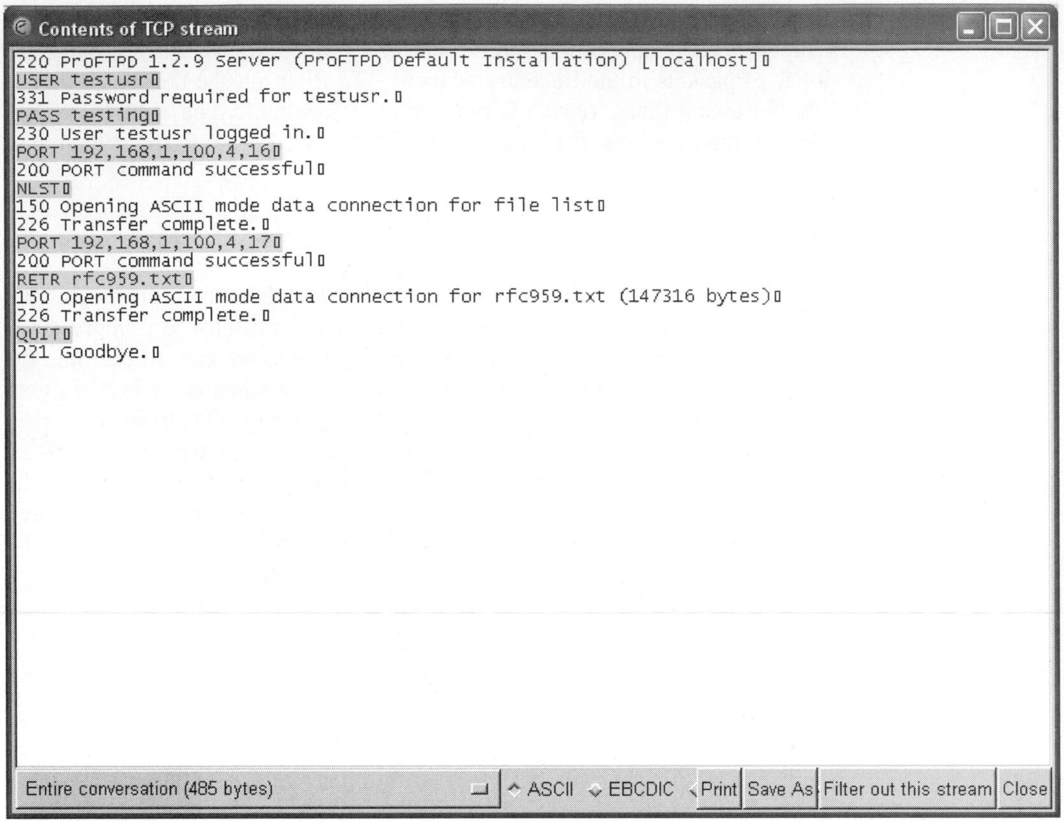

Figure 5.3.7: Single Data Frame Detail

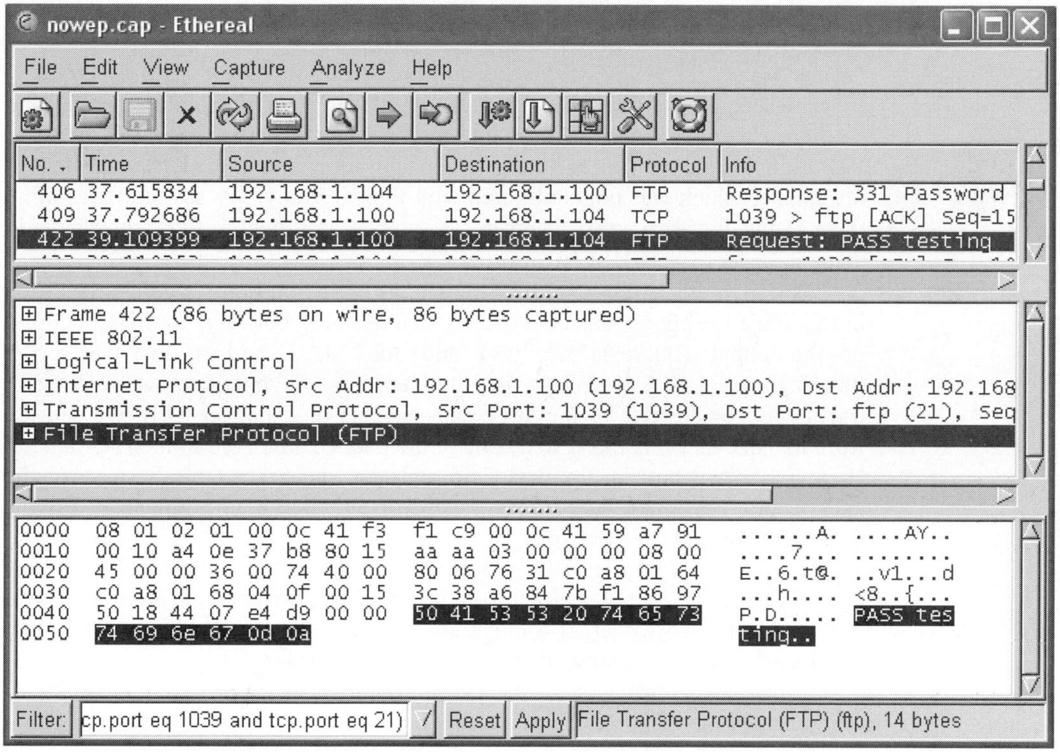

```
@ nowep.cap - Ethereal                                          [_][□][X]

File   Edit   View   Capture   Analyze   Help

[toolbar icons]

No. .  Time        Source           Destination      Protocol  Info
  406  37.615834   192.168.1.104    192.168.1.100    FTP       Response: 331 Password
  409  37.792686   192.168.1.100    192.168.1.104    TCP       1039 > ftp [ACK] Seq=15
  422  39.109399   192.168.1.100    192.168.1.104    FTP       Request: PASS testing

⊞ Frame 422 (86 bytes on wire, 86 bytes captured)
⊞ IEEE 802.11
⊞ Logical-Link Control
⊞ Internet Protocol, Src Addr: 192.168.1.100 (192.168.1.100), Dst Addr: 192.168
⊞ Transmission Control Protocol, Src Port: 1039 (1039), Dst Port: ftp (21), Seq
⊞ File Transfer Protocol (FTP)

0000  08 01 02 01 00 0c 41 f3  f1 c9 00 0c 41 59 a7 91   ......A. ....AY..
0010  00 10 a4 0e 37 b8 80 15  aa aa 03 00 00 00 08 00   ....7... ........
0020  45 00 00 36 00 74 40 00  80 06 76 31 c0 a8 01 64   E..6.t@. ..v1...d
0030  c0 a8 01 68 04 0f 00 15  3c 38 a6 84 7b f1 86 97   ...h.... <8..{...
0040  50 18 44 07 e4 d9 00 00  50 41 53 53 20 74 65 73   P.D..... PASS tes
0050  74 69 6e 67 0d 0a                                  ting..

Filter: cp.port eq 1039 and tcp.port eq 21)  /  Reset  Apply  File Transfer Protocol (FTP) (ftp), 14 bytes
```

DATA FRAMES

Let's also look in more detail at packet 422 itself. In the IEEE 802.11 section we can see that it has type 2 (or 10 binary) for data frame and a subtype of 0. Notice that this frame is sent from the wireless client with MAC address 00:0c:41:59:a7:91 and IP address 192.168.1.100. (Notice that the client's MAC address is Linksys also. It is a Linksys network interface card and not another access point.) It is sent to the wired FTP server at MAC address 00:10:a4:0e:37:b8 and IP Address 192.168.1.104. To reach a wired machine, the frame will need to be relayed by the wireless access point. Thus, the "To-DS" flag is set to one indicating that this packet should be relayed beyond the BSS and the third address field is set to the MAC address of the access point, 00:0c:41:f3:f1:c9. This field is labeled BSS Id by Ethereal.

The full protocol stack represented in this packet is the entire frame, IEEE 802.11, Logical Link Control, Internet Protocol, Transmission Control Protocol, and File Transfer Protocol. The Logical Link Control section is defined by IEEE 802.2. The LLC frame can be used with any 802 MAC layer to indicate the next higher level protocol which in this case is IP. It is also used to facilitate encapsulation of Ethernet.

WEP ENABLED

In our second configuration, we enabled WEP on our access point and configured the legitimate client with the WEP key. We then repeated the same FTP transfer as we did in the first configuration and traced the transfer on machine C which was not configured with the WEP key. We saved the resulting trace in the file **wep.cap**. (Remember to reset any display filters you have in place in order to see all of the new trace.)

Although this is the same FTP transfer as in the previous trace, there is little in this trace to suggest this. We can see data flowing between the MAC address of the client (00:0c:41:59:a7:91) and the MAC address of the server (00:10:a4:0e:37:b8). However, we cannot tell it is FTP traffic or even TCP or IP traffic. If we take one of the large data packets (e.g. packet 873), we can tell from the size that it is likely to be one of the packets involved in the file transfer. However, if we look in the data field, it is no longer readable because of the encryption. This may be bad for eavesdroppers but it is good news for the security of the wireless network.

If we look in the Frame Control Section, a data packet like 873, we can see that WEP flag is enabled. Interestingly, WEP is not enabled in the periodic beacon frames. However, if a client attempts to associate to the network they will be asked to demonstrate that they have the WEP key.

In this way, intruder machines such as our tracer cannot view the contents of messages on the network nor can they send data through the access point. They could launch a denial of service attack by constantly transmitting on all available frequencies. There is nothing that can done to prevent such an attack on a wireless network.

Figure 5.3.8: Data Encryption with WEP

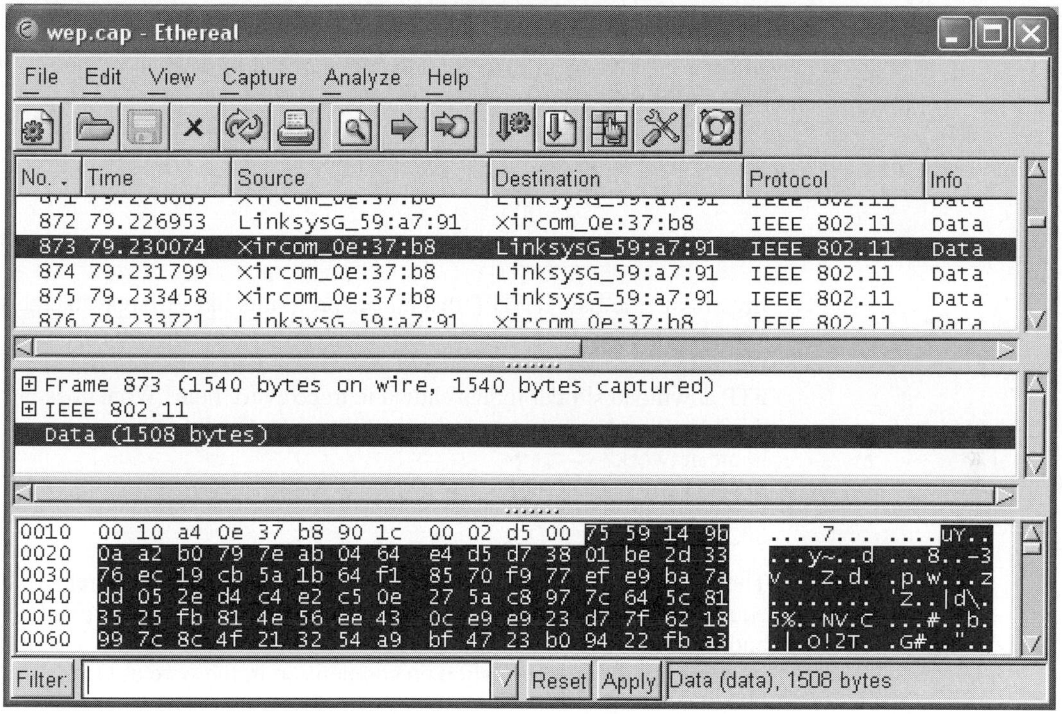

QUESTIONS

Answer the following questions. Refer to the files used in this exercise as necessary.

1. In **nowep.cap**, what percentage of the packets are beacons? What percentage of data sent? How do you know?

2. Not all the data frames in **nowep.cap** are part of the FTP stream, but most are. Write a filter to help you isolate the data frames from both **nowep.cap** and **wep.cap**. What is the total size of the data? What does this suggest about the overhead of WEP?

3. What is the SSID of our access point? Does it appear as if the default SSID has been changed?

4. We gave the MAC addresses for the access point, the FTP server and the legitimate client. Write a filter to find any other MAC addresses present in the trace. Examine the traffic from these MAC addresses.

What types of devices do you think these machines are (clients, access points,..)?

5. In Figure 5.3.2, we showed the access points within an ESS connected via wired connections to a network device. What would be the advantage of using an Ethernet hub over an Ethernet switch in this position? Could this connection be a wireless connection instead? What would be advantages and disadvantages of that? (Exercise 5.2 contains information on Ethernet hubs and switches.)

DISCUSSION AND INVESTIGATION

1. Investigate the flaw in WEP that allows programs like Airsnort to crack a WEP key given enough data. How much data must be captured? Estimate how long it would take to gather that data if the user did one FTP download similar to that shown in trace every hour. What does this say about how often you should change the WEP key on your home network?

2. Investigate proposals for wireless broadband such as WiMax or IEEE 802.16.

3. The Wi-Fi Alliance is a nonprofit organization that certifies wireless equipment for interoperability. In our traces, we saw an access point and a wireless card produced by the same vendor. Explain the importance of this certification on competition in the wireless market.

4. Search for estimates of how far away from a wireless access point you can go in a typical home or office environment. How about in the open?

RESOURCES

- GetIEEE802™, IEEE 802.11 Wireless, **http://standards.ieee.org/getieee802/802.11.html**

- Wi-Fi Alliance, **http://www.wi-fi.org/OpenSection/index.asp**

- Kismet, **http://www.kismetwireless.net**

- AirSnort, **http://airsnort.shmoo.com**

Section 6: Security

Introduction

Network security is an issue that cuts across the network protocol stack. Vulnerabilities exist in application layer protocols especially those like FTP and telnet that transmit user's data and even passwords in plain text over the network. Attackers can trick a TCP into accepting their data into an ongoing stream. IP addresses can be forged. Ethernet switches can be forced to act like hubs.

    The exercises in this section provide a detailed look at the types of attacks that can occur. Exercise 6.1 examines how network traffic can be encrypted at the application layer like in SSH or at the transport layer like in the SSL. It discusses the mechanics of exchanging secret keys over the network. Exercise 6.2 illustrates an attack known as TCP session stealing in which an attacker can terminate or hijack an ongoing TCP stream. This attack relies on IP spoofing or the forging of IP addresses. Exercise 6.3 discusses how malware like viruses and worms can enter a computer system and how they can turn a victim machine into the basis for future attacks. Many attacks rely on vulnerabilities in server software that respond to requests from remote clients. This exercise includes a trace of a machine infected with the Blaster worm.

    The exercises in this section will help you be a better network consumer by explaining the technical details of the potential risks as well as the advantages and disadvantages of possible defenses.

Security: Exercise **6.1**

Encryption

INTRODUCTION

The exercises in this book clearly demonstrate the kinds of information that malicious individuals can learn by sniffing traffic on a local network. Many protocols send both private data and passwords in clear text. One of the best ways to protect your privacy and the security of your systems is to replace applications that use plain text protocols like telnet and FTP with applications that encrypt data in transit. Encryption takes a plain text message and translates it into unreadable *cipher text*. The cipher text can only be decrypted or translated back into the original plain text message with a secret key.

There are two major types of cryptographic algorithms used to encrypt data —symmetric key cryptography and asymmetric key cryptography.

In symmetric key cryptography, both parties that are communicating must share a single secret key. If they establish this shared key in private, then they can use this shared secret to securely transmit over the network. The sending party encrypts the data using the agreed upon key and the receiver decrypts the data by reversing the encryption process. If a malicious third party were to learn the shared key, then they too could decrypt the data. Therefore, it is difficult to agree upon the shared secret key when all communication including key exchange takes place over the network.

In asymmetric key cryptography, communicating entities do not share a single secret key. Instead, each party generates a set of two keys; one key is called the private key and the other the public key. The private key is not shared with anyone, even when establishing a secure data channel. The public key can be shared with anyone, even attackers. These keys have the property that what one key encrypts the other can decrypt and vice versa. To send a private message to A, anyone can encrypt the message using A's public key, and no one but A will be able to decrypt it.

Asymmetric keys cryptography is based on the difficulty factoring large numbers. In particular, the private and public key pairs are computed by taking two very large prime numbers and multiplying them together. Multiplying two large prime numbers is a fast operation, but determining the factors of a large number is a slow process of trying the possible combinations.

Although factoring takes a long time on a single computer, it is easy to put many computers to work on the same problem; each trying a subset of the possible factors. With enough computing resources, it is possible to decrypt a message even without knowing the private key. However, the time and money required discourages all but the most dedicated and well-funded attackers. If someone were to discover a way to factor large numbers quickly, then encryption based on this technique would cease to be effective.

In addition to encryption, asymmetric key cryptography can also be used to digitally sign documents. Since an individual's private key is secret, they are the only ones that can encrypt a document with their private key. Anyone else can verify that they "signed" the document by decrypting it with the signer's public key.

In asymmetric cryptography, it is safe to send one's public key over the network. However, it can be difficult to safely determine that you have the correct public key for an individual. Consider for example, that an attacker might pretend to be A and then hand out their own public key rather than A's public key. Messages encrypted with the attacker's public key would be readable by the attacker even if meant only for A.

Asymmetric key algorithms are typically much slower than symmetric algorithms especially when encrypting/decrypting large amounts of data. As a result, many cryptosystems use asymmetric key cryptography only to safely transfer a shared secret key. This shared secret key called the *session key* is then used to encrypt the rest of the connection using a symmetric key algorithm.

Cryptosystems address the problem of safely determining the proper public key for an entity over the network in different ways. Some maintain a record of known public keys. The first time you interact with a new person or server, you must accept the public key they present. From then on, the system will warn you if they try to present a different public key. However, this only narrows the window of attack to the first connection; it does not solve the problem.

Other systems require that participants submit proof that their public key is authentic. Such proof typically takes the form of a digitally signed certificate. Trusted certification authorities will use their private key to encrypt a document that lists an individual's identity and their public key. Once again, this does not completely eliminate the problem. In order to prove that the certification authority signed the document, we must be sure that we have the correct public key for them. In addition, we must trust that the certification authority did a good job of validating each person's identity before issuing a certificate.

In this exercise, we will perform a variety of actions using plain text protocols and then perform an equivalent action using an encrypted data stream. Specifically, we will compare plain text protocols to protocols for encrypted data transfer like Secure Shell (SSH) and the Secure Socket Layer (SSL).

SSH or Secure Shell is an application layer protocol that provides secure remote login and file transfers. It encrypts and compresses transmitted data. SSH relies on asymmetric cryptography to exchange keys and then uses one of several possible symmetric key algorithms for data hiding.

There have been two main versions of SSH, SSH1, and SSH2, which are incompatible with each other. SSH1 is widely deployed but has some known problems. SSH2 was first introduced to avoid infringing on the patent for RSA, an important public key cryptosystem developed at MIT. Patent infringement is no longer a concern as the patent for RSA expired in 2000. However, SSH2 also fixes known flaws in SSH1.

SSL or the Secure Socket Layer works at the transport layer rather than at the application layer to encrypt data. SSL can be used in conjunction with unmodified plain text application protocols; anything written into a secure socket will be encrypted. SSL was originally proposed by Netscape and has since been renamed Transport Layer Security or TLS.

SSL or TLS is often used by web browsers and web servers to encrypt HTTP traffic. When you access a URL that begins with `https` rather than `http`, it is a good indication that the data is being encrypted. HTTPS connections are often used for on-line shopping or accessing private information with a web browser.

SSH is an application layer protocol. TLS is a layer between the application layer and the Transport layer. It can be used by any SSL-enabled application.

CONFIGURATION

The traces were taken on a client machine connected to the Internet by a cable modem router. The client makes a series of connections to a remote server using both plain text protocols like Telnet and HTTP and then it makes equivalent connections using encrypted protocols like SSH and SSL.

Figure 6.1.1: Exercise Configuration

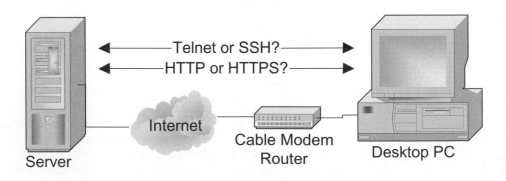

EXPERIMENT

In this experiment, we compare a plain text telnet session to an encrypted SSH connection. In both instances, we connected to a remote server and executed the same sequence of commands. A trace of the telnet session was saved in **telnet.cap** and the trace of the SSH session was saved in **ssh.cap**. You can open these files from the accompanying CD.

PLAIN TEXT TELNET SESSION

First, open the file **telnet.cap** and use Follow TCP Stream from the Analyze menu and examine the contents of the TCP stream. Telnet sends all data exchanged in clear text over the network. This includes everything the user types or views on their screen including the username and password, all commands executed and even the contents of files and directories viewed.

An attacker could capture this information using a network protocol analyze just like we did. Even if you protect your local network (e.g. physical security, switched networks, MAC registration, etc), an attacker could be listening on the remote server's network or to any intermediate network.

Figure 6.1.2: Transcript of Telnet Session

ENCRYPTED SSH SESSION

Now, open the file **ssh.cap** and use Follow TCP Stream from the Analyze menu and examine the contents of the TCP stream. The exact same actions were taken in this trace (type in username and password, cd public, ls, cs public_html/networks/book, ls, exit). However, with SSH, all the interactions are encrypted. The only data sent in plain text are handshake strings in which the client and server send information about the version of SSH being run.

In packet 8, the client responds by sending a session key. This session key is 148 bytes and is encrypted with the public key of the server. It would not be safe to send the session key in plain text over the network because attackers could decrypt the session if they knew this key. Once encrypted in the public key of the server, only the server's private key will decrypt it. The client knows the shared session key because it generated the key and the server knows the key once it decrypts it.

Figure 6.1.3: Transcript of SSH Session

Figure 6.1.4: SSH Key Negotiation

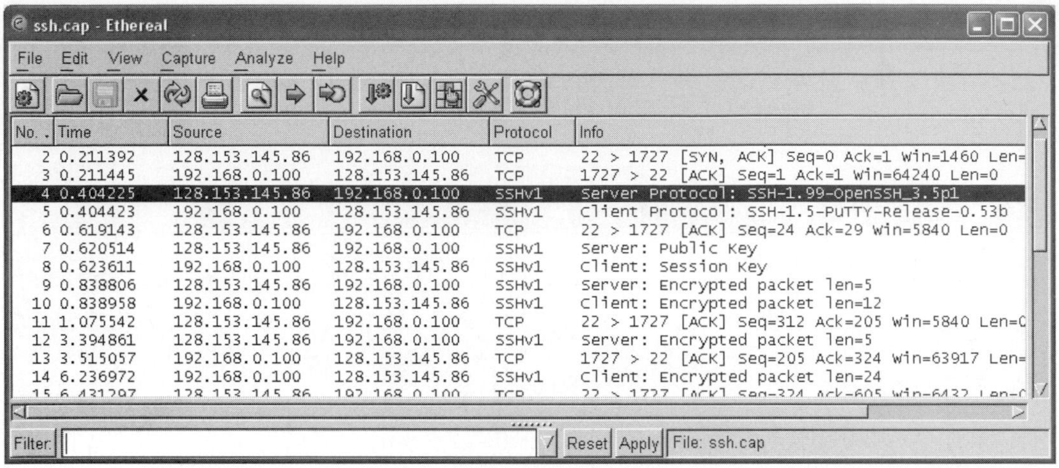

Packet 8 completes the key negotiation between client and server. After this point, all data is encrypted in the shared session key that is known only to the client and the server. This has several advantages. First, symmetric key encryption algorithms are faster than asymmetric key algorithms. Second, the session key changes with each new session and this limits the amount of data encrypted with a given key available to an attacker. If the same key was used for every connection, an attacker might be able to notice patterns in the encrypted data that could help him decrypt transmissions. This is especially true because an attacker can often predict what data was sent during certain portions of a connection. (e.g. the login prompt sent by the server). Given enough encrypted text and known plain text translations, an attacker might be able to decrypt data more easily.

ATTACKS AGAINST SSH

Now, let's examine in more detail what the SSH client and the SSH server exchange to allow them to decipher this encrypted stream. In packets 4 and 5, the server and client exchange plain text handshake messages identifying the version of SSH they are using. In this example, they are both using SSH1. The server is using SSH-1.99 and the client is using SSH-1.5.

In packet 7, the server sends its public key over the network. The key is 267 bytes long.

Recall that in asymmetric key cryptography, an entity's public key can be disclosed to anyone, even an attacker. So from the server's perspective announcing its public key over the network is safe. The SSH client will typically compare the public key to a locally stored copy and accept the key if it is the same. If it does not match, the SSH client will warn the user because this may indicate that an attacker is trying to pose as the real server.

If the SSH client does not have a copy of this server's key in their local database, then it has no way to check whether the key presented by the server is legitimate. Most SSH client's address this problem by asking the user if they want to accept the public key offered by the server. Once accepted, the key is stored in the local database. This narrows the window of opportunity for a possible attack to a user's first connection, but does not eliminate the possibility.

An attacker might get a user to accept their public key initially. However, it may be difficult for the attacker to pose as the legitimate server for long. For example, if the user logs into an attacker's machine that is posing as the real server, that machine would need to have a copy of all the user's data to continue the illusion. An attacker could gain passwords in this way, but would need to disconnect the user immediately to avoid detection.

Another more subtle attack is called a "man in the middle" attack. In this case, an attacker sits between a legitimate user and server. They first note the server's public key, and they provide the user with their own public key. When the user encrypts packets with the attacker's public key, the attacker can decrypt them and note all the information. They could even modify them, encrypt them in the server's real public key, and send them on to the server. In this way, the attacker does not need to possess all the resources of the server to pose as the server.

Although such attacks are possible, they still make the attacker's job much more difficult. Just like locks on the doors of a house do not prevent burglars from breaking a window. SSH does not prevent all kinds of attacks, but it does discourage casual attacks. This is often sufficient for all but the most valuable resources.

COMPARING HTTP AND HTTPS

Next, we compare a plain text HTTP session to an encrypted HTTPS session using TLS. In both instances, we fetched the same web page. A trace of the HTTP session was saved in **http.cap** and the trace of the encrypted HTTPS session was saved in **https.cap**. You can open these files from the accompanying CD.

First, open the file **http.cap** and use Follow TCP Stream from the Analyze menu and examine the contents of the TCP stream. All information sent by the web browser or web server is shown in plain text. In this case, we are simply fetching a static web page. However, in an on-line shopping example, we might see credit card information, usernames, passwords or other sensitive information.

Now open the file **https.cap** and use Follow TCP Stream from the Analyze menu and examine the contents of the TCP stream. In this case, all data exchanged in encrypted. There is no hint of the URLs requested or the actual data returned.

The encrypted stream in **https.cap** uses the Transport Layer Security Protocol (TLS). TLS is an extensible framework that allows the client and server to negotiate which cryptographic protocol to use and to exchange keys and other information needed to support the chosen protocol. At the lowest level, TLS consists of a series of records. The TLS Record Protocol takes plain text messages to be transferred, breaks them into smaller pieces if necessary, compresses them if desired, computes and appends a checksum, encrypts the resulting record and finally transmits. Above this lower layer record protocol, several other TLS protocols are implemented including a handshaking protocol, a protocol for changing cipers used and an application data protocol.

The client initiates the encrypted connection with a client hello record in packet 4. The client and server must negotiate the specific cryptographic algorithms to be used. In this client hello message, the client lists the options that it supports in order of preference. The client's first choice is SSL2_RC4_128_WITH_MD5 – Secure Socket Layer version 2, the RC4 stream cipher with a 128 bit key, and an MD5 checksum.

In packet 6, the server responds with four TLS records—a server hello, a certificate, a server key exchange, and a server hello done. In the server hello record, the server indicates that it has chosen to use one of the options listed by the client: TLS_DHE_RSA_WITH_AES_256_CBC_SHA. Notice that this was not the client's first choice.

Figure 6.1.5: Secure Socket Layer Client Hello

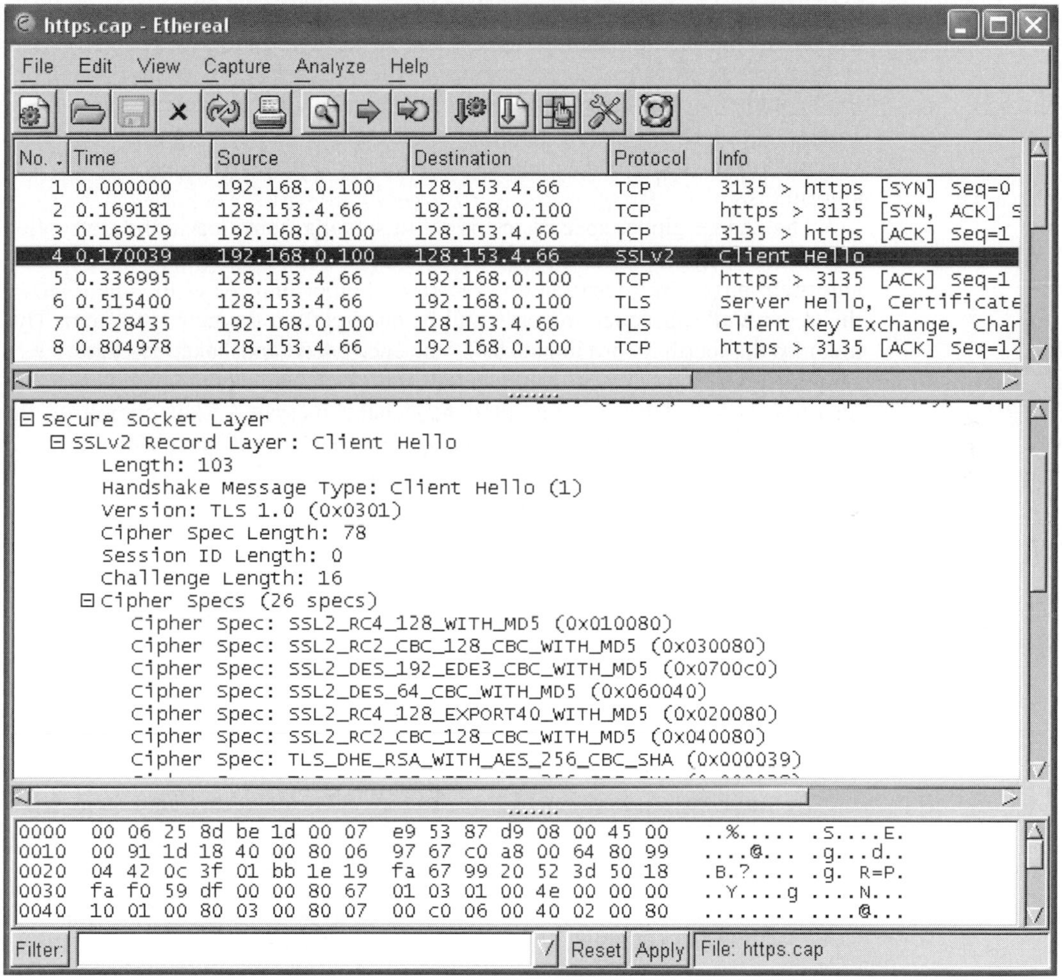

The Certificate record in packet 6 contains the server's X.509 certificate. This certificate contains the server's public key, information about the owner and location of the server (subject), and the certification authority who granted the certificate (issuer). Ethereal does not highlight these individual portions, but some of them (e.g. issuer and subject name) are in ASCII text.

The certificate also contains a digital signature. The issuer creates such a signature by encrypting a hash or checksum of the certificate information with their private key. If the signature can be decrypted with the issuer's public key, then only someone with access to the issuer's private key could have "signed" the document.

In packet 7, the client responds with 3 TLS records: a client key exchange, a change cipher spec, and an encrypted handshake message. In client key exchange, the client specifies a key known as the "premaster secret." The precise meaning of this secret depends on the encryption algorithm being used. For example, for RSA, it may be a secret encrypted with the server's public key. Just as in the SSH example, this allows the client and server to use a shared session key to encrypt data rather than the more expensive asymmetric key algorithms.

The change cipher spec record is set to signal a transition in the encryption algorithm being used. The change cipher spec record proposes a new encryption algorithm but is itself encrypted in the current algorithm. After the client writes this record, all subsequent records will be encrypted in the new algorithm. This includes the fourth record in packer 7, the encrypted handshake message.

In packet 9, the server also responds with a change cipher spec message of its own, followed by an encrypted handshake message. That completes the negotiation of the attributes of this encrypted channel. All data that follows is encrypted according to the agreed upon parameters.

QUESTIONS

Answer the following questions about the files **telnet.cap**, **ssh.cap**, **http.cap**, and **https.cap**.

1. The TCP sessions in **telnet.cap** and **ssh.cap** accomplish the exact same functionality. How much total data is sent from client to server and from server to client in each case? How many packets are sent in each direction in each case? What is the ratio of data transferred over telnet to that transferred over SSH? Does this surprise you? What does this suggest about the SSH stream?

2. How much of the SSH session is key exchange? What percentage is this of the total bytes transferred over the session? How does this affect your answer to Question 1?

3. Sketch the pattern of packet sizes sent between client to server in **telnet.cap**. Start with packet 12, which is the first set of actual data sent from server to client. Packet 12 sends 22 bytes of data from server to client. Packet 14 sends 404 bytes of data from server to client. Packet 14 is much bigger than packet 12. What is the purpose of packet 12? Or packet 14?

   If you knew what the client was doing, but could not see the contents of the packets, how could you guess the contents based on the pattern, size, and time the packets were sent? What would this imply about the effectiveness of an encryption algorithm that preserved message boundaries and sizes?

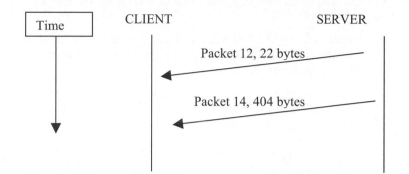

4. Try a similar analysis with the SSH session. For example, try to identify when the server returns the `ls` of the directory. What does this imply about the secrecy of an SSH session?

5. The TCP sessions in **http.cap** and **https.cap** accomplish the exact same functionality. How much total data is sent from client to server and from server to client in each case? How many packets are sent in each direction in each case? What is the ratio of data transferred over http to that transferred over https? How does this compare to your answer to question 1?

6. How much of the TLS session is key exchange? What percentage is this of the total bytes transferred over the session? What would the ratio between the two streams as computed in Question 5?

7. Examine the certificate presented by the server in **https.cap**. Determine the name of the certification authority that issued the certificate. You may need to search the web for the format of an X.509 certificate.

DISCUSSION AND INVESTIGATION

1. We have included a trace **ssh_slowtype.cap** in which we connected to a remote server using SSH and then proceeded to hit a single return key approximately every 10 seconds.

   i. Identify how many times we hit the return key. Explain your answer.

   ii. Is each return key encrypted identically? Why or why not? What does this say about ssh?

iii. Try establishing an https connection and then fetching the same web page over and over again. Will the response be the same each time (consider the first, second and third times)? Could you tell if someone had a previous copy of a page without decrypting the responses? Why or why not?

2. Could telnet and FTP be run over TLS? Why do you think people use ssh rather than telnet over TLS or scp rather than FTP over TLS? Explain your answer.

3. In the https trace, we saw the client send a list of encryption algorithms that it was willing to use. Investigate some of the algorithms in this list and explain how they differ.

RESOURCES

- Secure Shell (SECSH) IETF Working Group, **http://www.ietf.org/html.charters/secsh-charter.html**

- OpenSSH, **http://www.openssh.com**

- SSH Communications Security, Inc., **http://www.ssh.com**

- Transport Layer Security IETF Working Group, **http://www.ietf.org/html.charters/tls-charter.html**

- RFC 2246, The TLS Protocol Version 1.0, **ftp://ftp.rfc-editor.org/in-notes/rfc2246.txt**

- RFC 3546, Transport Layer Security (TLS) Extension, **ftp://ftp.rfc-editor.org/in-notes/rfc3546.txt**

- The SSL Protocol Version 3, Internet Draft, **http://wp.netscape.com/eng/ssl3/ssl-toc.html**

- OpenSSL Project, **http://www.openssl.org**

- Public-key Infrastructure (X.509) Working Group, **http://www.ietf.org/html.charters/pkix-charter.html**

Security: Exercise **6.2**

IP Spoofing and TCP Session Stealing

INTRODUCTION

In this exercise, we are going to discuss vulnerabilities in the Internet Protocol (IP) and the Transmission Control Protocol (TCP). Specifically, we are going to examine traces of IP Spoofing and TCP Session Stealing.

IP Spoofing refers to sending a packet with a forged source IP address. For example, a machine with IP address 192.168.0.1 could send a packet with source IP address 192.168.0.210. This is typically done through what is called the raw IP interface. IP packets that are formed by the operating system will be marked with the proper source IP address. However, application programs can use the raw IP interface to form and send any IP packet they want.

Using IP spoofing, attackers can send segments into an ongoing TCP stream by forming an IP packet with a matching source and destination IP address as well as source and destination port number. Recall from our Follow TCP stream exercises that these four numbers define a TCP connection. If an attacker sets these values correctly, then a receiver would accept the forged packet as belonging to the ongoing TCP stream.

A receiver will respond to a forged packet as if it belongs to the ongoing TCP stream. However, to actually steal the session, it must also set the sequence number properly. If it sends a packet with a sequence number that is too low, then the receiver will simply send an acknowledgment saying that it had already received this packet. If it sends a packet with a sequence number that is too high, the receiver may buffer the out of order data but will likely simply send a segment reiterating the sequence number that it is currently expecting. If, however, the attacker sends a packet with expected sequence number, she will succeed in "stealing the session."

Consider what the goal of such an attack might be. What type of packet might an attacker wish to send into a TCP stream? If an attacker sent a segment with the FIN or RST bit set, then she would succeed in closing the connection. This type of attack is called a denial of service attack. It does not gain illegitimate access to a resource, but it does prevent legitimate users from accessing the resource.

An attacker could also send a segment with actual data rather than simply the FIN or RST bit set. In this case, the data they sent would be accepted into the stream and delivered up to the receiving application. In this exercise, we will see that this can have serious consequences.

CONFIGURATION

The traces used in this exercise were taken on a private network that was not connected to the Internet. The exercise was conducted with the full knowledge and permission of all users involved.

Two desktop machines, one serving a legitimate telnet and FTP server and one serving as a legitimate client, are connected to the network. During the exercise, a third machine will connect to the network and launch an attack against these legitimate machines.

Figure 6.2.1: Exercise Configuration

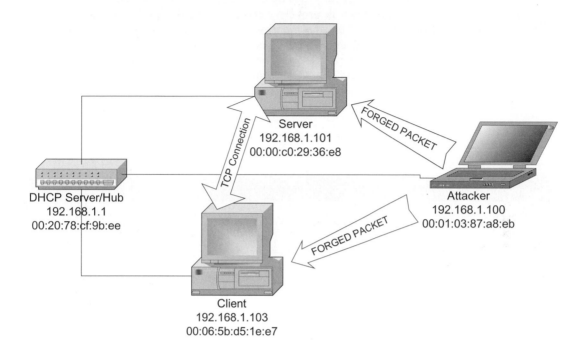

EXPERIMENT

The experiment consists of several telnet sessions from the legitimate client to the server. Each of these telnet sessions is attacked by a third machine using IP Spoofing and TCP Session Stealing. Some sessions are terminated with a FIN or RST. Other sessions are hijacked and data from the attacker is inserted into the stream. In addition, the attacker captures one user's password and uses it to FTP a file from the server.

We captured the entire attack sequence in a trace called **session_hijack.cap**. This file is rather large so we have also saved some of the individual connections in separate files: **telnet1_hijacked.cap**, **telnet2_fin.cap**, **telnet3_rst.cap**, **telnet4_hijacked.cap**, and **attacker_ftp.cap**. All of these files are available on the accompanying CD.

TCP SESSION HIJACKING

We will look first at **telnet1_hijacked.cap**. The SYN and the SYNACK are shown in packets 1 and 2. Notice that packet 1 is sent from IP Address 192.168.1.103 (the client) to IP address 192.168.1.101 (the server). If we examine the Ethernet frame headers, we see that the MAC address of the client is 00:06:5b:d5:1e:e7 (DellComp_d5:1e:e7) and the MAC address of the server is 00:00:c0:29:36:e8 (WesternD_29:36:e8). In the SYNACK packet, the source and destination addresses (IP and Ethernet) are reversed.

Figure 6.2.2: Connection Between Valid Client and Server

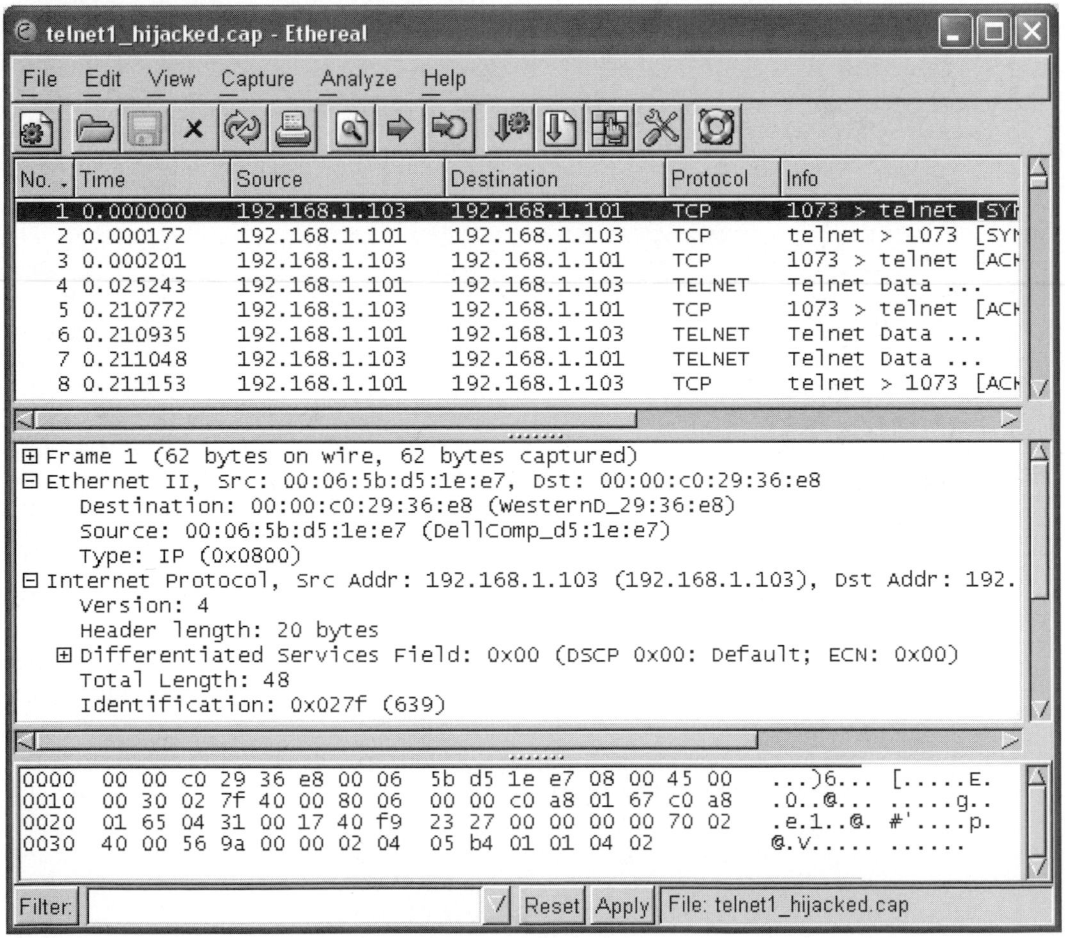

This TCP connection was isolated with the display filter (ip.addr eq 192.168.1.103 and ip.addr eq 192.168.1.101) and (tcp.port eq 1073 and tcp.port eq 23). There are a total of 98125 packets in this TCP connection. We would expect all of these to be sent from one of the two MAC addresses shown in the SYN and SYNACK packets. However, if we add these additional conditions on to the display filter, we find only 98123 packets. To isolate the two offending packets, we can use the following filter: !(eth.src eq 00:00:c0:29:36:e8) and !(eth.src eq 00:06:5b:d5:1e:e7).

These two packets both appear to be sent from IP address 192.168.1.103, the client. However, if we look at the Ethernet frame, we find that the source address is 00:01:03:87:a8:eb (3Com_87:a8:eb) and not the MAC address of our client, 00:06:5b:d5:1e:e7 (DellComp_d5:1e:e7). We have isolated two spoofed IP packets.

Figure 6.2.3: Packets from Attacker

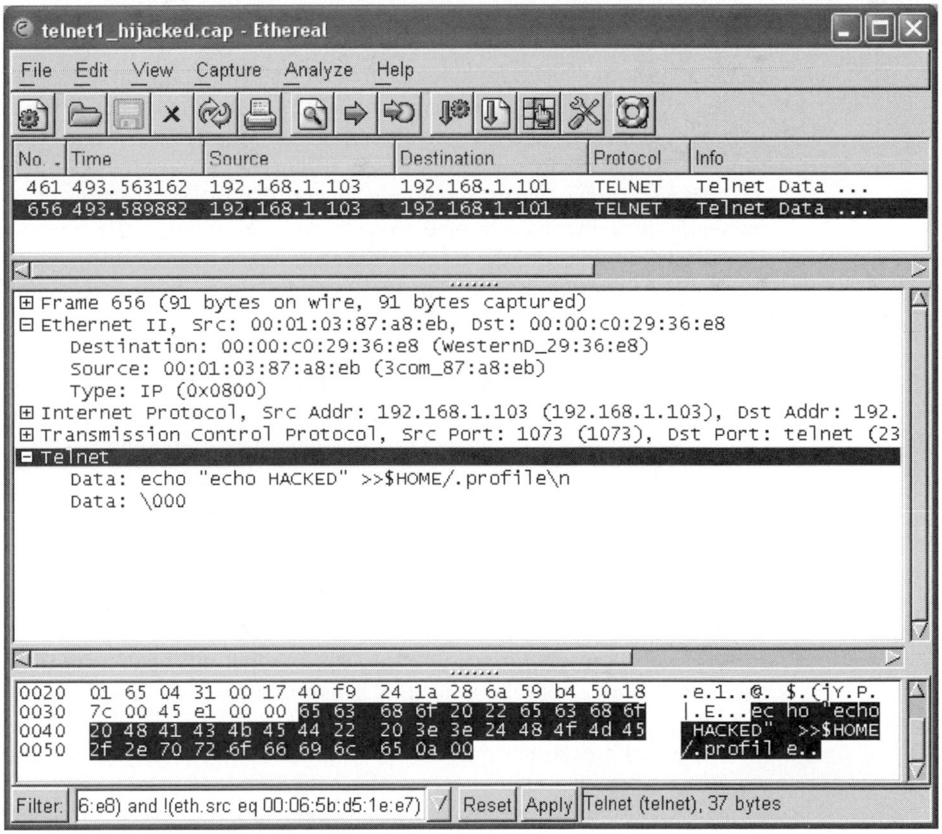

The first forged packet has sequence number 223 and contains 10 bytes of data. The second forged packet has sequence number 243 and contains 37 bytes of data.

Now, let's examine the impact of these forged packets. As we saw in Exercise 6.1, telnet sends each character typed by the user over the network. The keystrokes are then echoed back by the server to appear on the user's screen. Thus, the data sent by the attacker will be interpreted just as if the legitimate client had typed those characters.

In the first forged packet, there are 10 bytes of data that represent 10 ASCII characters, 8 ASCII 0x08 characters followed by 2 ASCII 0x0a characters. ASCII 0x08 represents a backspace and ASCII 0x0a represents a LINE FEED. When this is accepted into the TCP stream, the server will respond as if the user had typed backspace 8 times and then return twice. Although this may seem innocent enough, its purpose is to clear away whatever the legitimate user was typing and generate an empty command line. This will help ensure that the attackers next set of data will behave as expected rather than simply being added to the end of whatever command line the legitimate user was already typing.

In the second forged packet, there are 37 bytes of data containing the following command, echo "echo HACKED" >> $HOME/.profile. The command is followed by another ASCII 0x0a to enter the command. This will append the string "echo HACKED" to a special file in the user's home directory named .profile. In some command shells, the first action taken after a user logs in is to read this file and execute all commands found there. Users typically put a set of commands to prepare their working environment according to their preferences. Putting such commands in .profile means that the user need not manually type them each time they login. By placing the command "echo HACKED" in this file, the user will see the string "HACKED" printed to their screen when they login next. This will not work with all command shells and in fact, it does not work with the legitimate user's shell in this example. We will see in later sessions however that the string "echo HACKED" was indeed placed in the user's .profile file. It should be clear that the attacker could have used this technique to do more than simply place a string in a file. In fact, the attacker could have issued any command that the legitimate user could issue!

If the user had used an encrypted channel (like an SSH session) rather than a plain-text channel, the attacker still could have inserted data. However, it would be difficult for them to insert data that accomplishes a specific objective. Unless they broke the encryption scheme, they would simply be inserting garbage data into the stream.

If you examine the contents of the TCP stream using "Follow TCP Stream" in the Analyze menu, it is interesting to note that all input from the legitimate user comes one keystroke at a time. This input from the attacker comes in one packet.

Now, let's examine the impact of this attack on the legitimate client and server. Before the attack occurred, the client and server had successfully exchanged 460 packets. Notice that in packet 460, the server announces that it is expecting sequence number 233 (i.e. the acknowledgment number is set to 233). This is quite convenient for the attacker as it then knows exactly what sequence number to use.

Once the attacker has supplied sequence number 233 with its forged packet 461, the server sends an acknowledgement (packet 462) to the client indicating that it is ready for sequence number 243. However, the client knows it hasn't sent sequence numbers 233 through 242. Therefore, it responds with a 0 length packet with sequence number 233 (packet 463). After this, the client and server are never able to see eye to eye again! They proceed to argue back and forth; the server insisting that it wants sequence number 243, and the client insisting that it wants sequence number 233. This can be seen in the repeated duplicated acknowledgements from each side. This "argument" between client and server continues for over 95000 packets!

Figure 6.2.4: Disagreement Between Client and Server

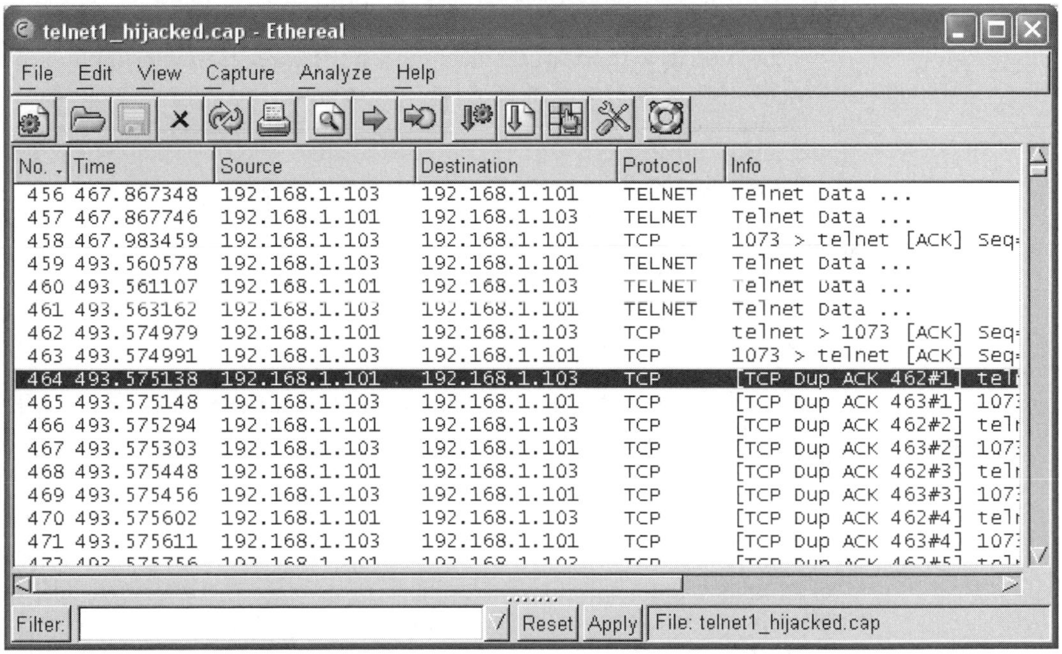

In the midst of this storm of duplicate acknowledgements, the attacker sends the second forged packet (packet 656). This packet has the sequence number 243, the sequence number expected by the server. The server accepts this packet and then sets the acknowledgement number of all its subsequent packets to 280. It then returns to the war of "duplicate acknowledgements" with the legitimate client.

TCP SESSION TERMINATION

In **telnet1_hijacked.cap**, the attacker succeeds both in using the "hijacked" session for his own purposes and in making it unusable for the legitimate client and server. In **telnet2_fin.cap**, **telnet3_rst.cap**, the attacker does not insert data into the TCP stream. Instead, he simply succeeds in terminating the connections.

In **telnet2_fin.cap**, the attacker sends packet 535 with the FIN bit set. This time the attacker poses as the server and sends the forged packet to the client. The client responds with its own FIN in packet 538. This is the first thing that the real server has heard of the connection termination so it attempts to respond with its own FIN in packet 540. When this reaches the client, the connection is already closed and the client machine responds by sending a packet with both a 0 advertised window and the RST bit set. This closes the connection on both sides and so we do not have a flood of duplicate acknowledgments as we saw in **telnet1_hijacked.cap**.

In **telnet3_rst.cap**, the attacker sends packet 339 with the RST bit set. The attacker once again poses as the server and sends the forged packet to the client. The client closes the connection immediately without the formal FIN/FINACK process. The server continues to send data in packet 340. When this data arrives, the client machine responds that the connection is closed.

The connection in **telnet4_hijacked.cap** is similar to the one seen in **telnet1_hijacked.cap**. If you examine the contents of the stream using Follow TCP Stream, you can see that the .profile file contains the string added by the first attack.

In **attacker_ftp.cap**, the attacker actually uses the user's password that he acquired by sniffing the network to make an FTP connection to the server and retrieve a file. For this connection, the attacker does not need IP Spoofing. He simply uses his own IP address, 192.168.0.100.

It is interesting to compare, from the attacker's point of view, the effectiveness of captured passwords to TCP session stealing. A captured password can be used to gain full access to a user's account. With a captured password, the attacker can connect with a full-featured, interactive telnet or FTP session rather than simply inserting a block of commands. However, telnet or FTP sessions tend to be logged. For example, it is typical for a server to print out the details of the users last login and users may get suspicious if they see that their last login in was from a machine they never use. On the other hand, TCP session stealing allows a connection to be hijacked even if the user relies on one-time passwords. In some systems, users are issued a list of passwords and each login uses a new password from the list rather than reusing the same password each time.

QUESTIONS

Answer the following questions about the files `session_hijack.cap`, `telnet1_hijacked.cap`, `telnet2_fin.cap`, `telnet3_rst.cap`, `telnet4_hijacked.cap`, and `attacker_ftp.cap`.

1. In each attack, a TCP packet is sent with the correct sequence number expected. Explain why the attacker is in a race against the legitimate sender. What does this suggest about the type of TCP stream that would be easiest to hijack?

2. In both `telnet1_hijacked.cap` and `telnet4_hijacked.cap`, the legitimate client and server exchange a long stream of duplicate acknowledgements in which they disagree over the correct sequence number to use. How long does the "fight" take in each of these traces? Approximately how many packets and how much data is transferred? Do you think it would be possible to detect an attack such as this by looking for this behavior?

3. Could the attacker do something to end the "fight" and allow the client and server to continue? Describe how this might be done. What are some problems with this approach? If you could do this, why might this be a more powerful tool?

4. We noted that when the attacker inserted data into a TCP stream, it contained many keystrokes at once (37 bytes). However, the real users seemed to enter one keystroke at a time. Do you think it would be possible to detect an attack such as this by looking for this behavior? ? If yes, why don't you think this is done? If no, then why wouldn't this be a good indication of an attack?

5. Write a packet filter to find all packets from the attacker in the big trace. How many packets are there?

6. Can you find the packets where the attacker joins the network and acquires an IP address via DHCP? What defense could have prevented this?

DISCUSSION AND INVESTIGATION

1. Why would an attacker need to be on the same shared local network with either the client or the server in order to perpetrate these attacks? Can you imagine any scenario in which such an attack could be used without this?

2. In these traces, when an attacker hijacked a telnet session, she executed a command to insert something in the user's .profile. Give some examples of worse things she could have done.

3. An attacker can insert data into an SSH session. However, an SSH session is still less vulnerable to a hijacking attack than a telnet session. Why is this? Is an SSH session also less vulnerable to the FIN and RST attacks? If so explain why? If not, what options do we have for defending against these attacks?

4. Investigate the IP Security Protocol (Ipsec)? How would it offer protection from TCP session stealing?

RESOURCES

- RFC 854, Telnet Protocol Specification, **ftp://ftp.rfc-editor.org/in-notes/rfc854.txt**

- IP Security Protocol (ipsec), **http://www.ietf.org/html.charters/ipsec-charter.html**

Security: Exercise **6.3**

System Vulnerabilities

INTRODUCTION

Computer systems are vulnerable to a wide variety of attacks from malicious software such as computer viruses or worms. Malicious software is generally referred to as *malware*. Malware varies significantly in its purpose and method of attack.

Malware often enters a computer system by tricking legitimate users into downloading it or otherwise introducing it into the system. Users may execute malware when they open an e-mail attachment, download a file from a web site or use a floppy disk containing infected files. Once executed, the malicious program typically runs with the legitimate user's full rights and privileges. For example, any file the user could delete, the malware can delete; any network connection the user could make, malware can make; any program the user could install, malware can install.

What do malware programs do with the power they acquire? Some programs simply want to irritate, perhaps by displaying a message to let the user know they've been attacked. However, other programs seek to destroy the system, perhaps by deleting key system files. In both these cases, users can easily detect that they have been attacked.

Some malware programs attempt to accomplish their goals without alerting users. For example, they may search the files on the computer for e-mail addresses or credit card numbers to send over the network to their creators. Others simply lurk unobtrusively but open a back door through which their creators can access and control the machine at will. Some attackers use controlled machines as a launching pad for further attacks; thus concealing their own identity.

Malware does not always enter a system through the "front door" by way of a legitimate user. Some kinds of malware try to sneak in through the "back door" by actively attacking weaknesses in the system. The major sources of such weaknesses are coding errors in server side software. By sending a request that the server is not expecting, an attacker can expose errors in the server. By sending a very carefully crafted request, an attacker can even trick a server into giving the attacker access to the system.

Server programs listen on open network ports waiting for clients to send requests. For example, web servers typically listen for requests on port 80. Each of these open ports represents a possible avenue of attack.

After studying application layer protocols like HTTP, it may seem hard to believe that an attacker could design a request that could gain them access to the server machine. If you send a GET request with strange parameters, the server will normally just reply with an error code, and will not allow an attacker access to the system. However, the requests sent by attackers are carefully crafted to actually insert code of their own into the servers address space and then cause the server to execute this code. A common technique to accomplish this is called a *buffer overflow attack*.

In a buffer overflow attack, an attacker sends a request that is bigger than the space the server has allocated to hold the incoming request. If the server program does not carefully check the size of each parameter, it may copy the big request outside the boundaries of the intended buffer. When it overflows the buffer, it begins to write into the address space of the server and can actually overwrite locations that instruct the server which code to execute next. If an attacker knows exactly what to send, the server will execute instructions contained in the request itself including instructions to open up a command shell for the attacker or copy a specific piece of malware into the system.

A buffer overflow attacker requires precise knowledge of the server program that is running. They must know how much space the program has allocated for incoming requests and exactly where to write the code being inserted. Attackers can easily obtain copies of the server applications to study and to practice attacks. They often target the default settings of the most popular server software packages because a large number of computers will be running with these precise settings.

Malware is often designed to actively spread itself to other vulnerable machines. For example, malware that enters through a buffer overflow attack often begins executing the same kind of attack on other machines. Malware may also search the computer for e-mail addresses and send copies of itself as an e-mail attachment.

In this exercise, we will examine the trace of a network application that probes for open ports or possible vulnerabilities in another system. We will also examine a trace of a machine that became infected with the Blaster worm. We will see how it actively tries to spread itself by attempting to exploit a vulnerability in the Windows Distributed Component Object Model (DCOM) Remote Procedure Call (RPC) interface.

CONFIGURATION

The traces in this exercise were taken in one of two configurations. In the first configuration, a desktop PC behind a firewall running DHCP scans the firewall for open ports. In the second configuration, we traced the network traffic generated from a desktop PC in a campus environment that was infected with the Blaster worm.

Figure 6.3.1: Exercise Configuration 1

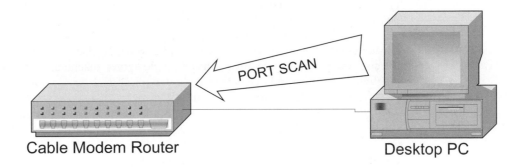

Figure 6.3.2: Exercise Configuration 2

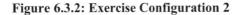

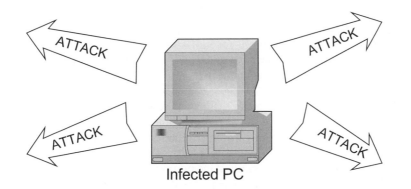

EXPERIMENT

PORT SCANS

In our first experiment, we used a tool called nmap to scan for open ports or possible vulnerabilities on another machine, 192.168.0.1. One open port, the HTTP port, was identified. We saved the resulting trace in the file **nmap.cap**.

A *port scan* program like nmap probes for open ports (i.e. vulnerabilities) by sending SYN messages on a large number of popular ports. In this case, SYN messages were sent to a total of 1658 ports. If server software is listening on those ports, it will respond with a SYN ACK. When the scan is complete, you have a "map" of the possible vulnerabilities in the system.

Port scans can be used to audit the security of your own machines, but it is considered an attack to perform a port scan on someone else's computer. In this exercise, we use nmap to investigate a single target machine, but it is also widely used to "map" a large network.

In the file **nmap.cap**, we use the filter `tcp.flags.syn == 1 && tcp.flags.ack ==0` to isolate the probe packets sent by nmap. The summary statistics show that it sent 6693 packets or between 3 and 4 SYN messages for each of the 1658 ports scanned. The scan does not proceed from low port number to high port number. It does not even issue all of the probes for a given port number together.

Notice that the nmap reuses the same source port for many probe packets. For example, 50210 is used as the source port for the probes shown in packets 15 through 44. If this were not a port scan, the operating system would typically assign a different ephemeral port for each connection.

Ethereal translates some of the well-known port numbers into a name. For example, it lists ftp for port 21. The Internet Assigned Numbers Authority (IANA) publishes a list of well-known port numbers. This list specifies the expected port number for common services to use. For example, port 80 is the well-known port used by web servers and port 25 is the well-known port used by outgoing e-mail servers. In general, well-known port numbers are in the range 0 to 1023, and on most systems only programs with root or administrator privileges can use these ports.

The list of well-known port numbers is a convention that allows users to locate services on remote computers more easily. Without this convention, each server would need to advertise its port number as well as its name or IP address. For example, a web server would need to advertise both its name (**www.foo.com**) and its port number (80). This convention does not prevent servers from listening on nonstandard ports. For example, you may have seen a URL that specifies an alternate port number (**http://www.foo.com:8080**).

Figure 6.3.3: Nmap Traffic

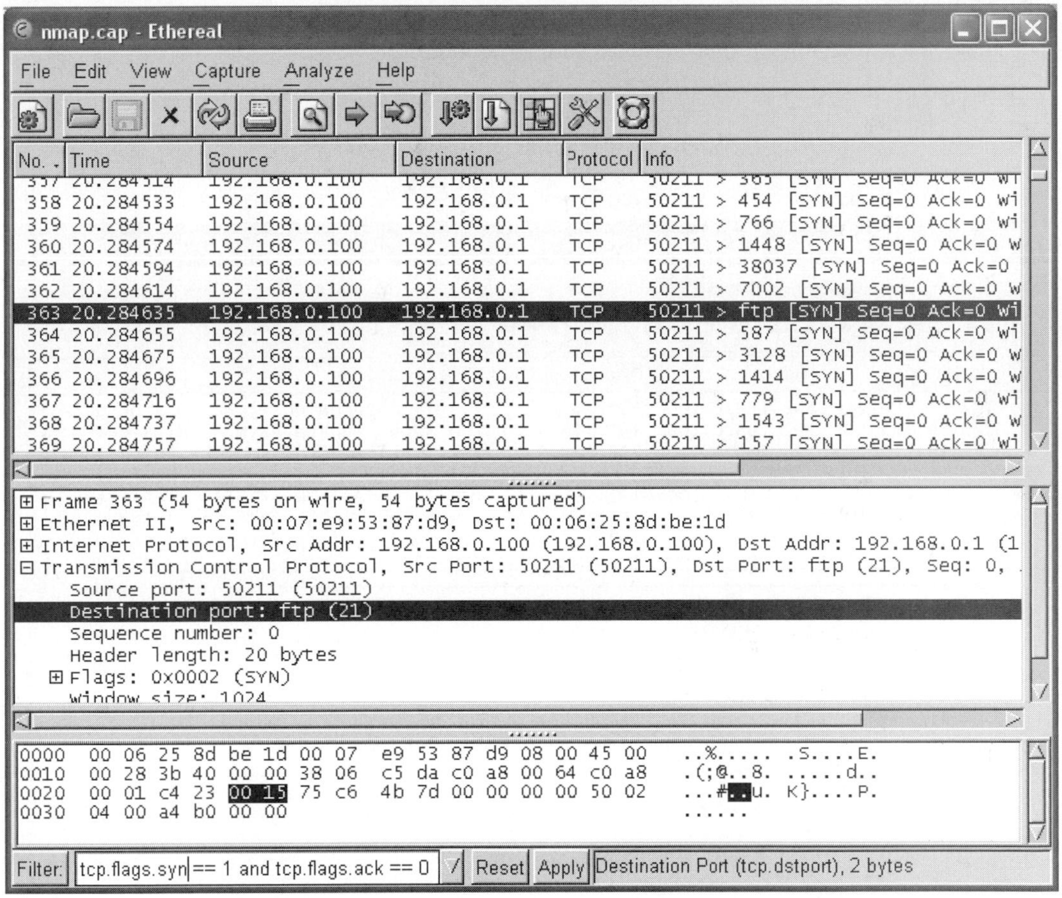

To identify any successful scans, we can use the filter `tcp.flags.syn == 1 && tcp.flags.ack ==1`. This identifies any SYNACK messages. From this filter, we know that the only open port is port 80. We can further isolate all the traffic to port 80 with the filter `tcp.port == 80`. Immediately after the target machine replies with a SYNACK, `nmap` responds by closing the connection by sending a segment with the RST bit set.

`nmap` can also be used to probe for clues about the type of machine and type of operating system running. It uses a technique to "fingerprint" systems by the differences in the way they implement Internet protocols. Most differences boil down to small differences in infrequently used or optional behavior. For example, nmap looks to see how the target system chooses its initial TCP

sequence numbers, which TCP options it supports and the data included in various ICMP error messages.

In the file **nmap_identify.cap**, we saved a trace of such a scan. We have highlighted packet 6780 which shows a single TCP segment that has the FIN, SYN, PSH, and URG flags all set. It is probing to see how the target machine will react to this strange condition.

Figure 6.3.4: System Fingerprinting

```
nmap_identify.cap - Ethereal                                          _ □ X

 File   Edit   View   Capture   Analyze   Help

No.    Time        Source          Destination      otoc  Info
  6777 97.289294   192.168.0.100   192.168.0.1      TCP   [TCP ZeroWindow] 38000 > http [RST
  6778 99.415550   192.168.0.100   192.168.0.1      TCP   38001 > http [SYN, ECN] Seq=0 Ack=
  6779 99.415600   192.168.0.100   192.168.0.1      TCP   [TCP Previous segment lost] 38002
  6780 99.415679   192.168.0.100   192.168.0.1      TCP   38003 > http [FIN, SYN, PSH, URG]
  6781 99.415753   192.168.0.100   192.168.0.1      TCP   [TCP Dup ACK 6713#4] [TCP Previous
  6786 99.416598   192.168.0.1     192.168.0.100    TCP   http > 38003 [RST, ACK] Seq=0 Ack=
  6789 100.917456  192.168.0.100   192.168.0.1      TCP   38001 > http [SYN, ECN] Seq=0 Ack=
  6790 100.917617  192.168.0.100   192.168.0.1      TCP   38002 > http [] Seq=1033084189 Ack=

□ Transmission Control Protocol, Src Port: 38003 (38003), Dst Port: http (80), Seq: 0,
     Source port: 38003 (38003)
     Destination port: http (80)
     Sequence number: 0
     Header length: 40 bytes
  □ Flags: 0x002b (FIN, SYN, PSH, URG)
       0... .... = Congestion Window Reduced (CWR): Not set
       .0.. .... = ECN-Echo: Not set
       ..1. .... = Urgent: Set
       ...0 .... = Acknowledgment: Not set
       .... 1... = Push: Set
       .... .0.. = Reset: Not set
       .... ..1. = Syn: Set
       .... ...1 = Fin: Set
     Window size: 4194304

0000   00 06 25 8d be 1d 00 07  e9 53 87 d9 08 00 45 00    ..%..... .S....E.
0010   00 3c ba 6c 00 00 37 06  47 9a c0 a8 00 64 c0 a8    .<.l..7. G....d..
0020   00 01 94 73 00 50 6d a1  7d 80 00 00 00 00 a0 2b    ...s.Pm. }......+
0030   10 00 b7 70 00 00 03 03  0a 01 02 04 01 09 08 0a    ...p.... ........
0040   3f 3f 3f 3f 00 00 00 00  00 00                      ????.... ..

Filter: tcp.port == 80                        ✓  Reset Apply  File: nmap_identify.cap
```

Port scan programs like nmap identify open ports and operating system types. From this information, it is not difficult to identify possible system vulnerabilities. For example, if nmap identifies a machine as a Linux machine and port 80 is open, an attacker could focus their efforts on attacks against the Apache web server. Although patches are often issued to counter known attacks, but this requires that system administrators patch their systems more rapidly than they are attacked.

BLASTER WORM

Although some attackers use information provided by port scanners to deliberately focus their attacks, some of the most costly attacks spread from machine to machine automatically. The W2.Blaster worm is an example of such an attack. The worm targeted a vulnerability in DCOM RPC that appeared only on machines running Windows 2000 and Windows XP. However, the Blaster worm did not attempt to specifically identify these machines. Instead, each infected machine would attack other machines by randomly generating IP addresses. Many machines attacked were not vulnerable, but the worm spread rapidly because there were so many Windows 2000 and XP machines.

In the file **blasterIsolated.cap**, we traced the network activity generated by a machine that was infected with the Blaster worm. Even though the user of this machine was running no network applications, the trace shows constant network traffic being generated. The only clue the user had to the presence of the worm was that their machine appeared to be running slowly due to this background activity. Without a network trace, they would not have known the source of the apparent slowdown.

The trace shows the infected machine, 128.153.22.191, sending a series of SYN messages to TCP port 135 (epmap) of random IP addresses. For example, packets 1 through 5 show such a message sent to IP addresses, 92.252.166.229, 92.252.166.226, 92.252.166.223, 92.252.166.221, and 92.252.166.220. The worm is not attempting to specifically target vulnerable machines, but rather to attack as many machines as quickly as possible in the hopes that some of the attacks will be successful.

Figure 6.3.5: Blaster Worm Attacking Random Machines

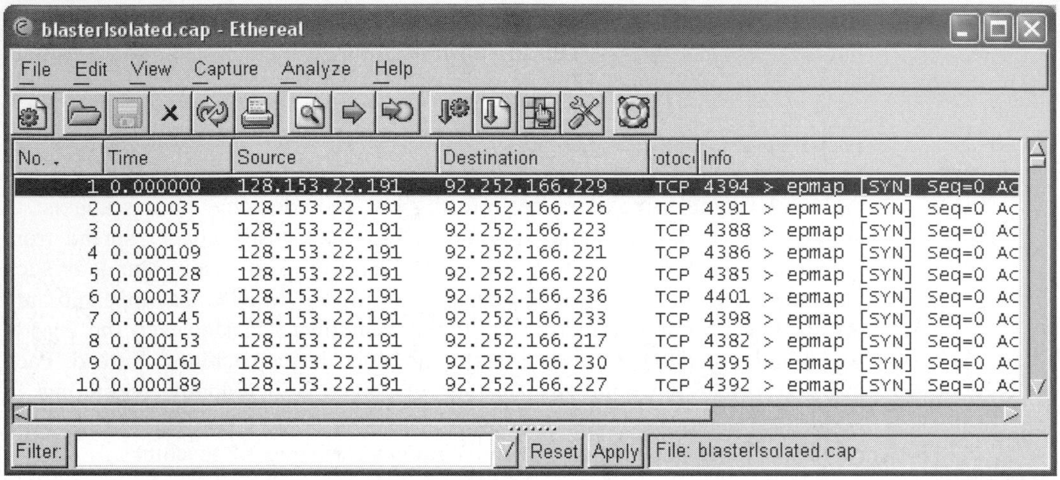

A successful attack would require several things. First, there must be a machine with the IP address chosen. Second, the machine must have TCP port 135 open. Third, the server listening on that port must be vulnerable to the attack. If you follow the TCP stream that begins with packet 1, you will see an example of a failed attack. There is a machine running with IP address 92.252.166.229, but it does not have port 135 open. If an attack is successful, the worm installs a copy of itself on the infected machine and the newly infected machine will begin attacking others in the same way.

The Blaster worm has other aspects to its attack. In addition to probing remote IP addresses, it would periodically launch a denial of service attack on the Microsoft Windows Update web server. Likely, this was done to make it difficult for unprotected machines to download the necessary patch once it was available.

The Blaster worm and others like it are more than a nuisance. Time and money must be spent to remove the virus from infected systems as well as patch them to prevent reinfection. Increased traffic on local networks and the Internet as a whole causes lost productivity. Authors of such worms, if identified, can be prosecuted for these damages.

QUESTIONS

Answer the following questions about the files **nmap.cap**, **nmap_identify.cap**, and **blasterIsolated.cap**.

1. In the file **nmap.cap**, how many probes are there for port 593? How many for port 135? What filters did you use to determine your answers?

2. In **nmap.cap**, if a probe for a given port is successful, does it continue probing? How do you know? How about in **nmap_identify.cap**? What do you think accounts for this difference?

3. Nmap does not probe well-known port numbers in numerical order. Although it probes a single port more than once, it does not issue these probes at the same time. Why do you think this is?

4. What is the largest port number scanned in **nmap.cap**? What set of filters can you use to quickly determine this? (Note: You should not need to spend time looking through long lists of packets.) Is this port number described in the IANA's list of port numbers? Can you find any other information on what applications use this port number?

5. Would the machine probed in **nmap.cap** have been vulnerable to the Blaster attack? Explain your answer.

6. In the file **blasterIsolated.cap**, what is the time between the first packet and the last packet? Estimate how many machines are attacked in that time. How many attack packets were sent? Did the infected machine send any network traffic besides attack packets? Explain your answer.

7. Consider the attack packet shown in packet 1. How many packets are sent in response? What filter did you use?

8. There are three possible outcomes when an attack packet is sent: no response, a "failed" attack, and a "successful" attack. There are no successful attacks shown in the trace. Can you characterize a failed attack? Of all the attack packets sent (Question 7), estimate how many received some response? What filter did you use to determine you answer? What percent of machines responded? What does this say about how fast it would likely spread if machines were not patched?

9. In the file **blasterIsolated.cap**, could you write a filter to isolate the probes that received no response? Why or why not? Explain your answer.

10. In the file **blasterIsolated.cap**, we did not include a trace of a successful attack. How can you verify this? Would there be problem with including such a trace?

DISCUSSION AND INVESTIGATION

1. Well-known ports are in the range of 0 to 1023. Registered ports are in the range of 1024 to 49151. Private or dynamic ports are in the range of 49152 to 65535. Use some Ethereal filters (no more than 5) to estimate how many ports in each range are scanned in **nmap.cap**. What filters did you use to do this? What percentage of each range appears to be covered? Why?

2. Anti-virus software typically relies on virus signatures that characterize an attack based on certain aspects of its behavior (how it enters the system, files it produces, network traffic it generates, even checksums of executable files involved). For anti-virus software to be effective, new signatures must be developed and distributed to anti-virus software running on client machines. Visit sites like CERT (**http://www.cert.org/**) or the Symantec Security Response Site (**http://www.symantec.com/avcenter/**) for information on the most recent and the most active threats. Choose several attacks and write a summary of their behavior and how systems can be protected.

RESOURCES

- Nmap, **http://www.insecure.org/nmap**

- Port Numbers, Internet Assigned Numbers Authority, **http://www.iana.org/assignments/port-numbers**

- Remote OS detection via TCP/IP Stack FingerPrinting, **http://www.insecure.org/nmap/nmap-fingerprinting-article.html**

- Symantec Security Response, **http://www.symantec.com/avcenter**

- Symantec Security Response to the W2.Blaster Worm, **http://securityresponse.symantec.com/avcenter/venc/data/w32.blaster.worm.html**

- CERT Coordination Center, **http://www.cert.org**

INDEX